Landscape and the Science Fiction Imaginary

Landscape and the Science Fiction Imaginary

John Timberlake

intellect Bristol, UK / Chicago, USA

First published in the UK in 2018 by
Intellect, The Mill, Parnall Road, Fishponds, Bristol, BS16 3JG, UK

First published in the USA in 2018 by
Intellect, The University of Chicago Press, 1427 E. 60th Street,
Chicago, IL 60637, USA

A catalogue record for this book is available from the
British Library.

Copy-editor: MPS Technologies
Cover designer: Alex Szumlas and John Timberlake
Indexer: Silvia Benvenuto
Production manager: Tim Mitchell
Typesetting: Contentra Technologies

Print ISBN: 978-1-78320-860-9
ePDF ISBN: 978-1-78320-862-3
ePUB ISBN: 978-1-78320-861-6

Printed and bound by TJ International Ltd, UK.

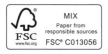

To my father, George Timberlake, who built jet engines,
read science fiction and walks the moors.

Contents

Acknowledgements ix

Introduction 1

Chapter 1: Land of the Giants: Size and Scale, Macroscopy 23
and Microscopy in the Landscapes of Science Fiction

Chapter 2: A Game in the Ruins: Landscape and Virtual Realities 49

Chapter 3: Blasted Heaths and Turbulent Energies: 75
Chris Foss's Accelerated Dream of Wessex

Chapter 4: An Unforgiveable Composure: The Apocalyptic 93
Imaginary Since Yosuke Yamahata's *Nagasaki*

Chapter 5: 'Suppositional Realism' and the Fictions of Science: 119
The Astronomical Landscapes of Pavel Klushantsev
and Chesley Bonestell

Chapter 6: Beyond the Periphery: Desert and Darkness 147

Conclusion: Where Otherwise Nothing Has Changed 169

References 177

Illustration Copyright Acknowledgements 183

Index 185

Acknowledgements

I would like to thank Alex Charnley, Matthew Cornford, Valeria Graziano and Juliet Steyn, all of whom gave invaluable feedback on either individual draft outlines or chapters of this book; Mark Bould and my two anonymous peer reviewers who read drafts of the book in their entirety.

I am grateful for the generous assistance of the astronomical artist Ron Miller; Mariecris Batlabayan, archivist at Bonestell LLC; Jeremy Cox at the Frederick and Frances Sommer Foundation, Arizona; Imogene Foss; Tasha Lutek, photography collection specialist at the Museum of Modern Art, New York, Debbie Walters, archivist at the White Sands Missile Base Museum, and Shogo Yamahata.

I would also like to thank Giles Bunch, Sonya Dyer, Keith Piper and Ben Wheele of the Middlesex University Science Fiction Research Cluster; Phil Healey, Eve Sevume Kauma and Kate Vasili for their support, help and advice respectively.

I am indebted, as ever, to Rachel Garfield for love and arguments, and Isaac Timberlake for his insights, filial devotion and ability to listen *ad tedium*.

One of the themes of Chapter 5, dealing with 'Nuclear war as false memory' was first presented as a paper discussing themes in my *Another Country* constructed photographs and my experience of the 9/11 attacks at the *Disturbing Pasts* Conference at the Museum für Völke Kunde, Vienna, in November 2012. That paper appears in the book *Disturbing Pasts* (Manchester University Press, 2017). The concept appears here in a reworked and expanded form; I am nevertheless indebted to Leon Wainwright of the Open University, Uilleam Blacker and the other conference organisers for that opportunity. Stimulating conversations with Joy Sleeman, Martin Myrone, Matthew Beaumont, Richard Misrach and Luke White in the course of preparing the *Landscape and Eschatology* conference at Tate Britain in 2012 (at which I presented a paper on Frederick Sommer) also provided early inspiration, and I thank all accordingly. I first started thinking about 'ocularity' when reviewing Mark Bould and China Miéville's edited collection Red Planets (Pluto, 2009) for the journal *Radical Philosophy* Issue 160. Again, I am grateful to the RP editorial collective, and in particular David Cunningham, Stewart Martin and Peter Osborne for that opportunity. I would also like to acknowledge the financial assistance provided by the Art & Creative Industries Faculty Research Funding Group at Middlesex University, and Tim Mitchell and all at Intellect Books for their enthusiasm for this project.

Introduction

Uneven Distribution and Terrifying Objects: The Science Fiction Imaginary and the Act of Landscaping

What might constitute a specifically 'science fiction imaginary'?

If, beyond any bald definition of narratives or visualizations constituted around scientism, 'science fiction' is a responsive montaging of scientific, social and technological development combined with a sense of historical agency, then Philip K. Dick might seem to have described the science fiction imaginary very well – and in an appropriately febrile manner – in these select lines from his 1962 novel *The Man in the High Castle*:

> Their view; it is cosmic. Not a man here, a child there, but an abstraction [...] the abstract is real, the actual is invisible to them [...] It is their sense of space and time. They see through the here, the now, into the vast black deep beyond, the unchanging. And that is fatal to life. Because eventually there will be no life; there was once only the dust particles in space, the hot hydrogen gases, nothing more, and it will come again. This is an interval, *ein Augenblick* [...] They want to be the agents, not the victims of history. They identify with God's power and believe they are godlike [...] their egos have expanded psychotically so that they cannot tell where they begin and the godhead leaves off.
>
> (2001: 45–46, original emphasis)

Of course, in these lines, Dick was not describing the science fiction imaginary per se – hence my imposition of opportune elisions – but rather the rocket-powered Nazi conquerors of his alternative 1960s, as seen through the eyes of an understandably disgusted Swedish envoy.

Nevertheless, I would plead that the reader allow my admittedly mischievous substitution on the following grounds: firstly, Dick's emphasis upon a sensibility led by visualization: Dick's Nazis 'view' and 'see' their relationship to the cosmos, and disregard that which is invisible; secondly, their mental state is characterized by an overblown anthropocentrist sense of outward self-importance, entangled with an inward desolation in the face of the realities of deep time and space; and, thirdly, as a result of this conflicted state, their collective ego (that category which Lacanian Psychoanalysis describes as the Imaginary) is destabilized by persistent attempts to correlate perpetually fugitive senses of self, place, and of course, history. Indeed, Fredric Jameson has argued that science fiction's 'historical situation' is key to differentiating it from other forms of fantasy (2005: 59). If twentieth-century Nazism can be viewed as the hysterical, obscene culmination of nineteenth-century European discourses on land, nation, eugenics, militarized imperialism and historical ends, then Dick's achievement lies in his successful re-visioning of those tenets beyond the technologies of the 1940s to the landscape of the 1960s. Of course, all of the above is certainly not to invoke some variant of Godwin's Law and proclaim all science fiction to be ultimately the result of febrile crypto-fascist imaginings. I invoke Dick's rocketship Nazis as an example of the contradictions of the science fiction imaginary, presented *in extremis*. Dick, I would suggest, outlines a certain complex that afflicts all of us who are prone to the fever dreams of speculation and conjecture around science, its evolution and its ends.

There are other, less distasteful ways of thinking of this issue of course. For example, in William Morris's romance *The House of the Wolfings*, we find a compelling image of history as landscape, which, as Tom Shippey (Morris 1980) has remarked, offers an image of 'a note of baffled yearning, even of homesickness, which many writers have drawn on since. This is especially true of science fiction' (introduction in Morris 1980: xvii–xviii). Morris's lines on the title page of the *House of the Wolfings* (1979) read as follows:

As still the dark road drives us on. / E'en so the world of men may turn

At even of some hurried day / And see the ancient glimmer burn / Across the waste that hath no way

As Shippey suggests, 'Morris was talking about history […] whilst writers of science fiction look to the future. Still, "the waste that has no way" has meaning for fantasists of either kind' (Morris 1980: xvii–xviii). Shippey's poignant example suggests an inward doubt and devastation as the obverse of that outward, overblown sense of historical agency Dick gives his Nazis: indeed, we might begin by thinking of the science fiction imaginary as an unstable one, vacillating between these two extremes.

Thus, the present book is about the way we might consider the interplay between the science fiction imaginary and landscape, specifically in relation to visualization: if we think of the imaginary spatially, located 'geographically' as a gap between the Real and the Symbolic; if, at the same time, we also consider, in the manner of a remark attributed to William Gibson,[1] namely that the 'future is already here, it is just not evenly distributed', then it is through the act of what W.J.T. Mitchell has called 'landscaping' (1994: 1) that fragments of the future are encountered, assimilated and historicized into the viewing subject's experience: 'What I have seen, with your eyes!' exclaims the replicant Roy Batty (Rutger Hauer) to Mr Chew, the ocularist, in Ridley Scott's film *Bladerunner* (1982), an adaptation of another novel of Dick's, *Do Androids Dream of Electric Sheep?* (1968).

In this book, I propose a neologism to talk about science fiction's particular relationship with landscape and its preoccupations with the visual: *ocularity*. What I mean by this is viewership that affects a relational artifice: relational in that it is shaped by a futurism based on the extrapolation of emergent technological tropes, grounded in historically extant forms.

In the alternative 1960s that his novel conjures, Dick's *Man in the High Castle* offers not only the story of an alternative political hegemony, but speculations on the 'might-have-beens' of its visual culture. Dick does this through describing the different affective visual investment of its characters in forms that are already familiar to the reader. Under the conditions of brutal occupation by Imperial Japan and Nazi Germany, an interest in visual abstraction emerges in America not in fine art painting – as it did under the post-1945 *Pax Americana* of our own world via Greenbergian Modernism – but rather in artisanal, handcrafted jewellery. Dick provides a convincing rationale as to why this might be so. The period in which Dick's novel is set sees an eviscerated American culture completely dominated by the cultural fascinations of its conquerors, who wish to see it as obsolete, but *authentic*. In the hegemony established by victorious Japan, a lucrative market has developed in collectable items of the authentic nineteenth-century 'Old West' – cowboy pistols and belt buckles, memorabilia of the 1860–65 Civil War and so on. As might be expected, this antiquarian obsession on the part of the conquering power with mining the past effectively prevents the development of any independent cultural power in the defeated nation, but at the same time causes its own internal problems – namely a burgeoning trade in fakes and forgeries, where collectible objects are manufactured in backstreet workshops, then worked over and treated by artisans to give them the patina of authenticity. Collectors' doubts about the authenticity of objects threaten the livelihood of the American petit-bourgeois dealerships and boutiques that have fed the tastes of the post-war Japanese ascendancy class of affluent professional connoisseurs. The turn towards abstract jewellery by dissident American artisans is therefore a way of negating a form of authenticity that is increasingly problematic due to its over reliance on historicism.

Dick's parable about visual culture, authenticity and the hierarchies of legitimacy that emerge as his novel unfolds has something to say about the position of genre and science fiction, and this is reflected, of course, in the 'novel within the novel' that *The Man in the High Castle* features: less successfully or succinctly, Ridley Scott's 2015 serialized and extended adaptation *The Man in the High Castle* attempted to find a suitable substitute in the form of 16mm films appropriate to his own cinematic medium. In Dick's novel, the messianic paranoid egoism of the world ruling Nazis is antagonized by their visualization of the vastness of deep space and deep time, whilst for those they and their ally oppress, small abstract fragments of metal ostensibly with no history, begin to make truth claims that historicized symbols of authenticity cannot, because the former allows for fantasies about the future. Dick's novel thereby shows both oppressed and oppressor relationally bound up into oscillating states of mind contingent upon their visual investments in the future: each attempts to seek justification by the affectation of a relational artificial viewpoint not only of the things around them, but how those things might shape the future. This is what I mean by 'ocularity'.

Fragments, Ur-Myths and Ur-Images

On the face of it, the remark attributed to William Gibson about an unevenly distributed future that I mentioned above can be seen as an apposite reference to the disparity in access to technology in a world of huge economic and social inequalities. However, I would also suggest that it acknowledges the inchoate, fragmented experience of the stuff of science fiction visualization itself. We catch glimpses of the future in our contemporary field of vision.

Uneven, fragmented or inchoate senses of self are the preserve of schizoid states. As such, we might suppose that the thrill of science fiction's visualizations, and the tremulous states they effect in the viewing subject, might poignantly remind us of formative mental states.

The pioneering psychoanalyst Melanie Klein (1882–1960) described a stage in childhood development where fragments of reality are embedded in the child's fantasy world. From the outset, speaking of the science fiction imaginary is to speak of an experience of its worlds in a manner analogous to that which Melanie Klein attributed to early infant development.

Central to the work of Klein was a conception of the development of what she termed 'object relations' and ego development. For Klein, this focused on clinical observation of infants being breast-fed. The newborn infant can only possibly experience the body of the mother in a fragmented, incoherent way. Without any sense of self, the newborn infant cannot relate to, or place itself in context to, its mother's body. Moreover, the same breast may, on different occasions, be the source of satisfaction or dissatisfaction, depending on the success or otherwise of the feed. As Klein puts it in her essay 'Mourning and Manic-Depressive States', originally published in 1940:

> In the baby, processes of introjection and projection, since they are dominated by aggression and anxieties which re-inforce each other, lead to fears of persecution by terrifying objects.
>
> ('Mourning and Manic-Depressive States', Mitchell 1991: 150)

> As regards normal development, it may be said that the course of ego development and object relations depends upon the degree to which an optimal balance between introjection and projection in the early stages of development can be achieved.
>
> (1991: 185)

Therefore, my proposal here is to think of the imaginary formed in and through science fiction as one that is fragmented and simultaneously shot through with anticipation and anxieties about the present and potential futures, and, as such, one that appeals because it resonates with the subject's formative experiences as Klein describes them. To see things *through* the ocularity that science fiction offers is to see the fragments of the present lodged within a fantasy of future historical time.

I should emphasize that my use of Klein in this way is not an attempt to suggest a geopolitical aspect to science fiction itself – some sort of metanarrative – reducing all the potentials of creativity to explicatory psychosexual familial narratives of infant development: as we have seen from my quotes above, there are constitutive elements within science fiction – time, for example – of which the nursing infant has no inkling. Time (as history) is central to envisioning both the future that might follow our past and present. This element of historical consciousness both distinguishes the science fictional form from other forms of fantasy, and simultaneously, establishes our place within it. However, my invocation of Melanie Klein here is pertinent to science fiction's historicism because, as Stephen Frosh has argued, for Klein,

> phantasy is not projected into the future as an ideal, [not] a substitutive response to external frustration, [but] the basic stuff of psychological functioning, without which there would be no mental processes at all.
>
> (1999: 24)

As Frosh goes onto argue, the radical implications of Kleinian theory do not end there. The emphasis upon fragmentation and phantasy in the work of Klein

> [...] refutes the simple individualism which begins with an integrated self and then examines what the social world makes of it. Instead the (real) social world is experienced through a conflicting screen of internal forces, which alter and shape it powerfully [...] this allows the theory to become dialectical, positing contradictions within as well as between each element in the inside-outside divide.
>
> (1999: 134)

Frosh therefore locates the significance of Klein's account in a combination of our conceptions of futurity and our constructions of a social world – the very stuff of science fiction. At the same time, Frosh's invocation of a dialectical, contradictory interplay in Klein evokes a sense of those fragments of the past that we inherit, as well as possible futures we might live.

In her book *The Dialectics of Seeing* (1989), Susan Buck-Morss elegantly parses the dialectical relationship between new and old across the antimonies of human and nature: 'In nature', she writes, 'the new is mythic, because its potential is not yet realized; in consciousness, the old is mythic, because its desires never were fulfilled' (1989: 116). In describing new and old in terms of myth, Buck-Morss links the concept of new and old to that of ideology. Buck-Morss's discussion of the past and the future arises from her scholarly discussion of Walter Benjamin's unfinished *Passagenwerk* (Arcades Project) that analysed the character of urban consumer capitalism. Through her discussion, however, via Benjamin's own work and that of Karl Marx, she traces the preponderance of images of a mythic past – the 'Ur-past' – to inform and shape images of a dreamed-of future. Through Benjamin, Buck-Morss argues that a collective Utopian imaginary 'cuts across the continuum of technology's historical development as the possibility of revolutionary rupture' (1989: 116). In other words, the *actual* development of technology challenges ideologically formed mythic pre-conceptions as to how that technology should be, whilst at the same time, leaps of the imagination strive to break technology from its own mythologies – of technologically determined, steadily paced evolutionary progress and, of course, its myth of ideological neutrality.

Central to this conception of dialectic is an image comprising a conflation of mythological pasts (the 'Ur-past') informing the images of the future. It is about future environments comprising societal, ecological, technological and historical elements. Buck-Morss describes this as a process by which collective, socially formed 'wish images' attach themselves 'as surface ornamentation' (1989: 117) to emergent technologies. As Buck-Morss points out, this was something observed by Marx in the 1840s – the tendency of a new revolutionary rupture to appear in the accoutrements of a mythic past can be seen in the revolutions in France of both 1789 and 1848, when revolutionaries adopted the iconography of the Roman Republic, or in the English Civil War, when Parliament and its radical supporters invoked the Book of Genesis against the absolute monarch Charles I. More prosaically, it is manifest in consumer technology in the forms of digital skeuomorphism, wherein digital interface icons not only mimic real-world objects, but more often than not are figured as older, more familiar forms – a twentieth-century television or telephone, for example.

However, what I want to suggest here is a way of imagining what is 'new' not merely as a counterpoint to such stylistic nostalgias. Rather, I want to argue that, in terms of visual culture and *representation*, we must try to think of 'the New' not as some sort of property hidden *within* an object, but, rather, as a context, or a moment, which creates fresh possibilities in the way extant forms are reconfigured such that they are perceived not only as transformed, but as potentially transformative.

The sense of the New I am proposing here, which draws upon the ideas of Ernst Bloch (1885–1977), also invests the 'old' – be that the extant or familiar – with potential meanings and possibilities it previously did not have. A good example of this is to be found in visual art, where, as Walter Benjamin argued, the avant-garde imagines the future using the media and forms of the present; in other words re-arranging the existing in such ways as it opens up the possibility of new meanings and interpretation. This is not to argue that new objects do not emerge – are *presented* to us – but *re*-presentation relies upon us already 'recognizing' an object – perhaps in the form that is estranged and uncanny, but resonates with a sense of belonging or familiarity. This is how – and why – we can talk about the 'return' of the new. This is also why, in this book, I am attaching such importance to, and placing the emphasis upon, the visual in science fiction, and in particular the landscapes which both present as oddly familiar and, at the same time, wondrously new.

This re-framing of the old or familiar in order to unleash new potential is a repeated aspect of science fiction – Orson Welles' infamous 're-imagining' of H.G. Wells' *The War of the Worlds* as a series of fake radio news reports spread mass panic in parts of 1930s America being perhaps the seminal example. This is also, most often, the juncture between two genres, namely science fiction and horror: an unspeakable past reawakens, requiring a futuristic solution. Arguably, this in itself should not surprise, since the corollary of what I have discussed above – namely contemporary capitalism's love of the past – would be the portrayal of the future as a hateful and dangerous realm. Yet in any case, 'science fiction' per se rarely appears in a pure form in visual culture. Rather, what we might think of as 'elements' of science fiction often appear in visual culture in a hybrid form: that is to say, inflected with other genres, not only horror such as the *Alien* franchise, but also tragedy (Fred Wilcox's 1956 film *Forbidden Planet*), noir and romance (Ridley Scott's 1982 film *Blade Runner*, Andrew Nicoll's 1997 *Gattaca*) and Utopian satire (Peter Weir's *The Truman Show*, 1998).

This book seeks to address science fiction as a genre dominated by visual conceptions. This, I argue, is true even in its literary forms: even in many non-illustrated science fiction novels and short stories, considerable time is often spent on describing how things would look to reader if s/he could see them. However, I should stress that my point here is not to argue that all science fiction writers are imagists. Clearly, some are very far from it. Indeed, to frame my discussion on the issue of science fiction's ocularity in that manner would be to wrongly focus the discussion on science fiction's literary forms, and this book is specifically not about science fiction literature per se. My point is that science fiction as an expanded field evokes or even elicits an excessive visual response, and that this visual response has peculiarly significant characteristics. In those cases where science fiction takes a non-imagist form, the lack of visual detail nevertheless elicits a desire for images to assuage a need within wider culture.

The ability to draw upon a wide range of recognizable historical tropes of imagery lies at the core of science fiction's ability to visualize recognizable forms in strange ways. This is why it is important not to focus on science fiction's *literary* form in isolation as some scholarly works tend to do, but to appraise the genre as one dominated by visualization. Indeed, I would suggest that a focus on the literary in science fiction at the expense of other forms fails to acknowledge the peculiar need for the visual that the 'unreal' quality of science fiction necessitates. Thus, for example, whilst Jameson (2005) argues that in the writings of Ovid, 'language is called upon to express the well nigh inexpressible' or conversely, that Philip K. Dick's writing on hallucinogenic drugs calls into question that same expressive capacity (2005: 262), he does not acknowledge that it is precisely the failure of words in much of literary science fiction – either through incapacity to express or chosen evasiveness by the author – which brings about an excess of visual pseudo realism – in illustrations, games and cinema CGI – in science fiction's expansive visual field. In Jameson, this seems particularly peculiar, since this is not the only occasion in which he dwells upon what he terms the lack of 'ontological density' for the reader of science fiction and pointing out that 'artifice and unbelievability […] is an unexpected source of strength' since it feeds a reflexive sense of estrangement in the reader in a way that would be 'disastrous in most realistic novels' (2005: 308). But therein, perhaps, lies also a reluctance to see beyond the limits of defining science fiction as a novel form, something which, by contrast, Darko Suvin was able to point to in his likening of certain forms of science fiction to 'anatomies' rather than novels per se. In his 1974 essay 'Science Fiction and Utopian Fiction', Suvin argued that utopian (and one might add dystopian) fictions, characterized by an interest in socio-political constructs, fall with the form and tradition of 'anatomy' (dealing more with states of mind than people per se). This argues for a close look at the particular role 'envisioning' description plays in science fiction – in Suvin's words, the tendency to create a 'vision of the world in terms of single intellectual pattern' (1988: 39).

Such unifying framings, are, of course, often the necessitated corollary of rupture and juxtaposition, and again, this leads us back to the realm of the visual, and the role of visualization that I explore in this book, addressing science fiction as a genre of visual culture in the forms of illustration and cinema that did arise to some extent – but not exclusively – from science fiction's literary forms, but now embraces much more. It is Darko Suvin who is widely credited with having first addressed science fiction as worthy of in-depth scholarly analysis and commentary. Suvin's central contribution to the particular function of the New within the genre – the concept of the 'novum' – is first fully expounded in his groundbreaking *Metamorphoses of Science Fiction: On the Poetics and History of a Literary Genre* (1974). Whilst many novels and short stories incorporate some element of revelatory 'new-ness' or surprise, for Suvin it is the dominance of this element in science fiction that is its key differentiating factor:

> SF [Science Fiction] *is distinguished by the narrative dominance or hegemony of a fictional novum (novelty, innovation) validated by cognitive logic.*
>
> (1979: 63, italics original)

Suvin binds this formulation of the novum to the genre's relationship to science in the following way:

> The novum is postulated on and validated by the post-Cartesian and post-Baconian scientific method. This does not mean that the novelty is primarily a matter of scientific facts or even hypotheses […] what differentiates SF [from other genres] is the presence of scientific cognition as the sign or correlative of a method [way, approach, sensibility] identical to that of a modern philosophy of science.
>
> (1979: 65)

It follows that the novum not only distinguishes the genre in relation to the New, but also gives the genre a specific relationship to anthropocentric time: Suvin sees the New itself as always a historical category, and the novum in science fiction is therefore 'born in history and judged in history' (1979: 80). Suvin's elegant formulation therefore neatly accounts for the three defining elements of the literary genre that have become the precepts for much defining critical work around literary science fiction. However, whilst the present book does pay some attention to literary examples in its discussion of the landscapes of science fiction, its principal focus is on the genre's visual forms, and, as such, the question has to be posed as to how the specifics of Suvin's novum might be applied to these. To answer that, we must go back to the work of Ernst Bloch, to whom Suvin acknowledges his indebtedness from the outset (1979: 64).

As I outlined above in my discussion of the New, Bloch's novum is integral to his conception of a Utopian impulse, or 'function' within art and literature – that of *Vor-Schein* or 'anticipatory illumination'. In the words of Jack Zipes, who co-translated *The Utopian Function of Art and Literature* into English for the 1988 edition published by MIT, anticipatory illumination is

> [...] a type of consciousness, formed by the impulse of hope, in which inklings of what they might become manifest themselves [...]. The anticipatory illumination is an image, a constellation, a configuration closely tied to the concrete utopias that are lit up on the frontal margins of reality and illuminate the possibilities of rearranging the social and political relations so they engender *Heimat*, Bloch's word for the home that we have all sensed but have never experienced or known.
>
> (Bloch 1988: xxxii–xxxiii)

The yearning invoked by a sense of home that we have never known might at this point seem an echo of Morris's 'Waste that has no way' – and, indeed, Bloch's *The Utopian Function of Art and Literature* is replete with allegories of horizons and pathways. Bloch writes of

> [...] an inner horizon which stretches vertically so to speak in self darkness [...] and an outer horizon of large breadth in the light of the world. Both horizons are filled with the same utopia.
>
> (1988: 155)

Whilst the absence of prospective horizon leads to a reality of 'the dead, namely naturalists and empiricists, who bury their dead ones here' when the

> [...] horizon is continuously kept in sight reality appears there as what it is concretely: as a network of paths of dialectical processes that take place in an unfinished world, in a world that would be totally unchangeable without the enormous future, the real possibilities within it.
>
> (1988: 155)

So in sharp contrast to Morris' wistfulness and loss of direction, Bloch's insistence on finding dialectical pathways and horizons emphatically rejects any melancholic or sentimental tone, or indeed, history as a waste with no way: when Bloch speaks of the anticipatory illumination in terms of a 'belated fragment' it is 'not sentimental ruin' (1988: 151) but rather *created in the work itself* – something that emerges as an element of incompleteness despite the skills of the artist, *transformed through the utopian pressure* (1988: 151, italics in original). For Bloch, uncertainty becomes the promise of transformatory possibilities: 'the course of the world is still undecided, unended, and so is the depth in all aesthetic information: this utopian element is the paradox in the aesthetic immanence' (1988: 153). As Jack Zipes has it, Bloch's concept of the novum, as 'the startling and unpredictable new is always at the forefront of human experience and indicates the qualitative reutilization of cultural heritage' (1988: xxxvii).

In a later transcribed public conversation with his friend Theodor Adorno, Bloch remarked specifically about both science fiction, and what he termed the *topos* of Utopia:

> Our epoch has brought with it an upgrading of the utopian – only it is not called this anymore. It is called 'science fiction' in technology […] but I believe that we live not very far from the topos of utopia, as far as the contents are concerned, and less far from utopia.
>
> (1988: 3)

Bloch appears here to conflate Utopia with science fiction per se, which is not something I wish to do. However, as Suvin argues, in a capitalist world preoccupied with temporal extrapolation (literary science fiction narratives are compelled to move things to the future to make them plausible), Bloch's sense of *topos* brought and subsequently fused a sense of spatiality to the temporal, to establish an *episteme*, in Suvin's words of 'spatiotemporal covariance, simulsequentialism, or humanist relativism and estrangement: in brief, one of alternate historical realities' (1979: 73–74).

Suvin's use of Bloch is limited to the literary, and, much of science fiction criticism has tended to focus on the written word as the key element in the genre. Returning to Bloch helps establish the possibility of thinking of the novum as something visual. In an insightful short essay 'From the Images of Science to Science Fiction' (2001), the science fiction writer and anthologist Gérard Klein specifically addresses the role of the image appearing as a visual phenomenon – a picture – in speculative fiction. In his essay, Klein seeks to differentiate science fiction in terms of its specifics from both science itself and what I have termed the fictions of science by recourse to conceptions of image and representation. Klein argues that science and philosophy throw up images (*eikons*), which, in turn, inspire representations (*eidons*). Klein uses the example of the image of Jupiter and its four largest moons, seen telescopically for the first time by Galileo, which, augmented by human imagination, resulted in the representation of large celestial bodies of various types orbited by smaller ones; Galileo, of course, duly imagined that the sun was similarly orbited by the Earth and the other planets, for which he was threatened with torture and death by the Roman Catholic Church. Crucially, Gérard Klein is able to use this as a point of differentiation between *eikons* and *eidons* insofar as it allows him to emphasize the role of creative imagination or embellishment in the making of representations:

> It is not enough to find an image of scientific origin in a work to classify it as science fiction. If that image is accessory and could, at least in principle, be excised without

the story breaking down, it is not science fiction. […] The following point should be emphasized: the image must have been elaborated in the imagination of the author.

(2000: 121)

Ultimately of course, Gérard Klein deploys his argument in order to take us back to science fiction literature, and give us a greater understanding of it, but the implications of his argument regarding literary imagery have clear ramifications beyond that, particularly in relation to what Quentin Meillassoux has referred to as a fundamental trait of 'Galileism' – the mathematization of nature (2008: 113). Klein's recourse to an imagist understanding of science fiction literature, and what he refers to as the influence on the likes of Jonathan Swift (who I discuss later in Chapter 1) and Voltaire of 'images emanating from science' (2001: 123) has a corollary: the extent to which images emanating from non-science fiction sources influence and condition the imagery of science fiction: in other words science fiction's 'Ur-images'. To this end, in this book it follows that I will sometimes have recourse to non-science fiction visual sources.

It is with this in mind that the present book explores the porous boundaries between the 'images emanating from science' and those emanating from elsewhere to examine the visual culture of science fiction in relation to landscape. At times this proceeds via that which is unseen: Cordwainer Smith declared Pierre-August Côt's *The Storm* (1880) to be the inspiration for his foundational short story Alpha Ralpha Boulevard (2003: 283). Côt's painting contains little landscape beyond that darkening background which surrounds his luminous figures, whereas Smith describes a sweeping vista of clouds, fields and titanic architectural structures – but I believe that is complimentary to my argument: the present book reads across the imagism of science fiction literary form and actual visual renderings, arguing that in either case, science fiction's visualization is central to its claims on the future.

In his essay 'On the Relationship between Imagery, Body and Mind' (1990), the psychologist David F. Marks pointed to the way images condition understanding: viewing Darwinian evolution as a tree of nature (as Darwin did in 1837) emphasizes the growth and divergence of species as 'branches' but suppresses conceptions of mechanisms of natural selection (1990: 18). As Marks observes, creative scientists, such as Darwin, are able to change their mental models or imagistic thinking more easily, allowing for paradigm shifts and revision. However, for the rest of us, a particularly dominant image may remain far longer; the supposed 'tree' image of evolution remains a popular myth, vulnerable to all manner of ill-founded criticism that the actual theory of Darwin and his scientific heirs are impervious to. Nevertheless, as Marks observes, Einstein was an advocate of Imagistic thinking as a liberatory tool, and an earlier example can be found in the work of Galileo's correspondent and interlocutor Johannes Kepler. In his catalogue raisonné of the painter Nicolas Poussin, the art historian Anthony Blunt (1907–83) pointed to the manner in which Poussin's landscape work of his late period reflected the relationship between the new images of scientific discovery, and at the same time, a complex range of allegorical imagery drawn from mythology. Blunt explains how another of Poussin's works, *Apollo and Daphne* (c. 1664), in which the god Mercury is seen stealing the arrows (a metaphor for light beams) from the sun god Apollo, can be read as a commentary upon Galileo's recent discovery that the planets shone not by self-generated light, but rather from the reflected light of the sun. As Blunt (1958: 351–352) observes, whilst Galileo himself was not prone to using mythical allusions in his discussions of the phases and transits of the inner planets Mercury and Venus, Kepler was prone to alluding to such, and Kepler's writing was well known within Poussin's circle in Rome. As I discuss in Chapter 1, Blunt argued that Johannes Kepler freely used mythical images to think through the phenomena of the intellectual or physical world in which he worked. Indeed, for Ernst Bloch, Kepler's achievement was all the more remarkable because of the way Kepler 're-utilized' these formative visual influences:

> It was widely known that Kepler's thought was originally tied to the animistic, especially to the class and qualitative past and essence of nature […] Kepler was not unaware of heritage, but rather that he had one in mind that was remarkably re-utilized.
>
> (1988: 60–61)

The imagery of science fiction can therefore likewise be seen as drawing on this legacy – its imagery thought of as the bricolage of scientific imagism: discarded or still in use, excessively far-fetched or extrapolatively imminent. Of course, in parsing any definition of science fiction, particularly in the context of critical histories of *representation*, one is also drawn to consider the effects of what, in historiographical terms, might be thought of as the 'fictions of science': for example, the discredited evolutionary theories of Jean-Baptiste Lamarck or Trofim Lysenko; various distal explanations of observed or presumed social phenomena that owe their formulations to ideologically informed assumptions, such as those about race and gender; or cultic belief systems arising from pseudo-scientific methodologies or *mythoses*. With regard to the visual cultures of science fiction, the delineation between the genre proper and such 'fictions of science' might seem particularly blurred: film directors and illustrators often seek to create a pseudo-realist effect not only through the presentation of evolved forms of extant or emergent contemporary technology or scientific discovery, but also by instrumentalizing extant ideological forms – Stanley Kubrick's *2001: A Space Odyssey* (1968) is a paradigmatic example of both. This should of course not be surprising since the two are arguably constitutive. As set out in the chapter outline below, this porous differentiation is a theme throughout the present book, and in particular is explored in more detail in Chapter 5 in relation to the work of two visual artists whose work was initially produced not as science fiction per se (although by various means intended or otherwise, it has been subsequently consumed as such), but rather as extrapolation.

As I explain in some of the forthcoming chapters, it is in this regard – the role of technological and ideological extrapolation in visual cultures of science fiction – that the need for critical examination and debate is most pressing. As I have noted above, both science fiction and the literary criticism around it are replete with visual terms such as 'image(s)', 'illustration', 'seeing' and 'viewing' – even the phrase 'landscape' crops up quite frequently. However, in the vast majority of cases, these words are, within the sense of the texts in which they appear, constrained to the role of literary description or metaphor. It would be wrong to dismiss this use of such loaded terms, since in many ways it points to the excess of visuality in science fiction – a point at which the visual obsessions of science fiction unconsciously or otherwise are revealed as Freudian slip.

Landscape Foregrounded

In the invention of stories, cinematic plotlines and protagonists, landscape is typically the passive setting rather than a protagonist in its own right. In this mode, the landscapes of science fiction are invariably passive and Kantian in their sublimity: they temporarily overwhelm the viewer/reader, as they do the story's protagonist, but ultimately are mastered by the viewer/protagonist's recourse to reason in the manner. Both the initial African watering holes and later Moonscapes of Kubrick's *2001* are the opportunity for initial human (or hominid) wonder, but serve merely as settings for formative moments in the story of the mastery of the Universe's secrets. Jean-Luc Picard, the captain of the USS Enterprise in the 1980s TV series *Star Trek: The Next Generation*, flexes the technology at his fingertips with his catch-phrase command 'Make it so!' and, in so doing, offers the anthropocentric corollary to the Kantian moment when the onlooker knows that despite the inestimable or unquantifiable of the sublime object with which s/he is confronted, reason dictates it must, indeed, be so. As in digital gaming, which I discuss in Chapter 2, the typical landscapes and starscapes, are constructed as incidental merely to facilitate the context for stupendous action, yet are typically rendered with considerable labour by teams of digital artists. If Christopher Nolan's *Interstellar* strikes a less confidently anthropocentric tone than either *Star Trek* or Kubrick, it is only at those points at which planetary eco-systems are seen to negate any putative anthropocentric function in supporting human development. To that end, other more willing planetary candidates for subjection have to be found. As Michael Marshall Smith has stated,

> [...] the two things for which science fiction is best known are these: the creation of new environments and the evocation of a sense of wonder [...] Science fiction has traditionally been about space – outer space, the space of distant planets and landscapes.
>
> (2002: xi)

As I suggest below via the work of Leo Marx, since landscape is not just spatiality, but embodies a sense of its histories, thinking of landscape allows us to keep both a sense of spatiality and temporality together, and it is the thesis of the present book that such a utopian impulse is pre-eminently constituted and articulated within the human temporal and spatial nexus – historical time, topographical space – that constitutes the basis of landscape generally, and the landscapes of science fiction particularly. The book therefore seeks to establish how and in what way the landscapes of science fiction may be considered in this context.

As Fredric Jameson argued in his 1981 *The Political Unconscious*: 'Even in preclass society […] collective consciousness is similarly organised around the perception of what threatens the survival of the group: […] the culture of pre-political society organises itself around the external threat of the nonhuman or of nature' (2002: 281).

So, in addition to what I have said above, if we are to take 'the science fiction imaginary' as that which, cognizant of human histories, desires the possibilities of an existence beyond the present socio-economic contingencies and conflicts, beyond contemporary limitations of scientific knowledge and technological abilities, then it is there that such desires re-encounter the symbolization of those natural threats indicated by Jameson.

The visualization of nature manifested in alien landscapes is one which gestures towards a possible Other beyond that around which the contemporary socio-economic subject is constituted – I say 'gesture' here since on many occasions for reasons that should be obvious, such visualizations remain grounded in Earth-like conceits. Nevertheless, as I suggest in Chapter 6, this gesture contained within the representation of science fiction landscapes, has a Levinasian aspect. Jameson's context of nature as external threat raises that fundamental antinomy that depictions of human figures in landscape evokes not only a sense of what is human and what is not but also, *mutatis mutandis*, some sense of being human in a future when such antimonies are negated.

The artist Jeff Wall, whose work has included large-scale landscape photographs in which events previously observed or reported to him are re-staged, has remarked that

> [a] picture tends towards the generic category of landscape as physical viewpoint moves further away from its primary motifs. I cannot resist seeing in this something analogous to the gesture of leave taking, or alternatively, of approach or encounter.
>
> (2007: 170)

'Leave taking' and 'approach' both connote last and first impressions – the sense of initial or summary visual categorization or classification. They also suggest distance – our embodied experience of spatiality. Within the visual realm of science fiction landscapes, this is a point marked by difference and rupture – an encounter with the new or alien, or a departure that leaves us with an unforgettable impression.

A central tenet of this book is that, as a generic category of its visual culture, the landscapes of science fiction are excessive. This excess is denoted in various ways, depending on the medium, but it is always considerable in its demands on human labour: in its literary form, an inordinate amount of words given over to invention and description; in cinema and gaming, the sophistication and inventiveness of rendering either in CGI or traditional matte painting and model making; in science fiction illustration, landscape, more often than not, exacts a considerable amount of effort from the artist as well as occupies a considerable portion of the overall composition.

Despite their established role as facilitators of action, the excessive aspect of the landscapes of science fiction posits them as traces of unspoken anxieties within the genre: for example, that which is non-anthropocentric, marked by geological time rather than merely the referents of human history. To begin to account for the excess of science fiction landscape, therefore, is to acknowledge the elephant in the room of science fiction. To consider how such landscapes are composed and consumed is to examine how we as humans might look afresh, without the comforts of familiarity or complacency. I want to argue here that the case for looking at the world as fragments of the present lodged within fantasies of future historical time can be made *via negativa*, insofar as the future is largely *absent* from much contemporary culture. As a result, such a way of seeing constitutes a radical act, in that it offers the possibility of viewing the world constructively. Moreover, as we can see in the natural sciences, the construction, of 'artificial eyes' – ones that move and scrutinize, and view from different angles, allow us to re-think in ways that allow for temporality, and positionality. As Oliver Morton (2002) says of the first Mars rover, Sojouner, in his book *Mapping Mars*:

> It was Sojourner, more than anything else, that turned the landing site in Ares Vallis into a place […]. Her slow movements brought time to the land, and time is as necessary to a sense of place as space is.
>
> (2002: 230)

Morton's suggestion that movement brings time to the land is something I want to think about and expand upon here: the idea that movement by the robot (as a cybernetic extension of its human controllers) brings a sense of place through its actions is an argument for the significance of agency. As Morton observes, this can apply as much to the sense of temporality as it does to one of spatiality. Either way, the sense of agency allows a view of the robot's actions as part of a fantasy of future potential – of robotics, and of Mars itself. In a catalogue essay entitled 'The Ideology of Space' published to accompany the 1991 Museum of Modern Art, New York exhibition *Denatured Visions: Landscape and Culture in Twentieth Century*, Leo Marx differentiated the notion of space from that of landscape, arguing that the notion of 'space' specifically applied to American ideologies of land. Leo Marx argued that 'landscape' specifically is tied to the emergence of that particular genre of painting in Holland (1991: 62). As Leo Marx also makes clear, the concept of 'Space' plays a crucial ideological role in the context of colonization: namely, the concept of 'Space', without time, excludes whatever was there prior to the 'discovery' of the space in question. In the context of the Americas, Leo Marx argues that the conception of 'Space' is therefore one which excludes the times and histories of peoples and places prior to the arrival of the European settlers. The framing of space in this way creates something that is timeless and unknown – the blank map of *terra incognita*.

That the construction of landscape conflates space and time perhaps reaches some sort of culmination in W.J.T. Mitchell's suggestion (1994: 1) that the word *landscape* be considered as a verb, rather than a noun. As I have indicated above, the corollary of this might be that the destruction of landscape – and in that sense I mean both the physical exploitation of land and the excising of the phrase – is predicated on the separation of the two. It is in that context that Mitchell asserts that landscape 'doesn't merely signify or symbolize power relations: it is and instrument of cultural power' (1994: 1). In doing so, Mitchell makes 'landscaping' an action in time, a corollarizing inversion of landscape as the sum of time and space.

Therefore, in visual terms, science fiction landscape works by way of that which Fredric Jameson has termed 'piquant montages' (2005:276) – the juxtaposition of the familiar with the uncanny, often in a series of overlapping framings and re-contextualizations. In fictions, cinema and the visual field general, folklore or urban myths are mined once more for fresh raw material. The fashion, appealing to the same demographic cinematically, is frequently as much about horror as science fiction, and arguably restarted in the 1990s by a horror film – *Blair Witch Project* (1998). However, films such as *Cloverfield* (2008), *Apollo 18* (2011) and *Troll Hunter* (2011) all follow a similar format, in which some recently discovered, illicitly made or previously suppressed amateur film or video footage is presented as a 'rediscovery' of reframed folklore memory: Godzilla-as-9/11 (*Cloverfield*), conspiracy theories surrounding the Apollo moon landings (*Apollo 18*) and, in the case of André Øvredal's tongue-in-cheek *Troll Hunter* (2011), giants re-framed in the context of an ongoing cover-up by the Norwegian government exposed by curious film students.

It is in this sense that, despite the repetition, what is 'new' is thrown up, revealed or exposed by the re-contextualization – the 're-staging' of the story, its settings, and the landscape or topography in which it unfolds.

Yet it is, therefore, precisely because of this that landscape should be such a central concern of this book. For the most part by definition 'in the background', landscape is arguably the element of the visual that, whilst never having gone away, is most often overlooked. In science fiction, even alien landscapes have to appear *natural* – insofar as they have to appear convincing – albeit presented in a manner suitably. It is precisely this aspect – how convincing the alien can be – that highlights the issue of realism. This brings me back to the issue of the visual, and the ocularity of science fiction, and why I am arguing here that it is important to think about science fiction beyond the literary. It is precisely the unreal, unconvincing aspect of science fiction – its inability to convince us of its fantasies in written word (in literature) and speech (in acting) – which drives the need for so much visual material: it is an excess, over, beyond and outside the confines of the written word. Of course, our culture is dominated by visual modes of representation in all sorts of ways, not just within science fiction, but science fiction, amongst all the genres, seems excessively preoccupied with this. Moreover, a complex consideration of the role of representation in science fiction beyond the literary not only revitalizes thinking around such issues as realism and the unconscious, but as I will demonstrate, it also collapses what I argue are essentially false differentiations within the literary genre itself, such as those made by advocates of 'hard' science fiction (fiction that is supposedly grounded in, and emphasizes the role of research into the natural sciences) and other forms, which are more concerned with social or cultural issues rather than the natural sciences per se. Much of, say, the work of the New Wave of science fiction writers in the late 1960s and 1970s would fall into the latter category, particularly those writers who, in the context of the revolutions and social movements of 1968–74, engaged with explorations of political and social Utopias and dystopias. Painting appears in science fiction in quite different guises: as illustrations, as backdrops (cinematic mattes) and as 'artist's impressions'. I differentiate this last category from illustration insofar that it plays a particular role in the extrapolations and speculations of science, but is nonetheless subject to shifts in its capacity for realism due to the relational shifts in the opacity of both media and technique, relative to historical conditions of reception. Painting's influence is also felt in terms of the recurrent figure/ground dyad: the figure – often alone, sometimes in a small group – surveying a scene of wonder or menace. As I discuss in Chapter 5, this trope owes much to histories of painting. The dyadic character of the image of the *Rückenfigur* (German, 'back figure') gazing upon an alien landscape has a *chiastic* character. *Chiasmus* is a rhetorical device usually associated with literature and poetry, which creates a two-sided argument. In chiasmus, two associated figures of speech are seen to 'cross over' and, in the process, one element is inverted to create a particular perception. A famous rhetorical example might be John F. Kennedy's 'Ask not what your country can do for you, but what you can do for your country'. Stylistically, chiasmus articulates a supposed balance within a text, but to a particular end: namely, it is reductive, with the second of the two phrases creating discursive closure. *Mutatis mutandis*, the device of chiasmus can also be applied to visual tropes. By counter-posing the anonymous individualized figure to the visual 'field' of the landscape, *Rückenfiguren* of contemporary science fiction qualitatively differ from those of an earlier age: no longer opening potential new horizons for humanity, but rather delineating the horizon of humanity's potential just as so-called 'archeological horizons' define the epochal extent of vanished civlizations within the strata. This, in turn leads me to consider how such chiastic devices can be seen to have a particular political and social role, of which, again, I shall say more in Chapter 5.

Genre, Immanence and Interpretation

Given the status of science fiction as genre, a significant proportion of this book addresses visual forms that in the West have occupied Pierre Bourdieu's 'Sphere of the Legitimizable' rather than the 'Sphere of Legitimacy' (1990: 96). In particular, I have spent time examining and thinking about works by artists designated 'commercial' rather than 'fine art', although some of that commercial work has been subsequently adopted by other fine artists by way of strategies of appropriation or mimesis. However, I have chosen not to interpret the outcomes of practitioners of those fine art strategies in this book, since they are adequately supported and explored by other commentators.

For my own part, as Pierre Bourdieu (1990) long ago established in his time as a Durkheimian sociologist, exploring the work of visual artists that might be said to be *legitimizable* rather than *legitimized* makes for a particularly rewarding experience in thinking through the formative pressures upon art practice, since they are less obscured by mystificatory assimilations of agency, cause and effect into narratives of either autobiographical or formalist purity (as if, one might add, such a purity of experience could ever exist for even the most financially liberated and culturally quarantined artist of whatever form). Whilst the present work is far from claiming any sort of Durkheimian field work as its methodology, I hope that the reader will see, particularly in those chapters in which I have devoted some space to biographical exposition, that I place significance and value upon the visual forms I examine in this book not only as a fan of science fiction, but because they are so clearly subject to what Jameson has, in literary criticism, termed the 'scandal of the extrinsic' (2002: 11).

As I hope is demonstrated in the following chapters, my critical appreciations of science fiction's visualizations of landscape has much recourse to thinking through such scandals, as well as what John Sallis (1987) has termed the 'place of the imagination within presentation' and how such presentations are mediated – the *Darstellung* of German Ideology. Jameson (2002) argues that for Louis Althusser, an understanding of *Darstellung* was the key epistemological concept in theorizing value. In *Reading Capital*, Jameson argues, Althusser suggests that *Darstellung*'s aim is to designate how structure is present (the mode of presence) *in* (which I take to mean 'by way of') its effects. Drawing on Althusser, Jameson argues that effects are not outside of the structure. What Jameson describes as Althusser's 'billiard ball' model of cause and effect allows us to think about structure as imminent in its effects: balls subjected to certain forces at certain angles roll in certain directions, collide with each other and rebound, producing concrete and absolutely contingent results, to the extent that 'the whole existence of the structure consists of its effects, and nothing outside its effects' (2002: 10). As Jameson observes, whilst this billiard ball model of cause and effect is Galilean/Newtonian in a way that is often seen as problematic or outmoded, it continues in various forms of technological determinism, most significantly, *qua* Buck-Morss, in the writings of Walter Benjamin that I mentioned earlier.

Science fiction imagery might be said to contain within it a reflexive duality: in relation to Gérard Klein's thesis referenced above, it reflects – sometimes *via negativa* – science's imagistic thinking, and, at the same time, in its form as commercial genre art, it seems explicitly subject to an extrinsic 'Galilean' process. To remark on this is not merely to indulge in quipping: as Jameson has also remarked, narratives of both allegorical and expressive causality are persistent because they are inscribed as a 'fundamental dimension of our collective thinking', and insouciance or hostility from the viewer to such is the manifestation of resistance to the reading and writing (or, for that matter, visualization, one might add) 'of the text of history within himself' (2002: 19).

Note

1 The provenance of this reported remark by Gibson is unclear, but seems to have been made on several occasions in variant forms. Gibson affirmed he had previously made the statement, and repeated it, during a discussion entitled 'The Science in Science Fiction', broadcast on National Public Radio in the United States, 30 November 1999.

Chapter 1

Land of the Giants: Size and Scale, Macroscopy and Microscopy in the Landscapes of Science Fiction

A Landscape of the Idea and the Idea of a Landscape

Juxtapositions of size persist as a recurrent element in the landscapes of science fiction. In Johannes Kepler's *Somnium*, a narrative published in 1634 (1967: vii) but probably written 25 years earlier, the narrator describes a flight 'as though he had been shot aloft by gunpowder to sail over mountains and seas' (1967: 16) to the small world of Levania (the Moon) which is inhabited by giants. Edward Rosen (1967) renders Kepler's original Latin thus:

> The whole of Levania does not exceed fourteen hundred German miles in circumference, that is, only a quarter of our earth. Nevertheless, it has very high mountains, as well as deep and wide valleys; to this extent, it is muych less of a perfect sphere than our earth is. Yet it is all porous and, so to say, perforated with caves and grottoes everywhere [...] these recesses are inhabitants' principle protection from heat and cold [...] Whatever is born on the land or moves about on the land attains a monstrous size. Growth is very rapid. Everything has a short life, since it develops such an immensely massive body.
>
> (1967: 27)

It is the *seeing* of discrepancies of scale in landscapes that are either miniaturized or outsized that introduces overtones of the uncanny or estrangement: the everyday rendered extraordinary and fantastical. Simple shifts in scale are a form of transformation which simultaneously preserves the particular iconicity of a representation, whilst fundamentally transforming the viewer's relationship with it. Shifts in scale are, arguably, a primal form of manipulation; children famously ignore perspective, to draw large those things which dominate their lived experience. Dramatic differentials in scale appear repeatedly in the landscapes of science fiction, either in their embodied form, as giants or more commonly as artefacts constructed by humans or alien others. A subcategory of this sense of the alien could be described as that of 'humans made alien by the passage of time': the trope of the Ozymandian artefact, originating in the distant past – particularly the pre-historic or the post-historic future. The manner and circumstances in which giants are located in science fiction originates in their place within an Arcadian 'landscape of the idea' and inversely, it is through the giant that an idea of landscape is constituted.

In his story *The Other World: The States and Empires of the Moon*, sometimes published as *Journey to the Moon* (1654), Cyrano De Bergerac's narrator is captured by beast-men – giants who lope and gallop on all fours – and taken to their city. The landscape of Cyrano's novel is simultaneously that of the Moon and also that of the Book of Genesis: for Cyrano suggests that the stories of the Creation, the Noachic flood and the Earthly paradise are those of interactions between the Earth and our satellite world, whose denizens, reciprocally, regard the Earth as *their* satellite.

Despite the ostensible familiarity of the biblical/lunar landscape – it is, apparently, that of his religious schooling – Cyrano's narrator finds he does not easily fit in. First castigated by Enoch the Just and expelled from the Garden of Eden, the Narrator's capture by giants takes place in the unknown terrain beyond, when the certainties of the Earthly paradise have been taken from him, reminding us, perhaps, that encounters with new landscapes inevitably raise doubts about belonging.

Cyrano's giant lunar captors make sport of him, attaching him to a lead for the entertainment of a baying mob. A bystander – a visitor from the Sun – eventually speaks to him in Greek, reminding him that much the same would happen to one of the beast-men should he find himself caught by humans. The ensuing dialogue further inscribes Cyrano's Moon as a mirror world to our own, and, *mutatis mutandis,* the passage between the two involves chiastic cross-overs and inversions. In the sky, we find the grounds of the Earthly Paradise; whilst the human qualities the solar visitor values are not the power and glory of kings, but the humility of hermits. In the Lunar landscape, sexual symbolism of the Narrator's world is likewise reversed or questioned: he is mistaken for the female of his species by his captors and ordered by their King to sleep with another captive man, in the hope they might mate; at court he finds Lunar aliens hanging metal phalluses on their belts as signs of fertility and life, instead of the death-symbolizing swords preferred by their Earthly counterparts.

A Freethinker, a materialist and a lover of both sexes, before becoming a writer, Cyrano had himself, famously, been a brave and adventurous soldier. His short life – he died at the age of 36 – was one that challenged both the territorial and the social precepts of a changing world, and encountered various ambitious constructions designed to reflect upon or effect such changes (from Atomist philosophical circles to the cannon, siege engines and explosive mines at the Siege of Arras). As in his personal life and his writing, so elsewhere: in general, it might seem that European landscapes of the seventeenth century are ones of inversions and reversals – a continent wracked by wars, popular insurgencies and autocratic reaction made all the more vicious by developing pyro-technologies. Intriguingly – but not unpredictably for a student of the materialist philosopher Pierre Gassendi – Cyrano proposes that stories of supernatural phenomena such as 'shades […] spectres, and phantoms' are, in fact, remembered past visits to Earth by these alien visitors from the Sun, who live for 'three or four thousand years'. Cyrano's worldview is one that therefore recognizes the power of Ur-myths.

Not surprisingly, given such a terrain of refractions and reversals, in Cyrano's *Journey to the Moon*, we find the figure of Diogenes referenced. An emphasis upon presentation of the historical event rather than the representation of history itself, reflected in the extolment of the hermit, similarly finds accord with the actions of the Cynics of the ancient world, who often sought to performatively invert or reverse the accepted orders, values and hierarchies of the world around them. The Cynics preferred action over theoretical reflection and an ascetic life of truth and virtue over the acquisition of wealth and power. In a fabled encounter between Diogenes and Alexander the Great, wherein, having been asked by his royal visitor if there is anything he wants, Diogenes requests that the young and brilliant military adventurer 'stands a little out of my sun' or 'stands away from the light'. Diogenes cuttingly contrasts the 'radiance' accorded to Alexander by the sycophants and politicians surrounding him to the actual radiance of the sun, and implies that Alexander 'the Great' is not only blind to that which really matters – the warmth and light of the true sun – but that his great presence, and the pomp which attends upon it, keeps the small commoners in shadow or darkness.

Yet if such a figure as Diogenes the Cynic can wander unimpeded through the landscapes of Cyrano the Materialist, a decade or so earlier we also find him in a painting by the Neo-Stoic painter Nicolas Poussin. There need not necessarily be an inconsistency here, insofar as Diogenes's rejection of pomp and his extolment of humility would appeal equally to each, to their respective interpretive ends: however, Diogenes, as a destabilizing figure, is left isolated in the pastoral landscapes of Poussin – whereas in Cyrano his legacy is made, by allusion, to speak to the throng in which the hero finds himself.

As Anthony Blunt (1958) remarks in his catalogue raisonné of Poussin, the artist went 'beyond the humanist conception of nature as something which can be controlled by man and made to act in accordance with his rationalist conception of the universe' (1958: 313). Poussin, Blunt argues, was an artist engaged with philosophy and the intellectual debates of his time, and, as such, his late landscapes became landscapes of ideas (1958: 4). It is in this context that Poussin's influential paintings, replete with juxtaposition and the perception of landscapes in which such are situated, repay close inspection in the context of my discussion here. Again, in contrast to Cyrano's giants, who live as a community, Poussin's giants are for the most part alone, or separated from the group: we see this in his 1648 painting, *Landscape with Polyphemus*, where the lone giant Cyclops sits atop a distant Mount Etna, with his back to us, wistfully playing his pipes in memory of his lost love.

The trope of the distant giant is one seen in many paintings. J. M. W. Turner uses it both with humanoid giants – for example his own painting of *Polyphemus Derided by Ulysses* (1829), and in his portrayal of a gigantic crocodilian dragon in *The Goddess of Discord Choosing the Apple of Contention in the Garden of the Hesperides* (1806). As with both Turner's and Poussin's portrayals of Polyphemus, the dragon here is shown basking on a distant mountain ridge, away from those it is charged by the gods with protecting. The dragon's relatively faint colours effectively render it aloof from any immediate discussion around choice of the goddess. Nevertheless, it remains present as figure of wider contexts: both underlying and overarching. In Robert Zemeckis's 1997 film *Contact*, based on both an original screenplay and intervening novel by Carl Sagan, the huge interstellar transportation device constructed on Earth at alien behest is first glimpsed from afar as a similarly faint pastel toned but ominous structure on a coastline, seemingly aloof from the controversies and politicking swirling around it, but nevertheless, now integral to the world, much like Turner's giant dragon.

Although most often formally defined by its novel form, giantism in science fiction visually emerges as a montage of epic and tragic elements juxtaposed against tropes of scalar normativity. Before man, Apollodorus (1998) writes, the Gigantes – born of a wrathful Ge (Gaia) – rose against the Olympian gods, before being cast down into the abyss of Tartaros, where their continuous writhing causes earthquakes in the world above. In the *Theogony* of Apollodorus, as of Hesiod, the Cyclopes, the one eyed giants are sired, like the Gigantes, by Uranus, the first ruler of the universe (1998: 27–29). Rejected by their father, the Cyclopes – who Virgil, in Book IV of his *Georgics*, calls 'Blacksmith Giants', and compares to industrious bees – become the makers of thunderbolts, and subsequently arm Zeus (Jupiter), the grandson of Uranus, in his battle against his father Cronos (Saturn).

The sense in both the stories of the Cyclopes and the Gigantes is that of giants as primordial, as having 'gone before' – having been born of the Earth before Man, and having worked and made things all through the Golden Age, before the labours of humans commenced, at the dawn of the Age of Silver. The mystery of that which is gigantic is therefore located in time – in its original creation and the subsequent disappearance – as well as in space, where only the indexical trace such as a footprint, ruin or ichnograph remains.

Although variously located by different classical authors in the central region of the Peloponnese peninsula, to the fields around the volcano Etna in Sicily, the definitive landscape of the pastoral ideal remains Arcadia. This sense of Arcadia differs in the hands of different authors, but the recuperation of Classical Greek culture and its re-introduction into Western European intellectual discourse during the Renaissance, reinstituted the concept of Arcadia as an ideal land, simple and rough-hewn, an ur-landscape that, of the Golden Age now lost, was ruled by an older god, Pan, the only god who, in classical legend, is killed. This conception of Arcadia as the landscape of the idea, of an original thought of the creation, inscribes the land of giants as one that, ruled by a god now vanished, presages the world of men in its entirety: it has been through a cycle we may or may not yet follow ourselves.

There are, however, other visual senses in which the gigantic is linked to an 'idea': insofar that the viewer *ideates* (imagines or conceives of an idea of something) through the incomplete visual hint; the traced or sketched outline, which indicates vastness through its incompleteness. Visual indicators of scale often work by being comparably incomplete – the building whose top is half lost in cloud, or the huge orbiting space station with diurnal and nocturnal halves, indicated by myriads of tiny lights. The figuration of the huge often requires a bisection – in Poussin's image of Polyphemus, for example, a line of birds crosses in the middle distance, intersecting with the mountainside upon which the giant sits; in Francisco Goya's (1746–1828) drawings and paintings made amidst the horrors of the Peninsula War, their feet are lost below the horizon. Whilst such visual conceits are repeated visual tropes of the sublime, what arises from this particular example is that giants and the gigantic remain unknowable and fragmented, because their entirety is too stupendous for human comprehension.

It is in this context of the incompleteness of depiction that colour also plays an important part when giants and humans are kept separate: that is to say in the depiction of the *separation* between the human and the giant, in its evocation of distance and size. Faintness, the juxtaposition of slight shifts in tone played off against one another, contributes to a sense of unreadability in distant giants as much as incompleteness of outline. There is a corollary to this in the experience of astronauts. Just as the conditions of earthly light – and the conventions of its depiction – dictate that which is large and distant is portrayed as increasingly bluish-grey, due to the effects of the refraction of the Earth's atmosphere. During the Apollo moon landings, astronauts reported some difficulties in judging distance because distant objects did not look fainter, nor was there a greater blue content to the colours of distant mountains in the way there is on Earth, because there was no atmosphere to 'dilute' the deep colours of shadows by refraction, and the shadow of a near object appeared as dark as the shadow of a mountain or hill a mile away.

Terrain, Technology and Precariousness: Traversing Landscapes on Giants' Shoulders

Science fiction landscapes do not, of course, limit depictions of the gigantic to the passively distant. But they do often conflate size with some form of detachment or elevation – and, as such, a moral or ethical shift. Shifts in size are accompanied by shifts in power – whether increased or diminished. The foregrounding of the gigantic however, is most frequently accompanied by a sense of precariousness or danger: the giant robot or mutant monster running amok, the crash-landing spaceship and so on. Just as I have drawn upon Poussin's image of Polyphemus in my discussion of the distant giant, there is a fascinating counterpoint to the tendency to locate the giant in the distance to be found in a late painting by the same artist, entitled *Blind Orion Seeking the Sun* (1658, Figure 1).

Poussin's painting places the giant in the foreground and amongst men, as he gropes his way, blinded by a cloud in front of his eyes, in search of the sun. The effect of this visual juxtaposition is bizarre, disturbing, uncanny: a giant man, being directed by a small man riding on his shoulders. This is not simply a matter of relative height – say, a seven-foot tall man carrying one who is four foot: here there is a scalar juxtaposition. Poussin's arrangement of the other figures in the painting allows the viewer to both feel sympathy for Orion, but not ultimately identify him as kindred. Rather Orion is presented as displaced from the group. Once the normative human height is established by reference to the onlookers, the man riding on his shoulders, the trees and so on, the viewers' relationship with Orion becomes somewhat reified – he is at least in part a thing. At this point in the myth, the giant Orion is blind to the world around him, and so has to be guided. In his search for the sun, Poussin's Orion is guided by Cedalion, who is the man standing upon his shoulders, steadying himself with his left hand upon the side of Orion's tousled head. Cedalion gestures forward with his other hand, but his gaze is downwards towards the top of Orion's head, as if he is speaking to the giant. The effort and concentration of the two, man and giant, as they make this precarious progress, is contrasted with the figure of the goddess Diana, who, despite her alien green skin and divine status, strikes a humanly relaxed pose – hand on hip, leaning with head quizzically propped, standing on a portion of the occulting clouds which precede Orion and Cedalion. The relative poses of Diana and Cedalion are telling: Diana, a deity of elemental force, remains indifferent, not merely looking on, but rather brazenly exhibiting the artless grace of her own divine powers by standing upon a cloud; Cedalion, by contrast, is actively piloting the giant. Diana's clouds are backlit by an unseen sun; their silver lining hints at a happy ending to the quest of Cedalion and Orion, but it also indicates her indifference to that of which she has plentiful supply: she has nothing of Orion's urgent need for the light, and can turn away from it if and when she pleases. Diana gazes on at the human-giant contraption as bemused by its contingent oneness: less a friend helping another, but a human-giant hybrid producing an unexpected symbiosis. Through their unlikely contrivance, the human can travel amidst the clouds, previously the exclusive preserve of the gods, whilst the giant can regain his vision.

Poussin shows Orion carrying his bow and wearing his quiver of arrows. His face, seen in profile, seems resolute, as if he is concentrating, carefully listening to the instructions of Cedalion. Although they proceed along a rough unpaved path, the landscape around them is hilly and wild – what in later centuries to that of Poussin would come to be regarded as 'Picturesque'. However, to Poussin's audience of 1658, such ciphers would signal the lack of human habitation and cultivation of the land, rather than a cultivated taste for a natural world being pushed back by industrialization, as it would come to do in the industrial age. In the foreground of Poussin's painting, broken and rotted tree stumps indicate both the lack of farming and the potential trip hazards to the barefooted Orion and his career ahead. As if to emphasize this, Orion's extended right foot steps into a shadow thrown by a rocky outcrop to the left of the picture – a step into the unknown. Despite being newly blinded, Poussin portrays Orion moving purposefully along the path. He could fall, but he is not shown to be falling. Later, his sight restored and his hunting skills invincible, Orion will threaten to hunt down every living creature on the Earth. Gaia, the Earth Mother, intervenes, sending a scorpion that fatally stings the hunter before irreversible damage is done.

It is said that, having been blinded and banished as punishment for sexually assaulting Merope, the daughter of his host Oenpion, at a drunken feast, Orion was pitied by Hephaestus, one of the sons of the goddess Hera, who himself is the god of craft, blacksmithing and technology. Cedalion, the youthful servant of Hephaestus, is befriended by Orion and is charged with guiding Orion towards the rising sun, riding upon the giant's shoulders. In this context, Cedalion, as a worker of the new technology of blacksmithing, appears atop Orion, the perfect armed hunter, as the pilot of a huge robotic killing machine, or 'mech' – akin to the Imperial AT-AT vehicles in Irvin Kershner's *The Empire Strikes Back* (1980), the giant 'Loader' exo-skeleton which enables Ellen Ripley to defeat the Alien queen in James Cameron's *Aliens* (1986), or the 'Amplified Mobility Platforms' of Cameron's later film *Avatar* (2009) but also, decades earlier, in Pavel Klushantsev's film *Planet of Storms* (USSR,

1961), where we find a giant robot carrying cosmonauts on its shoulders across a river of lava on the surface of Venus.

At once potentially invincible, but also potentially vulnerable, the extent of each opposite plays out as events unfold. In science fiction, Mechs are imagined as sophisticated machines, built of high tech materials no doubt, but ultimately, they are built from substances extracted from ores and wrought into shape. Interestingly, however, redolent of blind Orion relying on Cedalion's eyes and brain, Mechs are frequently portrayed as headless – their torsos boxes of weapons systems with arms (in both senses of the word) and legs. This is the case in the robotic versions such as those in Paul Verhoeven's *Robocop* (1987), the *Terminator* series of films, and also in their piloted form in James Cameron's *Avatar* (2009).

Again, thought of in this context, Cedalion's qualities as cultured human, elevated by the gods, are contrasted with Orion's diminished and impaired status. Like the Titans writhing below ground, Poussin's scruffy haired, bare chested Orion reflects the tones of his surroundings in the browns, blues and greys of his skin and musculature, and the dun colour of what little animal hide clothing he has contrasts sharply with the cultivation of Cedalion's bright yellow woven short robe. In contrast to the light touch of Cedalion's extended fingers against the side of his head, Orion grasps his bow firmly, in a fully formed fist that manages to convey both immense strength and the possibility of stress and ham fistedness: without showing his face fully, Poussin manages to portray Orion in a state of distress and dependency at being blind, but also in state of gritty determination to not be defeated by his affliction, and in this sense we see him lurching forward under Cedalion's guidance perhaps all too quickly. In the painting, three earthbound human figures look on at the giant-human combination. The closest, a bearded figure in blue robes holding a staff, looks up as if saying something: and perhaps, after all, Cedalion is not speaking to Orion, so much as waving to the figure below. A conversation along the lines of 'Are you sure you will be alright up there?' is then imaginable: a question which of course, the giant can have neither time nor truck with, since to journey thus is his only option, but to which Cedalion, by contrast, must respond collectively. This dynamic, again, sets human and giant apart: like an airship, or sail boat, its direction and fate multiply, determined by pilot and fortuitous gusts of wind, Orion has no choice, and his fate is determined by prior events. His new friends, the humans around him are merely chapters in a longer story. Like an oil tanker, it will take more than a slight nudge to the side of head, or a shout from below, to alter his overall course. Coming up the hill, the other two humans in the picture, perhaps travellers, seem to express incredulity, perhaps at the thought of the unlikelihood of the human-giant hybrid and its unlikely symbiosis lasting as far as the foot of the steep slope they have just climbed.

Thus the scion of technology attempts to martial and direct the force he is notionally in command of, and precarious progress is made. Although improved, the view ahead for the Orion-Cedalion combination is still uncertain and partial, in contradistinction, of course, to the purview afforded the goddess Diana. Cedalion and Orion are compelled then, to exalt in their precarious relationship, both with each other and the hazards of the world around them, and this lies at the core of the tragedy so unfolding. For if Orion is, as a giant, indifferent to the affairs of the miniscule humans around him, and even that of the human astride him, it is a *tragic* indifference, in that whilst his ultimate fate might, as a giant, lie elsewhere, for the meantime at least, his precarious existence and the vicissitudes of his companions and the journey he must make are bound up together. By contrast, the indifference of Diana is the indifference shown by the rugged landscape: the beauty of Poussin's distant crags and the tree filled gullies of the middle distance are *elementally* indifferent. This is an aspect of tragedy to which I will return later. Perhaps this contributes to its uncanny quality, and the strange lack of register in seeing two different scales of the human form occupying the same picture plane. Arguably this is something at the core of all conceptions of giants: a conflict between the macro and the micro in relation to space.

As with Cedalion perched atop Orion, giants and humans – or simply the big and the small – are portrayed as incapable of occupying the same place without precarious arrangements that can quickly descend into calamity or conflict. As I discuss below, Swift's *Gulliver's Travels* (1726) extrapolated this brilliantly to the political economy of mercantile exchange and imperial expansion. In André Øvredal's *Trollhunter* (2010), the root of the conflict between humans and trolls lies, again, in this question of the same landscape being occupied by two antagonistic scales of reference. In Øvredal's film, the giant trolls, the largest breed of which appears towards the end of the film is as large as a skyscraper, are portrayed as blight to the contemporary picturesque Norwegian landscape – a blight which requires extermination: this in turn necessitates a particularly dour form of pest control officer, versed in the taxonomy as well as the diverse biology and habits of trolls, as well as being tooled and trained in the science of their extermination. What makes *Trollhunter* particularly ecologically poignant in this respect is the way the creatures are portrayed as being integral to the landscape of Norway. As denizens of remote mountains, gullies, caves and forests, the trolls are clearly as much entitled to the landscape as humans. Moreover, as with Poussin's *Orion*, their colouration and texture makes them appear intrinsically part of the landscape.

The appearance of giants as a somehow integral, *native*, part of the landscape in this way emphasizes a sense of human alienation from the landscape. If an encounter with any landscape does, indeed, raise such questions as to what extent one might claim to 'belong', the supposition of giants is to suggest another older presence that has more claim to belonging than us: the possibility of some lost elder race that has gone before. In *The Georgics*, both the giant brothers Otus and Ephialtes, 'who leagued themselves to hack the heavens down' by stacking three mountains of Thessaly on top of each other, and the fields on the slopes of Mount Etna, formerly worked 'by the Cyclopes', are cited by Virgil as ancient legends associated with particular, real locations within the landscape (1999: 66–67). In contrast to Poussin's Neo-Stoicism, but in line with Cyrano's Materialism, Virgil's Epicurean philosophy leads him to embed these in the cycles of the seasons and the movement of the constellations, as counterpoints to the minutiae of human endeavours such as crop management and animal husbandry. In *The Georgics*, Virgil's reference to the Gigantes comes, therefore, directly after a happy image of a market goer returning from town with 'a lump of black pitch' or 'a whetstone ready dressed', traded for (olive) oil or 'cheap apples'; likewise, the Cyclopes appear after detailed advice on weather forecasting based on daily observations of the clouds, the moon and the sun.

Biblical references to giants are located principally in enigmatic references to the Nephilim, and, later, in more explicit accounts of the Rephaim. In both cases, there is again the sense that such giants are 'those who have gone before' – they were in some way 'there first' – and were subsequently defeated by the Israelites themselves, or that calamity befell them at the hands of an expeditious God for and on behalf of the Israelites. I want to suggest here that the enigma of the Nephilim, as they appear in the Bible, lies in their *tragic* indifference to the Israelites amidst the other elemental 'indifference' of the landscape.

In the context of science fiction, this sense of a mysterious other species or race of giant stature that has 'gone before' – as the Nephilim have – is typified in films such as Ridley Scott's *Alien* (1979). The early scenes of *Alien*, of course, deal directly with this sense of vanished giants, when the doomed human spaceship *Nostromo* sets down on an unknown planet. In a landscape of frozen lava fields and a howling Hadean atmosphere, which the ship's android science officer Ash (Ian Holm) describes as 'almost primordial', three members of the Nostromo crew set off in search of the origin of what they believe to be a distress signal. After trekking for some time in the planetary dawn, a huge derelict crescent structure on the horizon, revealed as an ancient spaceship, is found with a fossilized figure of elephantine proportions, the carcass of which a combination of taphonomic processes and the sedimentation of time seems to have melded to the titanic navigation device in which it is seated. It transpires that the giant fossil is an earlier victim of the malignancy the crew is about to encounter. Famously, the crew goes on to discover a chamber underneath the spaceship full of alien eggs – the inference is that either this is, in fact, the greater part of the spaceship itself, sunk beneath the tideline of frozen lava, or that this cavernous space was formed separately but has somehow become connected to the unfortunate space jockey's ship by way of a shaft, down through which the Alien's first victim, Executive Officer Kane (John Hurt) descends to his fate. Jameson (2005: 325) remarks that the 'two aliens' situation that is thus created in *Alien* (and, as he notes, also in A. E. Van Vogt's seminal short story 'Black Destroyer' to which the 1979 film bears strong similarity) is one of Freudian splitting, wherein the father is both the object of 'socially obligatory love and also of deep unconscious hostility and agressivity'. The alien other is thus sundered: one speculates that a possibly benign fossilized alien might well have protected the trespassing Kane and his comrades, or at least counselled them to the incipient danger, but the 'other half' – the malignancy of natural law imperatives wins out.

However, I want to focus here on a different reading, one which arises out of the psycho-analytical triad that is presented here, one that concentrates upon the landscape of the primordial planet – later, in James Cameron successful sequel *Aliens* (1986) given the nomenclature LV426 – as a land that was once one of giants that still harbours terrors of which the giants tried to tell, and suggest an accordant reading. To evoke the phrase 'land of the giants' in this way, inevitably but incidentally, evokes Irwin Allen's eponymous TV series of 1968–70 – and to an extent, so be it, for there are parallels here – but the unknown planet of *Alien* is a land in which the erotics found in the television series – of which I will deal in more detail later – is as extensively purged as is possible, so that only the most residual sense of the parental remains in the cipher of the fossilized space jockey – namely, like the Nephilim, that it was, bigger, older and 'went before' the human explorers. In *Alien*, the real of the planet's landscape – its stark *elemental* indifference to the travails of all life – is set against the *tragic* indifference of the unrousable alien parent to the diminutive human explorers, evocative perhaps of Edith Nesbit's short story 'The Deliverers of Their Country', from her 1900 collection *The Book of Dragons*, in which two children vainly try to awaken a graven effigy of Saint George to free England from a plague of dragons. It is between the real of the landscape, and the symbolic order of the dead giant that has gone before, that the insistent drives of Eros and Thanatos are synthesized into the egotist desires of the crew – from Kane's initial probing and avaricious curiosity to Ellen Ripley's release from the cycle of suffering and destruction into blissful sleep in the film's closing frames. If, therefore, we are asked to regard giants as an elder race, whose parental size infers our own immaturity, then giants become symbols of time, but also time's first victim: those who have gone before.

In this sense, both the similarity between the sinuous cords and folds of igneous rock that forms the planet's surface and the calciferous exoskeleton of H.R. Giger's fossilized alien signals an ultimate lack of differentiation between the two in the records of geological time: the truth of the grave. In this sense the space jockey has become part of the rock, its form merging with that of the planet, just as Orion's hue signals he is part of the Earth, but also, in the manner of those who have known God, privy to some greater ancient truth, which comes at the cost of transcending, in some fatally flawed manner, the smaller affairs of humans. This iconic similarities of the textures of landscape and those of older, ancient forms of life effectively evokes the sense of an ancient order perilously disturbed by the soft, younger flesh of humans, much in the manner of the chilling awakening of the giant bronze Titan, Talos, 'moulded by Hephaestus […] for all the world to see' in Don Chaffey's 1963 film *Jason and the Argonauts*.

The notions, therefore, of differentials in size or scale we find in science fiction are invariably bound up in the genre and its cultural precursors with *ideality*, reflected recursively throughout the genre itself in references to God or gods. Consider for example, H.G. Wells's *The Food of the Gods*, Asimov's *The Gods Themselves* (1972) or, in Kim Stanley Robinson's *Red Mars* (1992), the gently ironic evocation of some mythological 'Big Man' by secular scientists and atheist colonists when describing sublime aspects of a Martian landscape, the canyons and mountains of which are far bigger than their Earthly analogues.

This relationship with the landscape is therefore one of idealist *projection*, and also deferred or displaced responsibility. The gouged or damaged terrain, the despoiled landscape, are the sites of some externalized aspect of human endeavour made strange by its colossal aspect – the traces of titanic force unleashed, or the abandoned implements and engines of such, or the continued abode of a rejected Other.

One of the tragically ostracized giant children in Wells's *Food of the Gods,* which I explore below, is compelled to live in such an abandoned working – an English chalk pit – whilst elsewhere wars are fought across fields, and towns are overrun by giant vermin unwittingly nurtured by the same scientific concoction. The key affective element here of such giganticism is that moment of estrangement: the relational shift which makes the totality of the image simultaneously one in which the giant is seen to interact with its surroundings, whilst at the same time seem to be absorbed in a different register of activity due to the different view it has of that world. The interstellar *Herrenvolk* of Cordwainer Smith's *Alpha Ralpha Boulevard* (1961) encounter human-animal hybrids who have colonized abandoned subterranean sewers and service tunnels, whilst giddily exploring giant towers that rise over windy hills into the stratosphere of old Earth, abandoned for millennia and littered with the whitened bones of their distant ancestors.

Macro and Micro: Landscape Viewed by Large and Small

Imagine the following: a suburban area in England, some sunny weekend or bank holiday afternoon, a decade or more before World War I. Cumulus clouds of white and grey doves fleck the blue sky, their shadows moving with a stately pace over an intricate patchwork of fields, hedgerows, streets and factories. All the chimneys stream coal smoke. The world is largely made of wood, iron, steel, brick and stone. In the streets the smell of coal and horses is common, the smell of petrol is extremely rare. Down the cinder lane and across the small bridge that crosses the railway line, in the midst of a stretch of arable land, a crowd has gathered. Something quite extraordinary looms over them. The extraordinariness of this object lies both in its texture, form and colour, and also, most significantly, in its size and function.

Such a landscape is, of course, for the most part, the landscape of H. G. Wells. Warwick Goble (1862–1943), who produced contemporaneous illustrations for Wells's *War of the Worlds*, portrays this landscape partially occluded by the Martian tripods, in such a way that the Martian machines lean or lurch precariously into the picture frame, often from the top corner. Typically a purveyor of eroticized art nouveau nymphs, faeries and Orientalist themes, the landscapes that Goble produced for the serialization of *The War of the Worlds*, a full seventeen years before the outbreak of World War I, stand out from the rest of his oeuvre due to his repeated overlaying of recessional planes of flat shapes and silhouettes that seem to carry premonitions of the angular flat trench paintings of landscapes of C.W.R. Nevinson or Paul Nash. Produced seventeen years prior to World War I, Goble's lattice-legged tripods are fighting machines redolent of iron bridges and dock-cranes, frequently shown partially in the picture frame, partly out of it, leaning in from the top corner of the picture as if to remind the viewer that they have just arrived from the sky, their tentacles lashing across the picture frame, less in an endorsement of *Jugendstil* whiplashes and ogees that characterize his other work, than an aggressive sneering parody of them. Moreover, the flat rendering the hills of Surrey or the outline of Windsor Castle redraws the English landscape as schematic or stage flat. Later in the story as the Martians succumb to Earthly diseases, Goble portrays their war machines becoming flat silhouettes lodged in the landscape, as if monuments to their own demise.

According to Andy Sawyer (2005: 195) Wells never liked Goble's visualization of his machines. Certainly the novel suggests the Martian machines possess quick, lithe, whip like movements of grotesque efficiency. With hindsight, it is not only bridges and cranes that Goble evokes, but also the lattice and helical frames of the developing airships of the end of the nineteenth century and the beginning of the twentieth. Goble's own Martian flying machine slides amidst the clouds as a series of connected cruciforms and polygons, blotting out the sun as it spills its poisonous spores, but the illustration by A.C. Michael for Wells's *War in the Air*, published in *Pall Mall* in 1908, appear as near-future extrapolations of an already extant form: huge tear drop shape airships, their blunt noses escutcheoned with Teutonic imperial coats of arms, pushed by a single fast spinning propeller, glide in swarms over tiny terraced houses, church halls and distant factory chimneys far below, the facades of which are illuminated by the slanting sunlight that suggests the end of things. The horizon is lost in the hazy smog of a heavy industry that suddenly seems futile in the face of the coming of airpower. Indeed, the flatter, more distant airships in Michael's rendering seem ready to merge with the smog, as if opportunistically using the smoke of the city below as camouflage. In contrast to any traffic through the winding streets below, the airships in Michael's image seem to be confidently moving in straight lines, maintaining formation.

Collisions of Sky and Ground

The landscape of Wells – whether it be the expanding suburban sprawl that increasingly squeezed the rural corners of industrial Europe, or hills and estuaries further afield – is also the landscape frequently pictured in an extraordinary documentary book assembled and published in the late 1970s by the writer and novelist Len Deighton and Arnold Schwartzman, in a strangely fascinating documentary book entitled *Airshipwreck* (1977). In this book, Deighton and Schwartzman assembled an extraordinary sequence of rare photographs, showing those moments when machines of unprecedented scale and capability came crashing into the lives of ordinary folk: it relates the details of successive disasters which befell airships during their development and heyday, from Wölfert's first petrol powered dirigible of 1897 to the end of commercial airships epitomized by the *Hindenburg*'s fiery demise at Lakehurst, New Jersey, in 1936. The photographs reveal a parochial world of clogs and shawls, Edwardian Sunday best suits and frocks, bicycles and haywains, intersected by a new technology of aluminium, hydrogen envelopes and propellers (Figure 2). The still airborne portions of half deflated behemoths loom overhead whilst their tailfins lie crumpled on the ground: river barges lie at anchor whilst a huge silver torpedo shape that once lay poised like a pond-skater now lies ruptured and twisted amidships, awaiting a tow. Unearthly silver fabric reflects sunlight, whilst the lattice metal framework it tautly encased, wraps itself like a slain dragon around a hillside. These complex juxtapositions of the Edwardian industrialized world – and its pre-World War I optimisms in the efficaciousness of the mechanical – are, of course, deliriously played out in the genre of steampunk, that alter post-modernity that presents as the antinomy of William Gibson's cyberpunk fictions. Steampunk's emphasis upon visually intricate mechanism – contrivance, contraption, modes of dress – arguably present as an embodied visual excess in contrast to cyberpunk's disembodiments. However, my chief focus here is specifically on contrasts of scale, rather than stylization.

For Wells, it seems, the size and scale of the New was what distinguished it – from this flowed its revolutionary potential. To be big, in Wells's petty English landscape, is to have command, and to be superior. Size equates not only with power, but also speed and efficiency. It shaped his view of the future. Wells's lesser celebrated 1904 novel, *The Food of the Gods*, begins when two bungling scientists develop a growth stimulant, which, over time, is released into the ecological cycles of a comically petty late Victorian England. Although the so-called 'Boomfood' provokes a political response in the shape of the rise of a reactionary opportunist politician, the forces of the state and government per se are largely absent from Wells's novel. As a result, extant human affairs, and the extent of its territorializations are presented as Lilliputian and incapable of wielding any substantial power.

In the tradition of the ur-images of Arcadia, Wells too, deals with the ideality of giants. After describing in detail the initial plagues of giant weeds, fungi, wasps, rats and other vermin and their effect upon the human population, the novel focuses upon the gradual rise of children who have been raised upon the new food. Wells does this by describing two particular aspects: the first being the young giants' interactions with the landscape, and the second being their awakening moral revulsion at the social order they find around them. This is reflected in their treatment of that late Victorian landscape of small towns, meandering lanes and cinder path bridleways. As children and adolescents, the giants construct 'wheeled engines […] that no road in the world had room for, no bridge could bear […] capable of two hundred and fifty miles an hour'; at the same time they grow up, not only appalled by social injustice and gender discrimination, but determined to act, and to see such activism as fun:

> 'Doing nothing's just wicked. Can't we find out something the little people want done and do it for them – just for the fun of doing it?'

> 'Lots of them haven't houses fit to live in', said the second boy. 'Let's go and build 'em a house close up to London that will hold heaps and heaps of them and be ever so comfortable and nice[…] Fancy! They make their women – women who are going to be mothers – crawl about and scrub floors!'

> (2010: 144)

The story of Wells's young giants is therefore one of their idealist disregard for the material reality of the extent of landscape in which they emerge – one which cannot possibly accommodate them, and to re-landscape the world by seeing it with different eyes. With this in mind, the young giants – first through play, and later by design, set about energetically ignoring the topographic constraints around them, and so, in the process, colliding with the constraining social and legal factors also. Wells presents this as an inevitability borne of their physical condition. Not only do the giants assert that what they see is wrong with the world, and set about changing it, but rather, they are compelled from birth to live in conflict with the topographies and order they are born into, because the ocularity Wells bestows upon them renders extant scale physically restrictive and socially oppressive.

It is in keeping with the logics of his novel's structure that Wells should focus on the small world of South East England. Indeed, not only does Wells offer detailed descriptions of that landscape both as the rural patchwork of fields, villages and railways, prior to the advent of the Food, and subsequently as a transitional topography reshaped by giants – but he also reflexively frames his own authorial voice in that context – whilst the wider, international impact of Boomfood is alluded to, the wider world remains vague and sketchy, bereft of detailed description. Thus the retreat from the international contexts – an idealization of a lost unchanging peaceable England extolled, in the novel by the 'Reactionaries', is counter-posed to the progressive idealist projections of the giants.

As is clear from their concern over social injustice and poverty, Wells's giants are not blind to the greater issues played out within – and ultimately visually determined by – the landscape. Nevertheless, they are blind to its particular material details. In Wells's contrivance, of course, such materiality is necessarily bound up with matters of size. In one telling sequence, redolent of Goya's colossi, the young giant Caddles is visited by the local vicar, who finds his 'huge form seated upon a hill – brooding as it were upon the world'. Arriving at the place where the young giant is sitting, intent on remonstration, the vicar changes his mind and leaves unnoticed, pondering, as he does, that 'no-one on earth had the slightest idea what this great monster thought about when he saw fit to rest from his labours'. Because the respective engagements with the materiality of normative humans and the giants are, literally, incommensurate, there is no shared topology, and topology is, in Wells's novel, the prerequisite of any putative shared understanding. Because their material engagement is radically altered – reaching higher, seeing further, moving faster – not only is the giants' view of the landscape around them fundamentally different, but they are constantly imagining the *social* world around them as *potentially* different. Like the airships portrayed a few years later by A.C. Michael, the giants of Boomfood wish to travel in straight lines, cutting through the landscape, as well as moving over it. In this sense, and insofar as they imagine the ways in which it could be better, Wells's giants inhabit an ideal world of their own, composed of vectors and planes: but they are, as a result forced to repeatedly ground that ideality in the materiality of their surroundings, and work out solutions spawned by their own incompatibility with the world around them.

Wells's novel is one in which an emergent community – the giants – precipitates radical shifts in visualization and interaction with the landscape. The giants' radically transformative failure to appreciate the abstractions of normative convention and extant law is a direct consequence of the scalar shift in their constructed topography, and the ocular shift in Wells's imagining of how they would see the world differently:

> We see over their walls and over their protections; we look inadvertently into their upper windows; we look over their customs; their laws are no more than a net about our feet […].
>
> (2010: 157)

It is also their size that excludes them from both the extant architectures and the prevailing ideological apparatuses of schools and churches during their childhood. Wells describes how, for a while, the giant children are drawn out of curiosity to the schools and churches by the sound of the singing communities housed within, but they are discouraged from loitering outside, and, in time, are shown to withdraw first into introspection as on the occasion witnessed by the vicar above, and then towards a suitably larger scaled idealism particular to their own experience:

> 'It's all very well', said the second to the first, 'but I don't always just want to play about and plan. I want to do something *real* you know'.
>
> (2010: 144)

The differential in scale is therefore at the heart of this search for 'something real' which in turn creates an explosive disjuncture between the old world and the new arrivals. Insofar as scale is the cause of the giants' differentiation and their inability to adopt a normative reading of the landscape around them, it is also the means through which they seek integration and inclusion, albeit by *force majeure*.

Abstraction and Embodiment in Outsized Landscapes

Whereas Wells's giants grow to experience the landscape and metropolis of Edwardian England as an emergent community, Jonathan Swift's Gulliver experiences community from the outside – first gigantically, and then diminutively. Unlike Wells, Swift presupposes the possibility of meaningful exchange between the very big and the very small – a shared topology. Reflecting the concerns of a satirist aiming at the politics of his time, it might seem at first that Swift hardly mentions landscape at all; but in fact he does, and landscape appears in telling ways. Indeed, the inversions and reversals in scale between The Landscape of the Idea and an idea of landscape, which frame some of my core arguments in this chapter, are particularly notable in *Gulliver's Travels*. In Swift's political satire, the shift which occurs as Gulliver moves, first from England to Lilliput and back, and then, subsequently, from England to Brobdingnag, reflects this.

In Swift's description of Lilliput, where Gulliver finds himself a giant, the actual landscape is hardly described at all, as if its details are too small to be noticed. What references to landscape there are occur as abstractions: measurements of distance, relational comparisons and analogies of size and scale. Only briefly, when Gulliver is first swept ashore, is any sensate description given ('I lay down on the grass, which was very short and soft'). For the most part, the story of Lilliput, which is 1:12 in scale, is one of political absurdity and pointless wars, most famously, in a skit on the Protestant and Catholic eucharists, between the Lilliputians, who cut off the small end whenever they eat boiled eggs, and the inhabitants of Blefuscu, who are 'Big Endian' heretics. Seemingly as a deliberate point, Swift keeps description of Lilliput landscape to a minimum. Details of its flora, fauna or topography are passed over, in anticipation of a separate volume which the narrator, Gulliver, promises will soon be published. As such, the events and politics of Lilliput take place in a space quantified by relatives, but never described in particular detail.

In contrast to Lilliput, Gulliver's arrival in Brobdingnag finds him amongst giants, in whose company he is made to inhabit a range of landscapes, from the 'sharp pointed rocks' of the approaching coastline and the giant barley field into which he first wanders and is nearly trampled by a farmer, to, more tellingly, a topography of female bodies. Whereas in Lilliput, Gulliver is the ward of the King and the military, in Brobdingnag, Gulliver is protected by girls and women, first the farmer's daughter, and then the queen. He is kept in boxes and carrying cases, and played with as a doll. In Brobdingnag, Swift's narrative takes on a tone of disgust and revulsion in marked contrast to the airy abstraction of the Lilliput period. Everywhere, Gulliver is described as disgusted – by the giant lice and tumours on beggars, the thunderous noise of giant mouths eating and so on, but most significantly, he is disgusted by the 'landscape' of the bodies of the giant women who treat Gulliver as a sexual plaything to tease, placing him on their dressing table whilst they disrobe, and even allowing him to wander over their naked bodies. In contrast to the airy abstractions of Lilliput, in Brobdingnag, Swift wastes no time in portraying in detail the body odours, moles, skin blemishes, breasts and nipples of the giant women as objects of disgust and horror. This depressing misogyny is constitutive of a wider ideological nexus reflecting attitudes to both the human body and the environment. For example, when Gulliver is himself a giant man endowed by his relative size with great power, the diminutive landscape he inhabits has no meaning other than its measurements, and how this might relate to those of his homeland: as a result, abstractions such as politics, warfare and affairs of state become the chief elements in Gulliver's environment. In Lilliput, even the power of the body is described in terms of its feats and the application of its power, and what, therefore, is important to Gulliver is the *idea* of his own bodily powers and capacities. On the other hand, when he is made small, and so disempowered, the human body is not an abstract idea, but overwhelms and repels in all its corporeal reality. Like a newborn infant, Gulliver's experience of the women's bodies is fragmented and disjointed: a giant breast, a hairy mole, a giant nipple, but unlike the infant, he can find no comfort in that, because, as a grown man, his sexualized ideal of what he thinks a woman should be is undermined and destroyed by both the physical fragmented imminence he finds traumatic, and his own lack of patriarchal power over them.

There is, of course, an interesting coda to Swift's Brobdingnagian narrative in this respect. In the second half of the twentieth century, giants emerge in literature, televisual and cinematic science fiction, such as Richard Matheson's novel *The Shrinking Man* (1956, closely followed by a filmed version, *The Incredible Shrinking Man*, directed in 1957 by Jack Arnold), *Attack of the 50 Foot Woman* (1958, directed by Nathan Juran), *Fantastic Voyage* (a film directed by Richard Fleischer in 1966) and Irwin Allen's long running TV series *Land of the Giants*. The psychosexual landscape that to varying degrees unfolds in this context is one which draws directly upon the fantasy embodied in Swift's Brobdingnagian women. The conceits of this are clear enough: the diminished power a woman experiences within the wider social spaces of normative patriarchal social relations, is fantasized as reversed when the female body is enlarged to the point of becoming a landscape in its own right. Within such a domain the body of the giantess is fantasized as uncontrolled and uncontrollable. On the part of its devotees, this sexual fantasy is one of immersion and oblivion, drawing upon the pre-Oedipal experience of the mother's body as massive, enfolding and inchoate, and as such the fantasy offers the promise of release from the tyranny of normative gender roles. Such liberation is not afforded by the woman herself of course. In those narratives where a woman grows to 50 feet high, she remains the prisoner of her body, but, if captured or subdued, that body is now big enough to be roamed over and explored by others with absolute freedom. In Arnold's *The Incredible Shrinking Man*, a chance encounter with a radioactive cloud drifting across the ocean (the residual fallout of nuclear testing) causes a man in his prime to gradually shrink. Initially, the subtext is one of growing impotence and pity: gradually he becomes childlike in size in relation to his wife, and seeks comfort in a woman of diminutive proportions who works as an attraction in a circus 'freak show'. Thereafter, as the shrinking continues, the hero's domestic environment – to which he is confined for his own safety – becomes increasingly hostile and dangerous to him: at first his life is threatened by cats, then, as he shrinks further, from spiders and houseflies, until gradually he shrinks to an atomic level.

For all its preposterousness, *The Incredible Shrinking Man* creates a degree of affective pathos and melancholy, wherein at first the landscapes of public space and social interactions, then the domain of sexual relations and domestic contentment, and finally the actual building blocks of matter, become too overwhelming for the hero. Although it is the hero who ostensibly shrinks, *The Incredible Shrinking Man* is in many ways a story about a small landscape – suburban Middle America – feverishly growing preposterously large: the protagonist is defeated by the everyday environment. In this way, whilst retaining the psychosexual element of the fantasy, both Matheson's novel and Arnold's film stand out in their awareness of what each qualitative stage in the protagonist's reduction. As he drifts to the point of atomic size, fears of sexual impotence or becoming prey to household predators have long gone, and he becomes resigned to his place in the universe.

Similarly, in his travels through both Lilliput and Brobdingnag, what Gulliver sees – and, moreover, *how* he sees it – is directly linked to his corporeal size. This contrasts with what occurs in his subsequent visit to the flying island of Laputa. There, his size once more conforming to the norm, it is his subject position and intellectual concerns, rather than his body per se, which become the decisive factor in his marginalization, since they clearly are of little interest to his hosts. In contrast to his earlier voyages, in Gulliver's sojourn in Laputa, he encounters giant scale in the form of the aerial island itself, inhabited by detached intellectuals whose head slope one way or the other, and whose eyes are, symbolically, permanently askew, one looking upwards and the other turned inwards. The denizens of Laputa, all courtiers of a king, are fascinated by mathematics and astronomy, and morbidly obsessed with the possibility of cosmic cataclysm. Famously, the author's elaboration of this obsession – focusing on the possibility of the Earth catching fire if it is brushed by a passing comet's tail – led Swift to correctly guess the number of the then undiscovered Martian moons, more or less a century and a half before they were actually observed. However, the emphasis remains on Laputa as a totality, rather than a vehicle used by inhabitants: not only is the power driving the giant scale of Laputa (Swift describes it as about 'four miles and a half' in diameter) contained and bound up within the landscape of the island itself, but so are its denizens, so that they each reflect the other. In their own inimitable way, being 'of' this particular earth, and akin to the other colossi I have already discussed, the giant intellects of Laputa are sensorily deprived in fatal ways as much as blind Orion and his precarious passenger Cedalion.

On Laputa, the landscape is hollowed out, and artificial. At the centre lies a large chasm 'about fifty yards in diameter' into which astronomers 'may descend into a large dome'. The soil is no more than 'twelve feet deep' covering a massive smooth circular base. This hollow landscape is the container of anti-gravity machinery constructed of magnetite, which is controlled by the courtiers. The courtiers themselves wear ill-fitting clothes chiefly because their interest in abstract measurement and geometry has overtaken any understanding of practical craft. Artificiality seems both pronounced and pointless – beef and mutton cut into rhomboids and equilateral triangles might remind a contemporary science-fiction devotee of the obstinate insistence on octagonal sheets of paper in the 2004–09 remake of *Battlestar Galactica*. Indeed, the rarefied and technocratic interiors of all big starships owe something to the landscape of Laputa.

In a manner redolent, again, of Diogenes's encounter with Alexander, Gulliver first appreciates the true size of Laputa at the point where, moving towards him and descending from two miles in altitude, it eclipses the sun for 'six or seven minutes'.

On Laputa, the shape of the landscape itself allows water from precipitation to be garnered and recycled. Landscape therefore appears in Swift's story at this point as a construct, as artifice and cover, but also an ecological cycle. Nevertheless, landscape it most certainly is. It is notable that throughout, despite its perfectly circular plan and symmetries, its ability to float and be steered, Swift does not refer to Laputa as a coracle, vessel or ship; it is referred to only as an island. In parallels to the peripatetic existence of later Roman Emperors such as Hadrian, Laputa is compelled to constantly tour the empire over which it rules, reminding all of its presence. The island can be steered, and its altitude raised or lowered as desired, but not beyond the extent of the dominions below, or above an altitude of four miles. Seeing all, and with supposedly immense power, it is a topology imposed upon a larger terrain, and as such presents a witty allegory of Britain's expanding empire – and the imperium's reliance upon such – during Swift's age. Swift's description of Laputa involves the limitations of the seemingly limitless: in design, manufacture, scale and power, the floating island of Laputa is stupendous. Indeed, it is in order to effectively communicate this that Swift's choice of the word 'island' over that of ship or vessel seems right. Its form and capabilities make it the ultimate terror weapon. Yet, as Swift notes, despite Laputa's potential to literally descend from the clouds and crush beneath its smooth adamantine base any opposition or insurrection, fear of resultant damage to its base, and the consequent loss of the island's power to fly, prevents the King from ever exercising this capability. Instead, in prescient parallels with the Cold War and nuclear deterrence, Laputa's wars are proxy wars, not only of invisible forces (in this case magnetism) but feints and brinkmanship. As shown in Swift's account of the Lindalino rebellion, wherein an opposing city constructed large pointed towers topped with lodestone, likely to puncture or repel the descending island, the fear of mutually assured destruction prevents all-out war. Laputa is, therefore, a study of a tyrannical totalitarian rule by a technocracy which has detached itself from human affairs. This is true in both senses of the word: not only are the courtiers and functionaries narrowly interested in the arcane and the abstract, contemptuous and indifferent to the interests and concerns of Gulliver, but also, literally impotent, and Swift bawdily plays upon this by relating how the wives of the Laputian functionaries and ministers have, when given the opportunity, variously fled the island to take off with more virile lovers on the ground below.

Small as Delicate, Large as Ruinous: Size and Ecological Metaphor

The reluctance Swift accords with the King of Laputa in exercising his destructive power mirrors the earlier beneficence of Gulliver in Lilliput. In sharp contrast, the uprising and war against giants on the jungle planet Athshe, portrayed in Ursula Le Guin's 1973 novella *The Word for World Is Forest*, would seem a humourless but credible heir to Swift's political satire. In contrast to Gulliver's mere preconception of scale, the humans-as-giants arrive with a preconceived idea of a landscape and its uses. Le Guin conceived and wrote the novel in the shadow of the Vietnam War, and, unusually for her writing as a whole, the violence in *The Word for World Is Forest* is frequent, atrocious and bloody. As in some of her other stories, Le Guin posits as background a human diaspora scattered across various star systems, supposedly originating from an originary home planet, Hain, countless millennia ago. Therefore, the inhabitants of Athshe, although much smaller in stature, green and furry, are actually evolved humans, who nevertheless are forced to fight for recognition, equality and labour rights, when starships carrying their taller, furless, pink or brown skinned relatives from Earth arrive and inaugurate the militarized exploitation of their planet's resources on an industrial scale. As the title suggests, the Athsheans have no word for their world separate to that which names the forest that envelopes their small communes, nor do they suppress unconscious dreaming states of mind in favour of wakeful consciousness. Dreams are valorized and shared inter-communally as broadcast news. Therefore, just as the Athsheans immediately foresee (and in fact are unable to conceive anything other than) the complete ruination and impending planetary death wrought by the colonizers from Earth as the deforestation begins, so the violence of internment, rape and punitive mutilation inflicted upon individual Athsheans by 'rogue' colonial soldiers evokes an intuitive but lethal mass response from the native population, as the recurrent nightmares and revenge fantasies of one Athshean, Selver, whose wife died whilst being raped by an army captain, become the common property of the insurgent community as a whole.

In a 1980 foreword to a re-issue of her story, Le Guin seems somewhat abashed at the obviousness of Vietnam parallels. Yet it is for this very reason – the clarity with which the analogue is presented – that it is possible to discern some of the wider issues at work here in terms of the Vietnam analogue, in terms of landscape and destruction, and in terms of the montage and mimetic function of science fiction.

At the heart of Le Guin's vision of Athshean ecology is a collapsing antinomic pairings inherent within the normative Western conception landscape – that of consciousness and unconsciousness on the one hand and the putative opposition of geology to biology as separate categories on the other. For the Athsheans are unable to conceive the planet's rocky substrate separate to the living biosphere that surrounds it. This contrasts sharply with that of the invading giants – the humans – who arrive with a dyadic perception born of the earlier rapacious exploitation of Earth.

Le Guin's Athsheans are, of course, in their diminutive stature, the opposite of giants. It is the humans in the story who arrive, blindly blundering, destructive and ultimately not only defeated but beguiled by the forest-world. The Athsheans, derided as simple, primitive, irritatingly dreamy or duplicitous by the colonists, prove in the end the custodians of a deeper truth about planetary existence than the commanders of a fleet of starships.

As such, Le Guin portrays the humans-as-giants as barbarous thugs by way of their arrogant implementation of abstract categories: their pre-supposed taxonomies of human kind, their assumptions about the purpose of nature, life and ecological 'resources', and their dogmatic adherence to the predicates of a greater giant – the military industrial complex which they have constructed. The destruction of the Athshean world is precipitated by the drive to subject it to an imposed schema derived from a 'bigger picture'. As such, just as the Athsheans themselves make no distinction between their world and their forest, so the invaders, also, but in a terrible way, make no distinction between the Athsheans and the rest of the planet: they are categorized as fauna of the planet (and so a resource subject to manipulation and exploitation) rather than accorded human rights. Played out in Le Guin's novel are respective and contrasting refusals to differentiate that nonetheless mirror one another. This contention might carry with it echoes of Cyrano's tale, but the results are tragic rather than picaresque, and the key reason for this lies not only in the respective protagonists' view of the landscape around them, but in the actual fact of the landscape's own indifference to them. In an earlier short story by Le Guin, 'Vaster than Empires and

More Slow', as in Stanislaw Lem's *Solaris*, the biosphere itself is conscious, but in *The Word for World Is Forest*, there is no sense of anything other than the forested islands and seas of the world being non-sentient. Indeed, Le Guin goes out of her way to flag up similarities between Athshe and Earth, down to the fact that both have similar trees and plant forms. This indifference creates a third, tragic element in the story, equidistant from the conflicting ethics of the Federation troops and the Athsheans, yet transmuting the latter into the former: it is the battle over the land being despoiled by imperialist might that turns the Athsheans away from their earlier pacifism. Regarded as a necessary madman, Selver is proclaimed as a god (something greater in stature) by his people at the point he takes up arms and leads them to fight back. How (or if) he, or his people, ever recover from this terrible transmutation, is something we are left to ponder. *The Word for World Is Forest* is the macro-micro antinomy framed within the asymmetry of guerrilla warfare: Swift's gigantism of abstracted schematics finds an echo in the displaced jargon of superpower war machine versus the 'small lives' of localized insurgency. Within the purview of the hegemon, the small angry eyes of insurgents are viewed as those of the crazies: like Gulliver in Brobdingnag, however, those angry eyes stare back with disgust at that portion of the gigantic visible, only able to imagine the rest which is not. As Fredric Jameson has observed, the landscape of such asymmetrical war becomes that of estrangement, the shifting of the homely into the unhomely – 'in which the home village […] is transformed into unimaginable horror' (2013: 241). In Le Guin's novel, the sylvan island glades of 'New Tahiti' – the Federation troops' name for Athshe – become at first the site of jungle warfare, and then, in the end, an oubliette for a lunatic exile, as the Federation war criminal, Captain Davidson, is led by the Athsheans out of their dream – forest nexus, to a defoliated desert island of his own creation, to spend his remaining days in lonely madness.

In the background for his cover illustration for the 1980 UK paperback edition of Le Guin's novella, the English artist Peter Elson (1947–1998) evoked the Vietnam War, rendering an airborne view of green forest islands receding into the humid river delta haze under a yellow sky (Figure 3). However, above these tangled jungle coulisses, in place of the swarm of Vietnam era Huey helicopters, or A.C. Michael's phalanx of airships, Elson placed a rendering of a single 'hopper' – Le Guin's helicopter analogue – as if on some routine patrol. Elson's hopper is a wingless, quadruped bug, painted in a patchwork of blue and white, as if to emphasize its intrusive illegitimacy by chromatic contrast. All this is Elson's contrivance: Le Guin's description of the hoppers is brief and vague. Through the cockpit windscreen, the figure of a lone pilot hand desultorily resting on joystick is suggested, but half obscured by reflection. Beside him is an empty seat. Arrogantly defying the laws of physics, gravity and aerodynamics, the craft flies without rotors, wings or evidence of thrust; Elson's brush-marks render the merest shimmer of hot exhaust around some sort of side facing duct, suggesting an abundance of efficient power, lazily deployed. Elson's 'hopper' is small writ large: foregrounded, it dominates the picture frame as something much larger would. Its illustrational discrepancies with Le Guin's text – a common, at times almost *de rigeur* aspect of science fiction paperback illustration – but it is these combined elements – the hopper's significations of unlikely capabilities and the illustrator's efforts to supplement, through his work, the inadequacy of Le Guin's description, which produces a relational excess of imagery. Elson's work is typical of late 1970's science fiction hardware illustration. As such, it circulates the necessitated coding of its moment unaccounted for in Le Guin's story. It is therefore estranged from the story that it illustrates, whilst remaining loosely bound to it (this is an aspect of the montage-effect of science fiction visual forms which I will return to in Chapter 3).

The Landscape of Tragedy: Giants as Predecessors

The land of the giants is therefore a landscape of tragedy, more so than epic or comedic. In making this assertion, I am drawing upon Alenka Zupančič's capitulation: epic being where the subject – in my sense the landscape itself – narrates the universal, the essential, the absolute; tragedy being where the subjects enacts (or stages) those same categories, and, finally, comedy being where the subject is or becomes those (2008: 27–28). Again, like tragedy, the land of the giants is pre-determined: the mismatch between scales determines a tragic disjuncture – an inability to see that inevitably leads to catastrophe.

Frequently in this chapter, I have sought to draw analogies between the figure of the giant, and the parent. I have linked this to the situating of the figure of the giant in time, as well as space. Specifically, the giant person, or giant thing, is placed parenthetically to the human subject of the present: the giant as someone or something that has gone before, or which comes after. In this way, the idea of the giant as the successor to the human – in the manner of Wells – or the idea of the giant as the predecessor – in the manner of Apollodorus or Virgil – is closely bound up with the sense of the giant as the *other*, placed at the opposite end to ourselves, just as Cyrano's giants, whilst they might live contemporaneously with their human opposites, nevertheless exist in a mirror world placed in opposition to our own.

In his *The Interpretation of Dreams*, Sigmund Freud references the buried, convulsing Titans in stressing that '*the wish represented by the dream has to be an infantile one*' (1999: 363, Freud's own italics) preoccupied with the doings and attentions of parents. It might be an obvious point to argue that the shifts in scale in visualizations of the giant – whether it be from the giant to the diminutive, or the diminutive to the giant – are ones which seek to locate the peculiar size of human affairs in a matrix which dramatizes those foundational points of differentiation. But to summon up the figure of the giant – to awaken the giant either from the past, or to conjure its advent – is also to attempt to stir this imagined parent, or be aware of the danger of doing so. Irwin Allen's TV series *Land of the Giants* was premised largely on disappointingly repetitive permutations of what happened when the diminutive crew of the crashed spacecraft *Spindrift* stirred the 'slumber' of the giants and awakened them to their presence in a variety of scenarios. What the series missed was the opportunity to explore the complexity of the reversals such an awakening might incur.

The core interplay between what I have termed in this chapter the elemental indifference of the landscape, and the tragic indifference of the dead, is analogous to the dramatic mechanism of the classical Tragedy of Fate. In *The Interpretation of Dreams*, Freud points to Sophocles's *Oedipus Rex* as a typical example: whatever Oedipus's intentions or actions, his fate has been predetermined by the will of the gods who have shaped his world. If we are to see giants and the gigantic in this context, then it is to secularize that 'will of the gods' into those aspects of landscape and the world that are ontologically irreducible, and therefore unalterable by size. To do otherwise is to reverse such certainties.

A landscape of giants therefore contains a number of potent signifiers: the sense of environmental predetermination that will inevitably lead to calamities of mismatch in shape and size, combined with the sense, as with the Nephilim, that those with greater strengths than our own have recently departed for obscure reasons. Huge size is both a visual signifier of the incomprehensible and bodily estrangement. We might simultaneously recognize the outsize human figure or a giant tree, but also instinctively associate it with the passage of time. If, as I suggest in this and subsequent chapters in this book, that landscape is a nexus of our sense of spatiality of a place, and its temporality (the stories or histories we tell of it), then that which is outsize or reduced from the normative scale of things becomes a cipher of all that is irrational within that nexus.

Again, to evoke childhood experience here is not necessarily to reduce the discussion to familial archetypes: the uncanny estrangement of visualizing the gigantic, I would suggest, is bound up with the memory of both the dramatic shifts in scale we experience in growing, and also touches on traces in the unconscious of its somatic effects. A landscape of giants is one wherein the seeing subject projects those particularities onto a new and unsettling situation in the, perhaps vain, hope of recovering traces of 'those who have gone before'.

Big landscape is constituted via notions of 'big time' as much as 'big spaces'. This piquant scalar juxtaposition of both scale and time, and the magnitudinal sense of 'those who have gone before' are seen in the *vedute* (views) of Giovanni Battista Piranesi (1720–78). Piranesi is perhaps best known for his series of *carceri* – engravings, often pursued through several iterations of complexity and detail – in which massive piers, drawbridges, arches and windlasses of vast size are viewed as if from the floors of huge and fantastical dungeons.

Yet a sense of the fantastical is also found in Piranesi's *vedute* (views) of contemporary Rome, wherein, amidst what Luigi Ficacci (2006) describes as 'a fragmentary, chaotic Rome, devastated and dominated by archaic rurality' (2006: 30) are juxtaposed with the remnants of something mightier, more terrible, built by 'those who have gone before'. Arising from his work as an architect and archaeologist, Piranesi's etchings visualize the past Rome of the Republic and the Caesars, alongside the living city of his own time – imaginatively augmented interpretations of the city in which he lived. In this context it is not just Piranesi's prisons that signify – but also his detailed engravings of the particulars of paving and masonry, in which an unusual combination of three point perspective and painstaking detail communicates awe on the part of the artist and impels a sense of veneration on the part of the viewer.

As Ficacci remarks, Piranesi's images of Rome's future/past arose from an assiduous methodology that was 'conceptually analogous to the scientific method […] of enlightened scholars' (2006: 29). Therefore whilst both Piranesi's prisons and landscapes are clearly fictions, their construction is predicated upon the terms and precepts of the natural sciences, and, as such, represent a significant moment in the landscaping of science fiction, drawing themes of the gigantic into visual frameworks constructed around empirical observation and extrapolation.

Chapter 2

A Game in the Ruins: Landscape and Virtual Realities

That there was no Virtual Reality Revolution should come as no surprise: revolutions are, by their nature, predicated on the notion of historical rupture – wherein extant socio-economic forms and their attendant reified relations are supplanted by more humane ones. Virtual Reality (VR), predicated on the privileging of an enjoyment of endless *space* rather than the instrumentalization of the end (or aims) of historical *time*, would have no use for a revolution, and revolution could not be expressed through VR. As McKenzie Wark has suggested, 'computer games are the ruins not of a lost past but an impossible future […] Gamespace is built on the ruins of a future it proclaims in theory yet disavows in practice' (2007: 23). One might go further and suggest that the spatiality of VR precludes any future in the first place, but Wark's cipher of the ruin as a persistent, wrecked remainder of history is an attractive figure in this context, and one which I will pursue in this chapter.

Whilst various practitioners and artists within VR have not only spoken of Virtual Environments (VEs) as 'failed utopias' – in a lecture in Istanbul in 2014, the VR artist Jon Rafman used this very description, and declared that to be a motivating factor in his practice – the sense that such a utopia might have been a failed revolution is perhaps less clearly articulated. The differentiation is worth pursuing. Since Thomas More's conception, the notion of Utopia has denoted socio-spatial, as opposed to revolution's socio-historical. Nevertheless, the early 1990s saw many popular claims around the notion of the 'information technology revolution', and the discernable shift towards utopia – failed or otherwise – suggests a failure on the part of the technology or the human agents who sought to utilize it – to deliver transformative historical change in the manner such a phrase might have suggested.

A certain aspect of the science fiction imaginary has been a central element within video game development from the outset: students at MIT devised *Space War*, according to Simon Parkin, in 1961, using the university mainframe computer (2015: 89). The subsequent international phenomenon of Tomohiro Nishikado's *Space Invaders* in the late 1970s to early 1980s, followed by other similar games of growing sophistication – Atari's *Asteroids* and so on – reflects the continuing appetite for the subgenre of conflictual Space Opera, and their popularity was no doubt fed by the contemporary cinematic successes of the *Star Wars* trilogy and Glen A. Larson's *Battlestar Galactica* (1978). To date, the continuing development of the most successful MMOG, *EVE Online* – which Parkin, writing in *The Guardian* (2015a) described as 'the world's largest living work of science fiction' – is not only determined by the complex interplay of violence and politics that shapes an ever evolving online game of 7500 interconnected virtual star systems, but is shaped also by the real-world interplay between angry players and Crowd Control Productions (the software company that runs *EVE Online*), through the process of determining 'allowable actions'. The most famous example of this, the outcry following a complex factional conspiracy involving infiltration, assassination of a key online character and theft of virtual assets, resulted in the establishment of a Council of Stellar Management, 'a democratically elected player council' (2015: 73).

Of course, space opera does not form the majority of video games played in the way that perhaps *Space Invaders* or *Asteroids* might once have done, but its persistence attests to the presence of residual 'historical' progressivist claims within gaming that, as we have already seen, attend upon science fiction as a genre. Thus in this chapter my principle focus lies outside of space opera per se, concentrating upon broader themes of the ludic within landscape. An understanding of landscape as space *and* time suggests that virtual spaces such as *Second Life* – ones in which, as Rafman suggests, 'you can have symbols for all histories and cultures, all floating together, without any historical ground' (2014) – are self-diminishing in any claim on historical agency from the outset. That is not, of course, to suggest that all historical agents have to be conscious of their roles or effects, but it is of importance when, in the case of VEs such as *Second Life*, considerable value and emphasis is placed on its status as a user generated environment, facilitating all possible communities and the possibility of asocial, repressed desires being made expressible through it.

However, as Ghobolahan Olasina (2014) has suggested, the 'carry-over' of real-life situations into the virtual appear to predominate in relation to VEs such as *Second Life* and *Active Worlds*. In Olasina's surveys and focus groups of users of *Second Life* aged 18–25 in Nigeria and South Africa, users reported a landscape of 'clothing, shoes, flower vases, buildings, flowers, gardens, restaurants, mountains, waterfalls, water springs, fountains, rivers, swimming pools, cars, works of art, chairs, avatars (other humans) and clubs' (2014: 303). Real life structures and hierarchies were replicated: gender relations and behaviour, snobberies and rivalries. From his results, Olasina suggests that engagement with Virtual Worlds has yet to develop beyond entertainment:

VWs (Virtual Worlds) have the potential to become another extension of our environment like a sports field, shopping mall or place for social networking, entertainment and more, not only for youths but perhaps for people of all ages' […] [Virtual Worlds] fell short of expectations in terms of collaborative or educational use. Most participants in the survey regard *Second Life* as simply good for entertainment'.

(2014: 303–05)

This purported failure of VR to become an alternative natural world (as opposed to an Other to the natural world, which it eminently remains) only serves to highlight, *via negativa*, its more interesting function – namely that mediating our relationship with that natural world. Indeed, my thesis in this chapter is that VR effectively *augments* and defines the natural world: technologies which facilitate so-called Augmented Reality can in many ways be seen as an acceptance of this. Keiichi Matsuda's six minute short video *Hyper Reality* (2016, Figure 4) visualizes everyday commuting and shopping in a world augmented by some post-screen, brain implanted device, including glitches, drop-out and the possibilities of identity theft. Comprising one long Point of View shot, the hyped up garish saturation of AR emojis, pet avatars and online personal assistants is scattered with dreary moments when augmented reality crashes and the viewer is left beached and directionless in a dreary physical world devoid of even basic signage. As such, Matsuda's film suggests the proliferation of virtual augmentation would, through moments of sudden absence, *increase* even the most mundane resistances of the natural world.

Arguably, what VR and Augmented Reality does facilitate, sometimes positively, sometimes *via negativa*, is the suppression or inflation of certain relationships with the natural landscape and its *topos*, whether sensorial or perceptual – for example, the overcoming of certain physical resistances or impossibilities in order to *virtually realize* desires we might harbour in relation to those resistances. Whilst in activities such as gaming, the landscapes of VR can be seen as entirely expedient to the facilitation of gameplay, it would be entirely wrong to therefore dismiss them. The effects are real enough, arguably both in terms of driving technology itself – Murray Shanahan argues that 'the economic clout' of video gaming has driven computing power (2015: 43) – and, also, in terms of its perceived impact on human social relations: one of the former lawyers for Salah Abdeslam, accused of involvement in the terror attacks of 13 November 2015 in Paris, reportedly described him as 'the perfect example of the Grand Theft Auto generation, who thinks he lives in a video game' (*Metro*, 28 April 2016).

Just as Augmented Reality locates its facilitations within our sensory perceptions of the world around us, and is determined accordingly, VR in its ostensibly pure form – however fantastically and successfully it might eclipse the normative natural *topos* around us – continues to reflect the social constructions and pressures of that normative world. Those, like me, who experience the motion sickness inducing jolt of removing their VR headset and, in doing so, momentarily see the natural world around them with fresh eyes, might go so far as to read that jolt as a seam between the Virtual and normatively natural, along which the two are joined and contingently interactive. If, as a concept predicated on spatiality, Utopia obviates the predicates of temporality (just as, *mutatis mutandis*, revolution obviates the predicates of spatiality), Utopia can only be represented temporally as a *moment* indeterminate in length. A sense of *ruin* lingers in that space, its patina of excess temporality unmeasured, unspoken of and unaccounted for.

In thinking through VR's predilections for the ludic uses of space I would suggest recourse to a compelling image from a much earlier time, which contains these key thematic tropes: Francisco Goya's large early painting *El Juego de Pelota a Pala* (The Game of Pelota) of 1779 (Figure 5). I cite this painting because it can be seen to presciently comprise – and superbly order – many of the key desires of VR: its size (over 4 metres in length) lends itself to immersive viewing; it contains a mélange of competing historical signs; it shows Goya's extraordinary deft manipulation of space and perspective; and, foregrounded, it contains a compelling, seductive image of a community at play: no one figure or character sets a narrative in *The Game of Pelota* – the painting clearly foregrounds the collective. The game itself is seen played in the middle ground: the viewer of the painting finds him/herself on the fringes of a loose and relaxed crowd of spectators. Goya's setting for the ball game is redolent of Wark's description in that it shows a collective re-tooling of the ruins of one possible future. In Goya's painting, the ball game itself is being played against the backdrop of a blank wall of an indeterminate ruin: the players are shown arranged in the rectangular flat area that might have been the building's courtyard or basement. By virtue of its massive stepped shape and a crag caused by a missing portion, the ruined building's shape carries with it echoes of crenellation or the ancient ziggurats of some lost civilization. Distant hills lit by angled sunlight and blue shadows suggest either early morning or late afternoon. Both spectators and players are shown as understandably oblivious to this – they are shown either absorbed in the playing or watching, or engaged in the sorts of conversation, display and consumption that any mass spectator sports event might evince.

The parallels between team sports and video gaming are substantial, and increasing. As Parkin (2015) notes, a significant portion of the video gaming industry now involves the recruitment and training of professional 'eSports' players. Such players are not amateurs engaged in what Parkin has termed 'the quest for glory though the wager of public performance' (2015: 43) who, through MMOG technology, can display and record the posterity of his or her prowess, but, rather professional gamers, participating in cloistered training programmes in secluded accommodation with the aim of winning substantial million dollar cash prizes in world championships (2015: 45). As Parkin makes clear, the cultivation of 'a vibrant eSports league' (2015: 47) such as that surrounding Riot Games's product *League of Legends* 'is now so effective at drawing its players into a cycle of sport and improvement' (2015: 45) that it is analogous to that of Olympic sports.

Like Goya's ball players, the vast majority of gamers remain amateurs. However, this in itself does not in any way preclude modes of extreme, obsessive dedication: Parkin describes examples of players who have suffered physical deprivation or died after prolonged and obsessive immersion in their chosen games (2015: 13–30).

Landscapes Digitally Rendered and Landscapes Rendered as Digits

Away from the competitive and the confrontational, digital gaming and VR both emphasize landscape and location in interesting ways. Parkin points to a recent trend where 'video-game creators have turned their focus from obviously perilous scenarios to less extreme yet, for most equally alien places and systems in life' (2015: 63). Parkin cites as an example of the game *Oddworld*, produced by the eponymous company Oddworld Inhabitants. Arguably the impulsive desire not to fight or play, but simply to wander in a virtual landscape has been a common experience for a significant number of video-gamers. Indeed, some of the most compelling digital games to emerge with the increasingly sophisticated graphic capabilities of home computers in the early 1990s were games that were constituted entirely around a puzzling landscape and its interpretation – for example Robyn and Rand Miller's *Myst* (1993). *Myst*'s enigma was emphasized by the loneliness felt by the player – certainly this was the present author's lasting impression from his first experience of the game, played on a Macintosh Performa in 1996. The experience of loneliness in such an environment brings with it the sense of forbidden space or trespassing.

In early versions of *Myst*, the thin whisper of a slight breeze and faint sunlight created an expectant silence on an isolate island in an unnamed sea. Various buildings were locked or presented as inaccessible, whilst abandoned machinery – including a rusting rocket – were left for the lone player to investigate. Another early impression of playing the game was, of course, that of the collective authorship – I recall being very aware, the first time I began to explore *Myst*, that this was not the work of one artist or author, but that my putative isolation was the result of a collective effort of creation.

It is perhaps worth recalling the frangible awareness of digital community at that point that such a sense of collectivity versus the individual evoked: namely, one which, in the early days of the internet, was intermittently within and without one's reach. It was a sense contingent upon whether one either knew, or did not yet know, how to access the World Wide Web, whether one either had a secure modem connection, or did not, whether one either had sufficient RAM and a suitable graphics card to play certain games, or did not, and so on. Arguably such a frangible sense of community – not just online communities 'out there' but also behind one's experience of gaming, stalks still the landscapes of VR, contingent as it is upon both technological facility or obsolescence and whom one is actually engaging with.

Whilst Ken Hillis has effectively argued that VEs obviate the resistant – but dialectically productive – materiality of the natural world, suggesting that VR suggests the lived world 'need not be embraced but simply reprogrammed until it matches "our" desires' (1999: 203). *Myst* and its ilk can be seen as an attempt to create such resistances in the form of conundrum set within the landscape. To state this is not an attempt to dismiss Hillis' concern in one fell swoop: indeed, the developing academic field of VR/Gaming studies remains preoccupied with behavioural studies of gamers, and whilst debates continue over the methodological approaches, ontological claims and ethical implications of using the sheer wealth and granularity of data on human behaviour global phenomena such as Massively Multiplayer Online Games (MMOGs) afford, there remains a focus on optimizing the efficiencies with which gaming can be facilitated. Landscapes, arguably, exist in gaming simply in order to facilitate gratification – either immediate or otherwise – through the visual pleasures of wonderment or deferred through the process gamers refer to as 'grinding' – progressive journeying through successive levels of tasks or obstacle in pursuit of reward. As Torill Elvira Mortensen (2010) has argued, the landscapes of gaming are constructed to facilitate pleasure and *flow*. Mortensen draws this latter term from the work of Mihaly Csikszentmihalyi (1934–) wherein the notion of flow is associated with the pleasure of unalloyed concentration and absorption to the exclusion of other concerns. However, as

McKenzie Wark (2007) has pointed out in a *reductio ad Hitlerum* argument, such a sense of flow arising from exclusion of other concerns in relation to the act of landscaping need not necessarily have benign or morally elevated consequences, but might actually be a conscious attempt to evacuate spaces of those moral resistances:

> [Adolf] Eichmann made topography match the text of his orders [...] Topography is not only the means of producing spatial and social differentiation but of overcoming it, connecting a space of places with a space of flows.
>
> (2007: 105)

In this light, Hillis's concerns can be seen as integral to long established moral questions associated with mapping and picturing generally – what is represented, what is ignored, what is erased – the facilitation of power projection and territorialization that did not begin with digital virtual realities, but is now seen to be accelerated by them. This is also the point at which creation of a landscape by digital rendering (painting) sits contiguously with any given extant landscape being rendered (reduced) to digits. The conflation of reducing to number (an ontology which holds all is mathematizable) creates a blurring between what Helen Verran (2014) has described as the 'conflation of stake' in what she terms indexical numbers with iconic or symbolic ones. Verran's critique of what she terms 'Costanza's number' – a somewhat notorious attempt to quantify the Earth's resources as capital and thereby argue the value of protecting it – rejects conceptualizations of numbers as either universal abstraction or culturally relative social construction, in favour of thinking of numbers as a 'material-semiotic device' – inseparable from the situations wherein 'enumerated material entities come to life'. Verran therefore recognizes that the work numbers do is constitutive of the real. For Verran, numbers 'partially configure the ongoing emergence of our worlds' (2014: 111–12). However, Verran also argues that whilst 'enumerated entities are the real' (2014: 113) numbering is also engaged in representing order in the form of value. Since, ordering and valuing are not the same, Verran argues that ends are often confused with means and value attributed on the basis of spurious ontologies. Verran differentiates between ordinal numbers (conserving order) and cardinal numbers (conserving value) – in other words, a differentiation between numbers' participation in, and as, the real. As Verran suggests, switching between the two modes can be what she terms 'generative', 'as long as we know what we are doing'. The problem, Verran suggests, is that the dual moments in which number is used to generalize are often not sufficiently understood as fundamentally different (2014: 113). According to Verran, Ordinal numbers are frequently used to articulate economic flow, for example, GDP of a country or territory, the costs of reducing greenhouse gas emissions, etc. Amongst other things, ordinal numbers bring a given phenomenon within the purview of capitalist economics: 'the comforting idea that numbers carry within themselves everything that is needed to interpret their meaning' (2014: 118). Verran argues it is meaningless to try to value and hence quantify 'natural capital': zero natural capital is zero humanity (2014: 119).

The Space of Representation and the Re-presentation of Space: Virtual and Augmented Realities

As reflected in Goya's painting, wherein the madding crowd lays claim to the evacuated spaces of the Other, the collective ludic appeal of forbidden zones extends beyond those of a post apocalypse future, to territories and spaces that are unseen – the spaces of urban myth. To speak of myth in this sense is not to denigrate or dismiss, but rather to reinforce the ideological component of space-as-idea, or, as Ken Hillis has argued, that condition where a cultural willingness to accept images as equivalent, or truth of, what they represent – leads, via VR, to a juncture where 'truth might come to be identified with space itself' (1999: 201).

Goya's painting is an image of both active participation and active viewing. In the foreground nearest to us are eleven figures, one of whom holds a *frontennis* or racquet and, watched expectantly by the other players, is poised as if to resume playing. The ball lies motionless in on the pitch in front of him. One of the spectators in the foreground, leaning over a section of ruined wall, is calling out to him, forefinger partly extended, as if offering advice, or making a well-received humorous quip. Immediately to the right of the speaking spectator, on a higher rampart sits another, cutting a dash in beige breeches, red jacket, full cloak and hat, smoking whilst gazing towards us. To the right of him, there are six more spectators, two of whom are looking away from the game towards us, whilst the other four are clustered in pairs, talking.

As such, the game is shown as a moment of community affirmation, of shared ritualized communication and bonding, in a situation that seems quite ad hoc: as one would expect of a master such as Goya, the landscape is, on the one hand, in formal terms convincingly occupied by the players and spectators, who are placed in the composition in a convincing and natural way that would suggest the artist had observed such an event on many occasions. On the other hand, however, there is a sense in which the crowd and players are quite clearly displaced: this ruined building, perhaps situated outside the walls of the city in which they live, clearly bears the trace of some other, earlier history that they seem oblivious to. Indeed, there are therefore strong themes of displacement and appropriation running throughout Goya's painting. Whatever the ruined building once was, it quite clearly was not intended to facilitate sports. Similarly, the landscape in which the event is situated is one that might more usually be associated with classical genre scenes – the trees and hills are redolent of late Poussin paintings, depicting key moments in classical mythology or biblical stories. The feeling evoked by placing a ball game in this context is one of piquancy, which is only heightened further when one considers the ancestry of the game itself: pelota is a game of various forms and modes, some played with bats, racquets or hand attached scoops and some played with the gloved hand. In some societies, such as those of South America, playing was restricted to certain upper castes or classes. Whilst the players in Goya's painting are clearly of middling affluence – apart from the various cloaks and hats, they all wear stockings and culottes, for example – they are clearly not kings or dukes. Furthermore, as I have noted above, their location of play is improvised. Whether the comments of the spectator mentioned are welcome encouragement or given and received in the manner of cricketers' 'sledging', boxing 'trash talk' or some pre-internet 'trolling', it is part of a spatialized moment of wider ritualized communication that blurs the distinction between participant/player and non-participant/spectator in favour of acknowledged and reciprocated displays of presence, skill and wit. It is the special qualities of that moment which are highlighted by the surroundings and landscape.

Goya acknowledges what the players seem oblivious to older histories, represented by the ichnographic aspect of the ruin, that are either ignored or only acknowledged in terms of their momentary use, and beyond that, the cycle of trees in leaf and the unfathomable timelessness of ancient hills and God's heaven. Goya's focus on a movement *about* to happen – the poised figure with racquet is watched by all – seems like a minor but affirmative gesture towards the future in a picture replete with signs of the past. That such a gesture should be presented in the context of a game seems particularly prescient.

To *play* in the remnants of the past – rather than, say, to genuflect or ceremonialize – suggests more than mere indifference. Rather, playing in the ruins suggests a collective indifference to the requisites of memorialization and the affectation of ignoring ancestral or traditional dictates of utility and form in favour of one's own ability to rename, rethink or co-opt: Goya's players and spectators are 'in the zone' –immersed in Csikszentmihalyian *flow*. As such, they map a radically different set of references and requirements onto the landscape in which they are situated. Outside of game time, temporality as history or geology is reduced to nothing, whilst space is understood only in the terms of the pelota court and the makeshift seating for the spectator. If, as I have argued elsewhere in this book, landscape is to be understood as a relationship of space + time, then this surmounting of one set of 'space + time' relationship over another can be read as a form of virtual projection. Through his writings on skateboarding, the architectural theorist Iain Borden suggests presents us with a way of thinking of virtual landscape as a complex process of re-mapping and re-presentation of the resistances of natural space, using concepts of appropriation and the celebration of differentiation he finds in the writings of Henri Lefebvre (1901–91).

In Borden, skate culture can be seen as a 'lived relationship' between the skater and the urban topos, analogous to ideology in Althusser: a topographic projection or, following W.J.T Mitchell's exhortation to make landscaping a verb (1994: 1), a *re-landscaping*, determined by expediency, forgetting, ocular lacunae and re-imagining, of an extant map. A similar mindset can be seen at work in parkour. As with digital VE, the analogue virtuality of both skating and parkour can be seen as one in which the physical resistances of the natural world are repressed (a seemingly impossible architectural feature will be overcome) whilst specific social resistances are emphasized – modes of behaviour, speech, dress and so on:

> Skateboarding thus brings together a concern to live out an idealized present, trying to live outside of society while being simultaneously within its very heart.

> (1998: 39)

As with the expedient uses/appropriation of space, the ludic misuses and appropriations of history – the re-formulation and re-telling of stories to evince moments of pleasurable escape and relief – is a staple of science fiction and, in particular, the concept of games in science fiction. Freedom to roam at will, either via time-travel or simulation, allows for the suppression of historical contingency and the natural world in favour of vast but completely individualized utopias: no force is overwhelming or inevitable. In VR, the tropes of landscape are re-appropriated as extensions and requisites of the subjectivity.

In its portrayal of a game in a landscape, Goya's painting focuses our attention on one of the two modes of communication elucidated by Ken Hillis (1999: 61), namely, communication as a ritual rather than transmission (I leave aside, for the moment, the figure of the spectator transmitting advice or commentary to the player noted above). Hillis argues that ritual communication, which he situates as pre-literate, is about the maintenance of society *in* time. He distinguishes this from subsequent forms of communication as transmission over distance, beginning with the educated elite who writes and sends letters. Goya's ludic scene might therefore be seen as a moment in which a society is, indeed, affirmed or maintained through play, but its landscape setting is also one that entails the imposition of that society's distinct, autonomous sense of time upon previous, now disregarded ones: 'for the moment, this space will provide us with the time to play pelota'. This re-tooling of space and, with it, the suppression of received notions of time, has, of course, many parallels with contemporary digital gaming, where history is presented as – to borrow a phrase from Susan Sontag – a 'landscape of voluptuous extremes'.

Games such as *Metal Gear Solid*, whilst ostensibly constituted around restorationist fantasies wherein the player is the hero in a pseudo-historical quest to re-establish an old order, actually avoid real history in favour of scenic pastiche – effectively presenting a point where political history is subsumed into picturesque landscape. Arguably the antinomy of this turn towards time-as-picturesque – that where historical contingency is writ so large as to become prohibitive to any play at all – was explored in the landscapes of an earlier generation of writers in the form of the consequences and dangerous paradoxes of time-travel.

Ray Bradbury's short story 'A Sound of Thunder' (1954) describes a future where time-tourism has reduced a Jurassic swamp to a time-travelling sport in the form of big game hunt, with disastrous consequences for contemporary politics when a prehistoric butterfly is crushed prematurely. Science fiction's conceptualization of VR as a way of playing safely with history apparently free of any consequence might seem thus necessitated.

In February 2015, The Photographers' Gallery, London, staged an exhibition of work by James Bridle. Entitled *Seamless Transitions*, the exhibition comprised of highly detailed computer generated tours of three places in which conventional photography is banned: the Inflite Jet Centre at Stansted Airport – an exclusive terminal for the owners of private jets, also secretly used for deportations, the Special Immigrations Appeals Commission – a secret evidence court in London which has been determined by the Court of Justice of the European Union to violate defendants' right to a free trial and Harmondsworth Immigration Removal Centre – one of the networks of detention centres run by private companies holding men, women and children awaiting either deportation or the outcome of appeals for asylum. The title of Bridle's exhibition came from promotional material for Inflite Jet Centre, but the ambiguity in terms of the digital rendering – and the epochal move from the paradigms of analogue photography to those of digital rendering – is clear. As with the artist Victor Burgin's earlier exhibition *A Sense of Place* at Ambika P3, London, eighteen months earlier, digitally rendered images of landscapes and architecture constructed from verbal or textual information and research – in Bridle's case, eyewitness accounts, architectural plans and so on – have created spaces in which it is possible for the viewer to roam – playfully perhaps – in forbidden spaces. Whether in the form of Goya's ball players re-tooling the architectural ruin as playspace or Bridle and Burgin's respective investigative imaginings of the arguably unreachable or unrealized, conceptions of VR and architecture are intimately linked historically. Richard Gregory (1998) suggests that the first VR device was devised by the Renaissance architect Filippo Brunelleschi (1377–1446) to image his proposed cathedral for the city of Florence. Brunelleschi painted an image of the proposed building on a silvered surface, into which was bored a small viewing hole. Positioning himself behind his painted image (so that he faced the reverse side) Brunelleschi was able to peer through the hole towards a mirror that reflected the painting he had made. The silvered surface on which the image was painted reflected the sky and the environment, so that the mirror showed a composite image comprising reality augmented by the painted element. It is perhaps worth noting here that such a genealogy posits the architectural project as a moment of mediation between the *topos* and the human subject.

A Garden of Earth(l)y Delights: The Holodeck of *Star Trek: Voyager*

In the series *Star Trek: Voyager* (1995–2001) the 'holodeck' – an interactive VR zone serving the recreational whims of the crew of a lost star ship charting their way home through the distant 'Delta Quadrant' of the galaxy – increasingly comes to dominate and shape the lives of the lead characters. Whilst holodeck technology exists in the series predecessor *Star Trek: The Next Generation* and in the series *Star Trek: Deep Space Nine*, the Holodeck of *Voyager* was presented as a more central component of the diegesis – almost a character in its own right. Indeed, in *Star Trek: Deep Space Nine*, under the management of the Ferengi spiv Quark (Armin Shimerman), the insinuation is that the holodecks are largely operated as virtual brothels and what goes on in its interiors is hinted at but rarely shown. The premise of the holodeck is that it provides not only visual but other sensory stimulations, since, in the world of *Voyager*, the development of 'photonic' force field technology means holographic projections are no longer mere three-dimensional light shows: rather, they have become tangible and kinetic, presenting as solid to the touch.

Holographic beings present as sentient and, given sufficient computing support, are able to participate in human society. One of the lead characters, the ship's doctor (or Emergency Medical Hologram), is such a being – the human doctor having been killed at the outset of the series.

Voyager's holodeck presents the crew with the opportunity to re-define their relationships with one another and with their own sense of self-worth, from romantic breaks watching sunsets on planetary beaches and enjoying cocktail fuelled pool parties, to hanging out with appropriate languor in picturesque Parisian estaminets or participating in the supposed simple life of an idealized rural Irish village, the last complete with a chorus of comic characters. One of the leading characters in the series, Tom Parris, is able to indulge his obsession with twentieth-century Americana by playing the lead role in the adventures of Captain Proton, a Buster Crabbe-era *Flash Gordon* analogue, to such an extent that it confuses visiting aliens into becoming involved in an actual conflict. In another double episode, the Holodeck becomes Occupied France in World War II as a result of being requisitioned by the Hirojans, a reptilian species whose society revolves around ritualized hunting and the perfection of martial skills.

Absent from the original 1960s series, the holodecks of the later *Star Trek* series presented a paradigmatic ideal for the landscapes of VR – go anywhere, do anything in a perfect simulacrum. Considering the series as a whole, the conceit of the *Voyager* holodeck would appear parallel to traditional cautions against wine on the one hand or Clausewitz's famous dictum regarding war on the other: VR, it seems, exacerbates situations rather than ameliorates them and is the continuation of politics by other (i.e. ludic) means. It is in this sense that the Holodeck is presented as limited by its users. Having given the Hirojans permission to copy holodeck technology at the end of World War II episode in exchange for a ceasefire in an earlier conflict, in a later episode the captain of *Voyager*, Katherine Janeway, subsequently finds that the Hirojans have not resolved or dispelled any of their culturally determined preoccupations in the manner she had hoped. Rather, the Hirojans, who have expanded their hunting of sentient holographic humanoids, are found to be facing reciprocal, insurrectionary violence from their holographic prey, who are not only understandably furious about their treatment but have also succeeded in militarily gaining the upper hand. In another particularly poignant episode of season seven, entitled 'Human Error', Seven of Nine, a former 'assimilated' drone of the hive minded Borg who has joined the *Voyager* crew but continues to struggle to become human once more, is revealed to be using the Holodeck to live out fantasies of friendship, social acceptance and sexual intimacy with members of the crew whom she admires from a far but is unable to adequately connect with in real life. Seven of Nine's retreat, via the Holodeck, into an interior fantasy of emotional fulfilment is echoed by the surroundings she has commanded the Holodeck to create for her – a private quarters with sumptuously upholstered furnishings, candelabras and a grand piano. In reality she is unable to face large social gatherings or engage in light amusing conversation, in her VR fantasy she is eloquent, urbane and well liked.

Detail and Its Discontents

As evidenced in this and other episodes of *Voyager*, the defining feature of the Holodeck is its seamless replication of the natural world. Therein, I would argue, lies its continued status as the paradigmatic ideal of VR. Its denizens touch and feel as humans and other life-forms do and its seamless replication of (and interfaces with) the natural world are evinced by perfect detail. The issue of detail is an intrinsic part of VR's claim to realism. Hillis (1999: 71) suggests that 'many VR scientists and engineers' argue that the more accurate and numerous the data, the more realistic the representation. For Parkin the trend is historical as well as ethical:

> History has shown that the video-game medium curves towards photorealism. As the fidelity of our virtual worlds moves ever closer to that of our own, the moral duty of game makers arguably intensifies in kind [...] The go-to argument that video games are analogous to innocuous playground games of cops and robbers grows weaker as verisimilitude increases.
>
> (2015: 143)

Understandably, Parkin does not differentiate between virtual renderings of extant things (the accurate depiction of a thing) and the convincing portrayal of something invented. Arguably, the ability to convince and the ability to convincingly represent contain similar ethical questions. However, in his performative lecture given at the Moving Museum in Istanbul in September 2014, the artist Jon Rafman effectively proposed a dyad within VR, contrasting the environments of *Second Life* with that of Google Street View. Rafman was intimately involved with the development of both. Rafman describes Google Street View as 'one of the great documentary projects of our time', suggesting a natural evolution of the project from that of early street photography of the nineteenth and twentieth centuries. Although, as Rafman acknowledges, much of the imagery of Google Street View is by its nature quotidian and every day, he suggests that the concept 'had a sublime quality'. As an artist engaged with the environments of VR, Rafman began exploring Google Street View in 2007–08, comparing himself with the figures of both the late Romantic *flâneur*, and the early Romantic Wanderer. Rafman regards such a stance in relation to VR as ironic, acknowledging that the seeking of truth through union with reality, whether through closeness to nature or the transformational possibilities of the everyday, can only be ironic in the context of a VE.

At the same time as exploring Google Street View, Rafman has also explored *Second Life*. If, as Rafman suggests, the two are posed as a binary opposition, *Second Life* and Google Street View can indeed be seen as the *supplement* to each other: each accounting for an originary lack in a putative whole. However, in many ways we find both Google Street View and *Second Life* as various forms of realism other to natural – the former one that hinges on the veracity of photographic/photo-realist *representational* detail (qua Hillis, the 'transmission' of sufficient visual data to replicate the human retinal sensitivity to the natural world) and the latter, a realism which through the liberating anonymity of avatar, stages a ritualized performative communication. This latter model carries with it the notional sense of realism-as-liberation: 'finding/expressing oneself', 'being who you want to be', 'seeing the world as it really is' and so on. It is in this sense that, in VR environments such as those found in *Second Life* or even in Google Street Map, the viewer is required to do what is required by a Romantic artist's sketch – that is to say, if we are to pose VR as one side of a binary term, in which the natural world is the other, all forms of VR and CGI remain as a supplement to the originary lack the experiencing subject feels in response to the natural world.

Goya's *Game of Pelota* – desirous of moments of ritual communication, of ludic pleasure and of collective immersion – points to a collective desire to adapt that which is found in idyllic landscape – fresh air, the sublime ruin and so on – to the expediencies of fulfilling the needs of the desiring subject (in this case, a collective subject). It can also be read as an exhortation for the viewing subject to do likewise: in short, to play, in the face of the sublime expanse of geological time which reduces all momentary pleasure to insignificance, in spite of the implications of Ozymandian legacies of human history.

The paradigm of detail-as-truth is a Positivist one, directly akin to the extant paradigm in model making – the more correct detail a model has, the more accurate it is, the more convincing its truth claims as a model and as an accurate replication of its referent. Detail here can mean both accurate dimensions and precise replication of characteristics. Both professional and amateur model makers subscribe to the view that a model without detail is untruthful, unless that lack of detail is due to restrictions of scale (e.g. when the detail would require microscopic work too small to be effected, or seen) or, as, say, in the case of architectural models interferes with the promotion of a pristine aesthetic appeal. Model making in that sense bears the closest similarity to VR in its truth claims: the interpretation of photography has, in some cases, similarly rested on its capacity to record incidental detail as evidence of its truth. However, in the case of photography, the truth value of images has not always been contingent upon details per se – Robert Capa's images of US troops during the D Day Normandy beach landings, for example, are blurred, grainy and indistinct, yet it is precisely this lack of detail – variously attributed to darkroom mishaps, but quite possibly the result of incorrect exposure – that gives the images their veracity.

Hillis (1999) suggests that the surfeit of detail found in VR differentiates it from the experience of artworks (1999: 70–71). Using etymological analysis, Hillis proposes a taxonomy that differentiates three forms of visual experience: Conception, Perception and Sensation. For Hillis, *conception* implies the act of forming a notion or idea, whereas *perception* implies a single unified but more receptive condition. *Sensation*, Hillis' third category, is the one he links to impressions, which, following the eighteenth-century philosopher David Hume, he argues is the most powerful.

Using the example of a novel – but his argument could just as easily be applied to a drawing or painting – Hillis argues that VR is not an 'artist's conception' which the reader/viewer 'fills in' with his or her extrapolation of sensations. Rather, Hillis argues, in VR

> [...] sensation is brought into the conceptual orbit of the technology, leaving the tamed viewer with perception stripped of its active meanings [...] in VR, I rely on 'the kindness of strangers' as it were, who in their programming and software designs first conceive and represent this array to me in order that I might, after this fact, perceive its simulation.
>
> (1999: 71–72)

Thus for Hillis, VR is differentiated in that conception precedes perception, unlike in embodied reality, since 'the machine "thinks" the form of the image' (1999: 70).

It is here that Hillis locates the hubristic claims of VR: namely, its offer of a world designed-for-the-individual consumer or, as he puts it, 'the world as a condition of the subject' insofar as such an offer is conditional on users accepting 'as a moral good a reduction of the sensory interplay between people and their lived worlds to a concept of world picture, from which the non-human natural world has been excluded' (1999: 72).

However, with the benefit of hindsight, as VR stands in the present epoch, nearly two decades later, I would suggest there are problems with this formulation and the proposal that the question of detail in VR ensures a qualitative shift in modes of perception. Current VR packages – for example, Oculus Rift – provide an immersive visual experience that is no doubt impressive. But the rendering is not, at present, such that it is indistinguishable from the natural world. If anything, the forms, shapes and textures experienced in VR is one akin to a well-produced illustration – exactly the 'artist's conception' which Hillis differentiates VR from. Sensations of vertigo, loss of balance and so on are evoked through movement rather than detail per se. This is similarly the case in other gaming and VR platforms. Indeed, one of the interesting features of the forms VR and digital gaming environments have taken in the years since Hillis wrote his book is the noticeable frequent avoidance of the pursuit of super realism or photo realist rendering. Games such as *Grand Theft Auto* and *Metal Gear Solid* present stylized landscapes and characters more akin to those stylistic forms of rendering found in graphic novels or book jacket illustrations. This might simply be framed as the expedient form in terms of cost and computing power – flat graphics take far less bytes, less subdivisions in the rendering – than photorealist imaging does. However, as with all reductivist arguments, such a rationale fails to address the particularities of style that such games inherit from proto-forms and ur-images.

The picturing of landscapes and subjectivities in the graphic novel format is exactly the mode of expression that games such as *Grand Theft Auto* and *Metal Gear Solid* draw upon and, contra Hillis, the forms of viewership they engender are a component of the forms of experience they engender in gamers – moreover, I want to suggest, they are constitutive. It is true, of course, that remarkably detailed characters fashioned entirely from software such as Autodesk's Maya, make regular appearances in cinema, television series and games.

The games can, in some cases, be experienced in VR. However, whilst the surfeit of detail may create a seamless iconicity, in and of itself does not in itself determine a seamless interaction or reception. This is because human reaction has already been educated to a level of suspicion and scepticism. Whilst Hillis's 'filling in' may not always be necessary in terms of visual detail, 'filling in' in terms of the viewer's socially constructed suspension of disbelief is necessitated by the fantastical invention to which VR is used. The fantastically detailed and smoothly lifelike tiger that shares a raft with a boy in Ang Lee's film *Life of Pi* (2012) may have taken the work of hundreds of people to digitally construct, but ultimately its laboured virtual realism is tempered by the natural improbability that a real tiger could coexist on a boat with a young man for more than a short while without killing and eating him. Even at the level of detail of the tiger in *Life of Pi*, CGI raises that condition of deferral/difference that is highlighted in Derrida's concept of *difference* (1974): that is to say, the perception of the digital construct remains rooted in the logo centric emphasis upon speech/presence as privileged over writing/absence.

Virtual and Virtuous

The VE and the CGI construction are both experienced as writing/absence rather than presence/speech. That this might be the case in the context of the SFX rendering of the unlikely or impossible in, say, a science fiction or supernatural horror film is arguably a given, but what, I would argue, is more significant is the manner in which this written/absent character of CGI continues into VEs experienced in real time. *The Star Trek: Voyager* character Seven of Nine's storyline mentioned above perhaps illustrates this: at no time in her immersion in her fantasy life is she able to erase the haunting sense of lack in her real life – the two remain dyadic as much as they are constitutive. Seven of Nine's fantasy life is presented as problematic insofar as it is presented as one of indulgent excess that is regrettable given the paucity of sensuous and sensual pleasures within her life: she has created a fake world replete with pleasurable details, whilst the narrative of her own life is doleful.

For Wark (2007) the excess of visual detail is constitutive of gamespace, an entity distinct from previous pictorial spaces and one which erodes the traditional temporal device of the cinematic and the novelistic, namely, the storyline. Wark argues that in a gamespace

> The topographic – and telegraphic – flattened out the difference between topics while describing them in much more details. A tension arises between enriched description and the poverty of storyline, bursting to contain it [this is the visual excess I note elsewhere] The expansion of description nevertheless opened toward allegory […] towards a politics of allegory, of the writing and mapping of the world and also toward utopia, arresting the flux of the world in ideal form. Topology closes the frontiers of space within its lines and expands the dataset again, but by reducing data to equivalent calculable points it is able

to break with storyline as the principle of temporal order, replacing it with the algorithm. Storyline becomes gamespace.

(2007: 73)

Wark's description of an 'impoverished' temporal structure and an excess of visual detail arguably echoes that phenomenon which I have suggested is found in science fiction, but it is somewhat challenged by the procedurally generated, faux-naïf topography of games such as Markus Persson's surprise international hit *Minecraft*, where, as Parkin (2015) notes, the gamer's universe is 'procedurally generated, meaning that an algorithm places each asset – every hill, mountain, cave, river, sheep and so on – in a unique arrangement every time a new game is loaded, so that no two player's worlds are exactly alike' (2015: 83).

If, as Parkin seems to suggest, the virtue of *Minecraft* lies in the uniqueness of its landscapes, then it reflects upon the virtual subject within it. It might seem that such an environment – one's own private domain – will inevitably engender behaviour held to be virtuous by way of its individuality or quirkiness. One such example cited by Parkin (2015) is the endeavour by *Minecraft* gamer and YouTuber Kurt J. Mac, who, rather than 'mining and crafting' in the manner of other *Minecraft* empire builders, simply set out to walk as far as he could in a single direction, creating and enjoying the landscape as he does so.

Kurt J. Mac's walk amongst the cuboid terraced hills, valleys and seas of his own private *Minecraft* universe began in March 2011, and is still going on. His large following on YouTube – Mac has been posting 37 minute episodes in which he documents and reflects on his progress, answering posted questions from fans as he goes – bears some parallels to the devotees of Wilbur Mercer in Philip K. Dick's novel *Do Androids Dream of Electric Sheep?* In Dick's novel, millions tune in regularly via an 'empathy box' to see and feel the experience of a man pictured perpetually and laboriously climbing up a stony barren hill:

He saw at once a famous landscape, the old, brown barren ascent, with tufts of dried-out bonelike weeds poking slantedly into a dim and sunless sky. One single figure, more or less human in form, toiled its way up the hillside: an elderly man wearing a dull, featureless robe […] a rock, hurled at him, hit him on the arm. He felt the pain […] you felt it, too, he thought. Yes, the voices answered, we got hit on the left arm; it hurts like hell. He resumed walking, and all of them accompanied him immediately.

(2001: 19–20)

In Dick's novel, this never-ending narrative has become a shared adaptive coping strategy on the scale of a religion, wherein the devotees share the suffering of the old man: the avatar of the old man is a focus through which to share their hardships of a foundational landscape which is uncannily familiar but generic and recognizable as a universal experience, and through it, the wider truth of human suffering. However, the collective investment in Kurt J. Mac's subject position, like that of Wilbur Mercer, raises the question of what constitutes virtuousness amongst the inhabitants of virtual landscapes. Mac's discussions with his YouTube subscribers are boundaried and humane, and they seem to be marked by candour and honesty. As such, the act of 'conversational sharing' places him – and his place in his landscape – in marked contrast to the lonely asociality of Seven of Nine or the ruthless competitors in professional e-sports. Parkin persuasively argues that the figure of the 'gamer' – as opposed to 'player' or 'sportsperson' – is interpellated in a particular way, depicted (and self-acknowledged) as 'a contemporary nerd group, a mildly downtrodden crowd, shunned by the jocks and achievers' (2015: 110). As Parkin notes, despite the considerable efforts by software producers to broaden the appeal of video gaming (and despite some success in doing so)

> In truth, it's gamers who fit within the demographic who benefit the most: here, within the artifice of community, they find a place to belong, a place where they fit, are understood and are free to be themselves, and together with likeminded people, enjoy a sense of collective power.
>
> (2015: 112)

Whilst this demographic continues to largely extol the traditional stereotypes of representation within games through narratives of violence and power, with its accompanying heteronormative gendering and sexualization, the figure of the lone pilgrim presents us with both an experiment in the delineations of virtuality and virtue. As with Poussin's painting of Diogenes that I mentioned in Chapter 1, we can see in the figure of Mac the virtuous figure of the Holy Fool: his asceticism is represented not only in his reclusive existence (refusing to play the kind of game for which *Minecraft* was constructed) and the pilgrim (in Mac's case, he has been accompanied some of the way on his journey by a tame *Minecraft* wolf) but also, in its blocky naïve toy-town renderings, in the simplicity of the *Minecraft* landscape itself. Arguably Kurt J. Mac's self-imposed exile journey is a private landscape (an individual moving through a procedurally generated topos) made public (via YouTube), there are other cases of abandoned virtual landscapes, either empty of all inhabitants, or home to a handful of avatars. As Parkin notes, some long established MMOG games such as *Meridian 59* now consist of depopulated spaces with a very small continuing virtual community.

'Live in Your World, Play in Ours': Retreat and Detachment in Landscapes of Virtual Reality

Whilst the advent of MMOGs and other networked forms arguably eclipse the solipsistic predictions of VE reflected in the story of *Star Trek Voyager's* Seven of Nine related above, what Ken Hillis terms 'the world as a condition of the subject' (1999: 72) might seem to remain one of retreat of the type *Meridian 59* evokes. Visualizing artificial landscapes requires time and visualizing landscape as an artifice – as a construct borne of the accretions of human effort and shaping, also requires an appreciation of time. Goya's *A Game of Pelota* presents a fantastical layered landscape of symbols inhabited by working people at leisure. Although the space in which *A Game of Pelota* is played would appear to be a co-opted space, rather than a garden per se, the painting was produced contemporaneously with the growth of ambitious landscape gardening in Europe. As a landscape co-opted out of expediency – or, more correctly perhaps, a space that has been *landscaped* by the imaginations of present occupants into a playing area, the setting for Goya's painting is one where an ideal has been mapped on to an extant *topos* to facilitate an alternative space for its occupants – in other words, a space imagined for *retreat* from the pressures and obligations of working life.

Retreat as a necessary setting, not for the realization of alternative social forms (revolution) but, rather, for the *imagining* of such alternative worlds through gaming and leisure is intimately bound up with both notions of both the virtual and the *virtuous*. David Harvey (2000) recalls that Bernard Le Bovier de Fontenelle devised the conceit of conversations with an elegant lady in a garden, 'away from the hurly burly of daily life' in order to expound his *Conversations on the Plurality of Worlds*. Harvey argues that we must think of similar conversational devices if we are to 'uncover possible alternatives to the social world we currently inhabit' (2000: 199).

The idea of landscape as a retreat – indeed, the Landscape of the Idea as retreat – is of course, one that can be traced back, via pastoral drama, to Ovid. In her 2008 essay 'Peace and Tranquility of Mind: The Theme of Retreat and Poussin's Landscapes', the art historian Claire Pace identifies Nicholas Poussin's late paintings, painted between 1657 and 1665, as ones in which 'the forms of nature dominate and mythological beings are reintroduced – although they are almost abstractions – as metaphors or allegories for the processes of nature' (2008: 73–87). Pace suggests that retreat from public life – whether in disgrace following a shift in political alliances, falling out of favour with or the death of a patron – is a cult that has seen various historical revivals. This is, of course, a common place within our own epoch – it is not unusual for the disgraced or exposed politician to pose for the media contritely in the cultivated landscape of a domestic garden setting, before asking for privacy and time for reflection, and in the British Civil Service, 'garden leave' or 'gardening leave' is an established euphemism for suspension from employment.

A key element in the positioning of the subject in the cult of retreat is that of detachment – 'viewing from a distance' and maintaining a posture of *otium cum dignitate* ('leisure with dignity'). Another key aspect to retreat is the *topos* of the garden: this is landscape as haven from the conflicts, stresses and potential indignities of public (and particularly political) life, and also landscape formed to the needs of the subject, not independent of that subject's needs:

> While there is always a danger that this might degenerate into the production of unrealizable dreams, getting the historical and geographical materialism right should help convert those dreams into prospects that really do matter.
>
> (Harvey 2000: 199–200)

However, I also want to suggest parallels here with the subjective and topographical constructions of gaming and VR: this might, initially, seem an odd comparison, when thinking about the dungeons and dragons or ludic eroticism of many games, but Kurt J. Mac's *Minecraft* odyssey, which I have cited above, might seem a suitable example here, predicated on the decision to withdraw from the mining and crafting the game 'expects' in favour of a more abstract calling. The use of avatars generally, of course, remains one of distancing – arguably, the virtual avatar allows for the maintenance of the actual player's leisure with dignity by virtue of its superhuman powers, its expendability and regenerative capabilities, sparing as it does the human indignities of actual sweated travails and challenges. Similarly, whilst the landscapes of gaming are easily read as sports-fields, constructed to optimize the flow of play, they are also gardens of retreat: to quote an early 1990s Sony PlayStation slogan: 'Live in your world, play in ours'. Clearly, such a slogan offers a notion of retreat constituted upon an antinomy – gaming on the one hand, the 'rest of life' on the other – that is hard to sustain in relation to the lived relations of an exponentially expanded digital life that we have seen developed since Sony used such a slogan. Whilst in the 1990s, one might have feasibly retreated to virtual estates to recover one's dignity and, ultimately, virtue, the pervasive aspect of VR, VEs and ultimately, the possibilities of Artificial Intelligence within those (which I discuss further below) has led to any posited lines of differentiation becoming increasingly permeable and necessitating a dialectical, rather than an antinomic approach.

Time, Space, Power and Play

For Harvey, it is the subject-position of the architect that lives the contradiction of what he sees as 'dialectical utopianism' (2000: 203) between a materially determined consciousness and a transcendent imagination. 'Many revolutionary movements,' Harvey notes, 'did not or could not free themselves from ways of thinking embedded in the material circumstances of their past' (2000: 203). 'The architect is not a free agent […]. Doing architecture' suggests Harvey, 'is an embedded, spatio-temporal practice' (2000: 204). One might draw a qualified parallel here and say the same of games designers and the builders of virtual worlds: for though one might for a moment imagine that games designers are free to construct landscapes of any form or kind, they too must accept the predicates of culturally embedded forms in order that their environments are inhabitable – not only by the perhaps superhuman denizens they imagine to live there, but the capacity of the human player to imagine martial and utilize whatever powers his or her avatar is endowed with.

Harvey's insistence that '[t]he production of space *and time* must be incorporated into Utopian thought' (2000: 182, my emphasis) acknowledges a dystopian disembodiment of the spatial-temporal nexus that seems perilously close to disintegration. One aspect of this is the manner in which VEs and social media hugely enhances the possibility of community over and beyond the dissemination of information: to use just one example, a radical campaign or group advocating a particular lifestyle that in past times would have spent much of its time proselytizing by handing out leaflets on street corners and debating its adversaries, might now focus more on building its community according to the dictates of its aesthetics and ethics rather than attempting to evangelize, recruit, defeat its opponents and seize state power. The possibility of creating other worlds rather than changing the extant one brings with it a renewed emphasis upon community, but also, potentially, a retreat from the perceived imperatives of historical agency. Harvey's suggestion seems to point away from this, back towards a sense of human history as a continuing project.

The disintegration of the link between an environment and extant notions of time is termed 'chronoslip' by Simon Parkin (2015). Parkin argues that gaming environments are absorptive in a way that cinema, TV box sets or even novels are not. He suggests that this is because games are 'active rather than passive media' and 'do not suppress freewill' in the way the latter do. He argues that 'games achieve chronoslip because they replace the real world with new one that moves to its own laws of physics and time. This reality engages us totally, and we synchronise with its tempo'. Parkin argues that video gamers are not so much time wasters, because the gamer is not idle. Rather, he sees them as

[…] time killers: they destroy Time. And they are accomplished killers, often leaving little trace of their handiwork; we remain oblivious to time's passing.

(2015: 20–21)

In this context, Harvey's insistence upon the recognition of spatial and temporal factors in the construction of Utopias seems particularly compelling, extolling the necessity of a socio-historical serpent in every Edenic garden.

The Construction of Landscape and Artifices of Intelligence

Computing power has been driven by various impulses at various times. As Richard Rhodes (1995) observes, mathematical computation power was, in the 1950s, driven by H-Bomb development, whereas in other decades some have argued the internet's development was driven by pornography. Murray Shanahan (2015) argues that it is the 'economic clout' of video game consumers which has, in recent years, driven increasing computing power – 'the demand for an ever more photorealistic gaming experience' requiring high detail renderings of landscapes and their denizens. Arguably, the impulse to push computing to visualize is at least decades older: in 1964, NASA's Mariner 4 spacecraft made 21 complete pictures of the surface of Mars, combining television camera capture and a digital tape recorder. The tape recorder had a storage capacity of 5.24 million *bits*. Since a bit – or *binary digit* – is one eighth of a byte, in contemporary parlance this entire storage space would be around 655 kb. Once the recorded data had been played back and transmitted back to Earth in binary code, NASA employees, impatient to see the results, pinned the resulting numbered strips to a display board and hand coloured the correct tonal values using coloured pastels to obtain pictures. This extraordinary moment in which collective 'brigade painting' transcription was organized to hand finish digital data perhaps stands as a peculiar moment of human-cybernetic ocularism.

Murray Shanahan (2015) posits the possibility of future VEs as places in which Artificial Intelligence is constituted. As Shanahan points out with reference to studies of animal intelligence (2015: 78), any understanding of intelligence that effectively isolates the brain from an embodied experience of the world is fallacious and quite possibly incapable of mechanically replicating human brain function let alone creating Artificial Intelligence, regardless of computational power: a computer isolated in a room could never be more than a brain in a jar, if that. However, if landscape is constituted by human presence (W.J.T. Mitchell's 'landscaping' as a transformative positionality, constituted around ur-forms) we can imagine an emergent artificial intelligence, its basic structure modelled on sliced and scanned organic brains but accelerated and modified, moving through a VE, assimilating and embodying the data it harvests.

To what extent one might regard such an entity as a single subject is a moot point – Shanahan suggests a collective paralleling of multiple computers – arguably this presents us with an effect of field rather than figure and ground, where that which is normatively regarded as an interior creative life of the subject is exteriorized as a nexus of functions. The extent that such a series of processes give the appearance of a conscious subject without a sense of self as such remains to be established. In due course, such an entity, drawing upon trillions of bytes not in an ordered computational manner, but in 'messy' forms, would in all probability exhibit diverse modes of behaviour indistinguishable from those we recognize in the extant natural world as instinct, intuition and common sense.

One should, of course, avoid inscribing dire warnings about the future when it comes to evaluating the impacts of new technology. But if we are to use landscape as both, the *object* of Virtuality and its metaphor, then issues of aim or direction are arguably particularly pertinent. This is not something which is instituted at some putative future point in which all of humanity is subsumed into a VE, but rather an issue which is emergent in the contemporary world. Linear narratives were germane to the Modernist sensibility, and *vice versa*: revolutions might have been made possible within a conception of history defined by a linear progressivism, and individual goals were also more easily defined. In an analogue world, an author, artist or musician might seek acknowledgement through institutional validation by overcoming real-world resistances of all kinds and succeed through such acknowledgment or remain in obscurity accordingly through established hierarchies of legitimation – a respected publisher, a prestigious record label, a famous gallery. On the other hand, when everything is readily mediated and disseminated digitally, goals are harder to define compared with old Modernist paradigms (even though this latter situation is arguably more democratic) because there might seem to be a superabundance – and therefore inflationary surplus – in the subject's investment in its own interpellation. The ability to produce completely immersive alternatives to the natural world and a commitment to an endless play in a myriad of possible worlds is to abjure the ethical imperatives of the natural world. In Marlowe's *Doctor Faustus*, unlimited power ultimately leads to nothing more than banal tricks and infantile mischief. If we consider *landscaping* as an ethical ordering of the natural world, then the virtual world might seem to negate such ethical investment.

In his discussion on Artificial Intelligence, Shanahan (2015) suggests that a fundamental schism will occur at the point where one might work for an Artificial Intelligence boss:

> Such an AI would be perfectly capable of using emotive language in imitation of humans. But it wouldn't do so out of empathy. Nor would it be out of deceptive malice. It would be for purely instrumental reasons.

(2015: 113)

Shanahan's argument might seem compelling, but if we are to take his 'purely instrumental reasons' as the key point of differentiation, then we could reasonably argue that Artificial Intelligence is already presaged in the landscapes of contemporary capitalism, albeit in reified human, rather than digital forms. For example, Shanahan's fears that a company managed by computer would lack actual empathy and only use empathetic phrasing in order to increase performance might seem less a spectral futurological fear to employees in many forms of sweated or indentured labour across the globe, but even in those countries where labour conditions have been successfully improved by combinations of trade unions campaigns and reforming legislation, ostensibly humane conversational phrasing in our day to day interactions with commercial enterprises has long been employed for purely market based goals of, say, increasing sales through customer brand loyalty or enhancing productivity. Commonly encountered characteristics of 'caring employers' from motivational pep-talks and employee training courses to various perks and discounts on company products can all be attributed to enhancing efficiency and productivity of employees, rather than actual empathy. The artificial 'have a nice day' scripting of the verbal interactions of call centre and fast food chain employees, in which neither employee nor customer has any empathic investment, are perhaps the most frequently encountered examples of this.

It is easy to conflate virtual and artificial, but of course there is an important distinction to be made between the two. Whilst *artificial* can connote insincerity or affectation, it principally denotes that which is produced by human craft when such is to be distinguished from occurring in nature. That something might be crafted suggests the possibility of mastery on the part of the maker. *Virtual*, on the other hand, denotes that which is for practical purposes, though not in name or strict definition (OED): one might have 'virtual intelligence' insofar that any human encountering it may find it indistinguishable from real intelligence, without it actually being 'true' artificial intelligence. Virtual landscapes inhabited by avatars of computers able to emulate human intelligence – or, indeed, even if only through speed of processing, are able to create the impression of surpassing human intelligence – would no doubt create a crisis in both confidence and belonging amongst human participants, whatever extra or super powers the human's avatar was virtually endowed with. The Edenic appeal of VEs might at that point wither somewhat– and lead to a human exodus from them.

If we are to make use of Goya's image of ludic energy amidst the ruins, then perhaps it behoves to imagine the manner in which random uncontrollable resistances are wrought into the landscapes of gamespace, and how ethical consequences would flow from that. That, I would suggest, allows us to imagine such resistances as temporal rather than spatial – as per Wark's point regarding the erosion of the temporal storyline by gamespace I cited above, it might seem that a linear temporality through which such resistances are encountered ('I came to a mountain, and I climbed it' and so on) is necessary if one is to avoid the situation where any number of possibilities ultimately generates insufferable banality. Surveying technological potentials being unleashed in the twentieth century, Adorno (in Bloch 1988) argued much the same:

> However, insofar as these dreams have been realized, they all operate as though the best thing about them had been forgotten – one is not happy about them. As they have been realized, the dreams themselves have assumed a peculiar character of sobriety, of the spirit of positivism, and beyond that, boredom.
>
> (1988: 2)

Boredom, it might seem, is the ultimate outcome of the endless production of spatial possibilities. Landscape, insofar as it can reassert the resistances of the temporal as well as the spatial, might overcome that, but only, I would suggest, in those cases where the encounter with landscape is unavoidably temporal as well as spatial.

As I have argued in this chapter, VEs tend to suppress that temporal resistance. The intriguing possibility that, in the future, Virtual or Augmented Reality technologies might be used via massive amounts of data streamed from robot probes to allow human interaction with the alien landscapes of other planets, which would be inhospitable to actual human bodily presence, might allow such. Likewise, as Parkin (2015) has noted, VR allows for the creation of empathic games, wherein players are able to explore the possible motivations and mindsets of different subject positions, from the struggle of someone disclosing their sexuality in a heteronormative world to forensic recreations of notorious crimes. Whilst the latter has been the subject of frequent controversy, the authors might not necessarily be motivated to create such games out of spurious motives. The forensic restaging of events is arguably a form of play, in order to understand. Goya's great painting seems to have great power not least because across the centuries, successive generations of viewers have been able to empathize with the players and spectators he convincingly renders.

Towards the end of Olaf Stapledon's *Last and First Men* (1930) – a groundbreaking science fiction novel, which charts an imagined future history of successive species of human over aeons of time – a voice addresses the reader. The voice Stapledon conjures is a collective one, from a far future species of humanity that has come to terms with its ultimate cosmic doom. The voice is in no way bitter or apprehensive, but wise, rational and benevolent. The voice informs the reader that through unknown technologies this evolved human collectivity has been able to enter the minds of ancestors and, in doing so, they 'seek to afford intuitions of truth and of value', they are 'engaged upon the great enterprise of becoming lovingly acquainted with the past, the human past, in every detail [...] not the least of them, not the worst of them, shall be left out of this great work of understanding and admiration' (1999: 297–98). If, following the quote from Harvey already cited, the production of space and time must be incorporated into Utopian thought (2000: 182), then one might also argue that the Utopias of VR be produced as spatio-temporal embodiments. As with robotic streaming, Stapledon's vision might be appropriate here in its suggestion of just such a landscaping – of history, human experience and the possibilities of empathy through virtual play.

Chapter 3

Blasted Heaths and Turbulent Energies: Chris Foss's Accelerated
Dream of Wessex

My father, who was born in 1937, spent his working class childhood in the poorer area of a Lancashire cotton and coal town. He recalls a marvellous sight he once saw as a boy, shortly after World War II ended: at the end of the steep cobbled street in which he lived, a large horse-drawn flatbed wagon paused at a standstill for a moment, bearing a large ring of bright polished metal, steadied with ropes and wedges, half covered with a tarpaulin. An older brother informed him it was a part of a jet engine, being transferred between train stations, on its way to the Rolls-Royce factory in a nearby town, where, by coincidence, as an adult, my father would go on to spend his entire working life.

To those for whom it remains a living memory, the passage of time reveals a poignant truth of the twentieth century: namely, how its visual manifestations were constituted as sharp juxtapositions of memories of the nineteenth century and the imagined forms of the twenty first. Arguably, juxtapositions are to be found in any age of transition, but the twentieth century sees this process intensified: there was a time when jet engines were borne on horse-drawn wooden wagons.

The future rests on understandings of the past. Faced with such juxtapositions, one might be tempted to wonder how the visual forms of the twentieth century could possibly be dominated by anything other than the cut-up, the montage and the surreal. Outside of science fiction, this cultural phenomenon was the basis of the foundational works of Walter Benjamin (1892–1940) and Siegfried Kracauer (1889–1966). Yet the visual culture of science fiction provides fascinating cases-in-point: a plethora of 'what if' antimonies. Consider, for example, the antithesis of such dramatic juxtapositions of modernity – the baroque fantasies of steampunk. Steampunk ironically inhabits the scientism and mechanical ingenuity of the Victorian age (for invariably, the flavour of steampunk is that of a synthetic British Empire at the height of its power) to the point where it eclipses that which was peculiarly revolutionary about twentieth-century Modernism, as if to deny not only Modernism's technological distinctiveness, but also to obviate the necessary ruptures and juxtapositions of its visual culture in favour of endless extrapolations of Victoriana. Nevertheless, the twentieth century synthesized its own signs of the future: aluminium, hydraulics, circuitry and combustion chambers superseded iron, pulleys, signals and boilers.

In this chapter, I want to explore a particular moment of what we might think of as montaging, which is manifested not in the normative form of the cut-up photograph but in the painted and airbrushed landscape work of a particular illustrator, Chris Foss (b. 1946), who excelled in combining visual references to contemporary machines to create wildly improbable but visually convincing images of landscapes and hardware. In doing so,

I want to consider Foss' images as a radical dystopic rejection of the established modes of representation into which they suddenly emerged, and the role of formative encounters in landscapes specific to that era. I will examine the roots of that rejection in the light of two impulses that are constitutive of each other: on the one hand, what we might now understand as *accelerationism* and on the other, what George Steiner defines as *'ennui'* (1974), which in turn gave rise to what I will suggest is the querulous, impatient vision of an accelerated dysfunctional industrial future under consideration.

Juxtaposition, Montage and the 'Artist's Impression'

To establish what is at stake here, I want to briefly review the place occupied by certain illustrative forms in the technological optimism of Britain in the post-World War II economic boom: the period that was ending at the point at which Chris Foss's illustrations attained such remarkable popularity and commercial success. One of the defining tropes of the visual culture of that aerospace engineering, which my father first glimpsed in the startling juxtaposition with which I opened the chapter, was what is commonly referred to as the 'artist's impression' or sometimes the 'artist's concept': in Britain, in the 1960s, those extrapolative impressions of what the British statesman and Prime Minister Harold Wilson (1916–1995) referred to as 'the white heat of technology', harnessed for the common good. Corporations such as Rolls-Royce, British Aerospace, Lockheed-Martin, Boeing, Dassault and Dornier regularly issued composited images – paintings superimposed on photographs – of their soon-to-be released aircrafts, engines, rockets and satellites, for press releases, brochures and promotional posters. These 'artist's impressions' can be seen as part of a wider culture of optimistic extrapolative ideology arising from the prolonged post-World War II economic boom in Western economies that extended from the early 1950s to the early 1970s. Kubrick's *2001: A Space Odyssey*, for example, contains a number of piquant visual examples of this extrapolative optimism: a space shuttle operated by Pan-Am, at the time a major transatlantic airline; the twelve or more BBC television channels shown at a time (1968) when the BBC operated only two. Again (and analogous to the occlusions Steampunk ironizes) an interesting aspect of such extrapolations is the suggestion of uninterrupted, continuous development of extant paradigms and polities: in reality, Pan Am actually collapsed 10 years before the film's titular year, moon bases and human missions to Jupiter have so far proved unaffordable and of course, more prosaically, the BBC has not been afforded a monopoly of channels in the manner perhaps implicit in Kubrick's celebrated film.

The tropes of such artist's impressions in relation to extrapolation are worth thinking through in detail. Their visual conceits are founded on the formal logics of extant forms and ideological assumptions ('it is natural, given current trends of development to assume that x will grow to become $2x$ and furthermore, that $2x$ will embody, in an enhanced but recognizable form, the characteristics of x'). As such, the artist's impression typically mobilizes a set of immediately recognizable signifiers of realism – easily readable, detailed renditions of lighting, modelling and shadow; and, finally, in the depiction of the novum itself, an element of visual frisson – high key underpainting, vertiginous or sweeping perspective and so on. The novum of the speculative artist's impression is therefore one that does not depart from or contravene contemporaneous presumptions of science in the artist's time, but rather affirms extant ideologically determined assumptions of progress through extrapolation. I will examine the relationship between ideology and extrapolation further later in the present book.

However, in this chapter I want to explore two particular elements relating to the artist's impression, the first of which emerges from the specifics of its form – namely its montaging aspect, which is used to pursue a project of credible extrapolation; and secondly, I aim to examine a point at which the tropes of the artist's impression become exaggerated to the extent that a qualitative shift away from extrapolation occurs. This break with the precepts of extrapolation is marked not by a radical break with illustrative techniques as such, but rather by dint of excessive use of extant tropes and increasingly exaggerated juxtapositions. At the same time, however, the method of producing such images – for example, the superimposition of painted elements over stock photographic backdrops – produces an effect more similar to photomontage than collage or montage, insofar, as Bürger (1984: 76) suggests, the montage is obscured or made harder to spot.

As Bürger makes clear, any technical procedure for making pictures 'is not semantically reducible to invariant meanings' (1984: 79). However, in the context of extrapolative illustration, there is a noticeable point of disjuncture at which the combination of montaging, authenticating detail and realism are used in such an unlikely way that whilst the tropes of illustrative realism are maintained, the image that is produced might oscillate between the credible and *in*credible – a point, perhaps of inversion, where a combination of the illustrative tropes of realism and extant signifiers of technology are deployed to signal something that nevertheless appears *un*real and preposterous. In those situations where one medium – say painting – is superimposed upon a photographic backdrop, this might be an effect of the 'seam' between the two media, but, in a picture unified by medium or techniques, it might be one in which motifs that trigger cognition within the viewer are re-presented in such a manner that the credibility they signify seems exaggerated to a point of extremes. This latter case might be seen as one of accelerationist absurdity – *jouissance* perhaps – analogous to Surrealism. In science fiction, it is clearly seen in the work of Chris Foss where lurid colour, epochal juxtapositions and the quantitative agglomeration of signifying detail produces a qualitatively explosive negation of the tropes of credible extrapolative science fiction, in favour of an exciting juxtaposition of the 'realistic' and the incredible.

The science fiction imagery of Foss emerged onto the British paperback market in the early 1970s, and in many ways can be seen to both embody juxtaposition and estrangement of everyday scuffed and worn technology – trains, ships, earthmovers – to effect a sharp break with the optimism of the preceding era and, as I will argue below, a radically perverse re-thinking of elements of the 'artist's impression' in the forms I have described above. Foss's images, produced mainly in acrylic paint – although he also produced works in ink, pencil and wash – were impactful and distinctive, quickly spawning imitators. Foss's work typically featured vast lumpy starships, banded with bright colours and glittering with tiny windows, spewing smoke and incandescent vapour trails, set against bleak post-industrial landscapes scarred by quarrying, catastrophe and pollution. What stands out about Foss's landscapes is their sense of place. Whilst soil might be blue and the skies bright red, the topographies themselves are composed of familiar elements. Where vegetation is portrayed, it takes the forms of blasted heaths, sparse tussocks of sea grass, spiked cacti or monstrous, mutated succulents sprouting from rocky wastes – all the commonplaces of science fiction, but rendered with a curious familiarity. Accordingly, his wasp-striped starships are redolent of engorged oil tankers, dock cranes, earth-movers and diesel trains. In Foss's paintings, the human figure is often tiny, dwarfed by technological artifacts. When shown close up, the human figure in Foss's work is either a passive onlooker, surprised as the rest of us, or shown struggling to remain in control of technological malfunction, possibly being blasted, ejected or sundered at the moment of explosion or impact.

Analogous to the peculiar figure of the jet engine on the horse cart I began with, Foss locates the origins of his work within the juxtapositions of a particular foundational landscape: an airfield named Tarrant Rushton, near Wimborne in Dorset. The airfield was established in 1943 (Tanner 2006: 44–45) and, in the years following the end of World War II, was the site of early experiments in air-to-air refuelling of fighter aircraft which subsequently revolutionized military air capabilities. Foss's early encounters with aircraft parts, abandoned hangars amidst this ancient landscape, proved poignant and affecting (conversation with author, 20 January 2016).

Given his subsequent influence on the genre, Chris Foss's initial encounter with science fiction per se seems tangential and limited. He asserts he had no interest in reading science fiction novels, which he found 'boring' and was initially employed as a jobbing commercial artist on a wide range of paper back genre fiction, including Westerns and war paperbacks in a commercial studio. It was, by his own account, 'two or three years' before the science fiction work 'got started' (conversation with author, 20 January 2016). Having studied architecture at Magdalene College, Oxford, he left before graduating, ostensibly rejecting what he saw as the uninspiring prevailing concrete block modernism (Figure 6) typified by the work of John Meunier (conversation with author, 20 January 2016). Despite this rejection, he subsequently not only retained but also developed an affinity for concrete itself on his own terms: working for a while in the studio of architectural sculptor George William Mitchell, he became familiar with concrete casting and still loves working with concrete: 'It's there forever' (conversation with author, 20 January 2016). Concrete Brutalism therefore re-emerges in Foss's imagery albeit in a somewhat neurotic form: in Foss's imagery, space stations are re-imagined as concrete fortifications that appear to conflate 1960s Brutalism with Hitler's Atlantic Wall, the post-war remnants of the latter, as Angus Wells has described, Foss encountered during family visits to Guernsey (1977: 6).

These fortified forms are often augmented by tribal or runic markings, but not necessarily of the kind one might associate with twentieth century dictatorship: elements redolent of Aztec or Mayan relics abound also. This last element is perhaps unsurprising, given the immense popularity of the theorems and conjectures of the likes of Eric von Däniken and other exponents of ancient-astronaut pseudo-archaeology during the 1960s and 1970s. Yet the locations remain resolutely those of Wessex – moorland *tors* and rocky outcrops figure repeatedly in his work, as do quarries, towers, shafts and bunkers. Foss built his landscapes up around the spaceship (interview with author, 20 January 2016) as if from a remembered repertoire of forms.

As a commercial artist, Foss became friends with Michael Johnson. Strong influences of Pop Art can be seen in the work of both artists of the time: flatness, angularity, cropping and frame breaking. Foss has suggested Johnson was the superior figure artist of the two. At this time, Graham Sutherland, Paul Nash and John Piper were influences (interview with author, 20 January 2016) and strong echoes of the Surrealist juxtapositions, desolate landscapes and twisted metallic forms found in those artists' work seem to re-appear in Foss's work. These appear less as fragments of the past projected into the future than as fragments of the decaying present inflated or accelerated: a recurrent aspect of Foss's work – and its visual appeal – perhaps lies in its deployment of contemporary tropes. Foss's work would seem to effectively hover around the notion of an imminent future by deploying familiar tropes of the present and past to construct an absurdist realism. An early painting by Foss, entitled *LYDD*, painted in 1971 (Figure 7), highlights the relationship between landscape and technology. In the foreground of the picture, a trapezoid prism object, predominantly bluish-grey but marked with small flashes of yellow and white, squats on a cement apron overgrown with weeds. The object is illuminated with small lights and displays an octagonal decal on one of its faces, containing opposing equilateral triangles and what appear to be initials. The background shows a rail siding and a gantry crane. Flatbed railcars are lined up, ready to be loaded. Both the structure and landscape are specific: although the gantry has since been updated, the siding still exists, located on the outskirts of the small town of Lydd in Kent, England. The gantry is used to load nuclear flasks on to the railcars for transportation to and from the nearby nuclear power stations at Dungeness, a hauntingly bleak shingle headland on the Kent coast. In Foss's picture, the trapezoid object in the foreground seems the only activated object: along with the lights, a thin column of vapour rises from a vent in the top. Yet its base, like the gaps and cracks in the cement, is overgrown with weeds. The effect of this is to suggest the trapezoid has been there for a considerable period of time. The positing of extant alien presences in the English landscape is a trope found in the fictions of writers such as John Wyndham and Nigel Kneale. Arguably, it reflects the unease and anxieties of the changed Britain post-1945: the landscape as metaphor for neuroses within the national psyche; the threat of potentially uncontrollable new technologies; the appearance of off-limits military installations, in some cases under the control of the United States rather than the British government. Moreover, given the influence of English Modernist landscape artists such as Sutherland and Nash, I would suggest that what resonates here is a distorted sense of *genius loci* – specifically, a displaced sense of spirit of place, which I will explore further in the conclusion to this chapter.

As is common in the field of commercial work, pressing deadlines and expediencies dictated by the demands of art directors meant that *LYDD* was subsequently partially painted over, becoming a new work, *Astounding Analog Reader*, for Sphere Books a year later in 1972. In this later iteration, the yellow sky appears re-painted black and dotted with a scattering of stars and the squat structure replaced with a hovering vehicle of some kind, dotted with yellow lights and emitting gases. In the background, the rail gantry remains. The landscape of *LYDD* seems situated as an account of formative influences on the cusp of what Foss subsequently became famous for. However, I would suggest that what *LYDD* lacks, in comparison to his subsequent work, is the sense of accelerationist jouissance that drives his subsequent imaginings to such feverish levels. As the work developed through the 1970s, Foss's machines no longer merely sat in his landscapes, but bounded, crashed and soared over and through them. Of the hundreds of book covers, cinema conceptualizations and magazine illustrations Chris Foss produced during his career, the following will suffice for this discussion: the 1977 Corgi paperback edition of J.T. McIntosh's *Norman Conquest 2066* (Figure 8) and the 1986 Panther edition of Isaac Asimov's *Earth Is Room Enough* (Figure 9).

Foss's cover for *Norman Conquest 2066* shows a brown rocky coastal landscape, lit by a large, pale yellow star, the disc of which is haloed in a miasmic khaki sky that darkens towards the zenith, through which, despite the daylight and the murk, a scattering of other stars can be seen. Beyond the shoreline, in the bottom right hand corner of the image, a pale luminous ocean can be seen, whilst at the opposite left hand side of the picture, the land rises to an escarpment of broken rocky outcrops. The impression of a warm, heavy, polluted atmosphere hanging over a barren landscape is confirmed by the three foreground elements, consisting of two spaceships and a cluster of buildings. The less prominent spaceship is high overhead, in the background: banded in greys and blacks, it most resembles the cab and boom of a large dockyard crane or perhaps a rotor-less helicopter left only half complete: a latticed scaffolding tail extends to its rear, serving as some sort of exhaust for the means of propulsion, spewing black smoke in the spaceship's wake. As it cruises across the sky towards the horizon, its contrail about to draw a chord across the disc of the sun, a large number 9, seen upside down as a '6' and smaller, along with less legible lettering can be seen on its underbelly. Smaller latticed booms project out from the upper reaches of its starboard side, whilst an antenna projects forward in the direction of travel.

In the middle ground of the picture, a huge bronze coloured metal squat tower rises, its column and cupola speckled with tiny windows and lights, sprouting various antennae rendered as straight, white lines, from the sides and the roof. On the roof there are also a set of brown nodules, whilst in the walls and sides of the cupola and trunk of the tower, a series of vents or slots are situated, their interiors shadowed. Another smaller tower, resembling a bunker, can be seen some way off, whether it is separate or contiguous with the main tower is impossible to determine because a clear view is obscured by the larger, foreground spaceship which is caught as if rushing forward, leaping out of the lower centre of the picture plane towards the right. Naturally, it is this larger, centre stage spaceship that seizes the viewer's attention first, although I have chosen to address it here after other elements of the picture. In many ways, this spaceship typifies Chris Foss's work: a huge, ungainly looking spacecraft, striped in yellow and black circles and bands, speckled, like the tower behind it, with portholes and antennae, caught in a moment of dynamic rupture with its setting. Foss's spaceships seem to shake and rupture the air or space around them: he frequently underpainted with an airbrush to create an aura of vapour or a corona, which would then appear to surround the spaceship, rendered by hand on top. This 'aura' serves the dual pictorial function of lifting the foreground figure (the spaceship) from its backdrop, whilst simultaneously suggesting a physical disturbance caused by the spaceship's power and velocity. In *Norman Conquest 2066*, the yellow and black spaceship surging forward towards us out of the picture displays seven large trapezoidal fins – two respectively projecting upwards and downwards, surmount the nose, whilst others at the ventral, pectoral and anal sections – along with a gaping air-intake and a blank large circle insignia give the spaceship a decidedly ichthyoid character, so that its shape, colouration and flying conflate echoes of both fish and wasp, whilst steadfastly retaining the common metallic signifiers of twentieth-century aircraft, ships, locomotives and heavy plant machinery. This colourful banding was another key element in Foss's signature style – the bright, warning colours that are common to both bulldozers and stinging insects. In the case of the foreground spacecraft in *Norman Conquest 2066*, the presupposition of symmetry in the viewer – albeit, admittedly, not always a given in Chris Foss's work – might suggest that the spacecraft is supposed to have at least nine fins in total, three on the far side being out of view, but, as the spaceship is thrusting forward, the fragments of even more fins and panels are shown shattering and breaking off from the spacecraft, scattering in the its wake, suggesting it once had even more. Like the '9' mentioned on the more distant spaceship above, the letter 'P' seen here is common in Foss's images of this time, in this case on the ventral and tail fins of the spaceship, although for the most part, the letters and numerals that liberally adorn Chris Foss's aero- and astronautical hardware often read as reversed or inverted mutations of what would appear to be Latin, Arab and Hebrew ancestors, as if his vehicles defy the rules of grammar as much as those of gravity and aerodynamics. On the nose, the letter 'T' followed by other unknown hieroglyphs suggests that a human-alien multiculturalism is the norm for spacecraft insignia. The final element I want to draw attention to in this extended description is that which lies between the onrushing yellow and black spacecraft and the bronze tower, and is another typical element of Foss's compositions: a bank of cloud – in this case the profusion of exhaust from the advancing spaceship lingering around the bright circular portal at the base of the tower from whence it appears to have just exited – rendered with an airbrush in a mottle of browns, greys and white. Foss's clouds and miasmas were almost invariably rendered thus, the flocculence built up with successive undulations, waves and squiggles of spray paint that often merges with other sprayed elements – in this case the spaceship's aura and streaks of atmospheric vortices from the fins on the spaceship nose. All these signifiers – the blind fish eye circle and gaping intake, the shattering fins, the mutating texts, the polluted, seemingly artificially coloured atmospheres, the momentum of the spaceships – suggest systems and structures out of normative human control: in Foss's imagery, the future is presented to the viewer of the 1970s as a moment in which things are too big, too fast, too poisoned, too dangerous for that viewer to control.

The signifying roots of what extrapolative elements there are in Foss's technology have grown and mutated, as if in fever dreams, to gigantic size, whilst the landscapes in which they run amok have been reduced and pummelled to that of deserts and quarries in order to accommodate their energy and violence. Of course, it is not hard to find those elements in the context of the period in which Chris Foss's illustrations emerged: the early 1970s oil crisis, an age of sudden sharp economic recession, Foss's paintings of rampaging spaceships and the occasional tiny figures of onlookers in them present an addled, anti-humanist rupture away from the predicated humanist apotheoses of, say, Gene Roddenberry's *Star Trek* or Kubrick's *2001* or the confident manifest-destiny-in-space illustrations of the previous generation of space illustrations, predicting colonies on the Moon and such. This break is not just evident in the content of the illustration or the manner in which it is relayed, but also functionally: in Foss's paintings, the quantity of 'relational excess' of visual imagery I referred to in Chapter 1 is here accelerated to the point of qualitative transformation. That is to say that there is no direct relationship at all between Foss's image *on* the cover and J. T. McIntosh's story *between* the covers. The painting has broken free of any illustrative function, though it still notionally occupies the place of such.

Foss's covers proved very popular and boosted sales (conversation with author, 20 January 2016). Indeed, as Foss's images emerged as a new style in the 1970s, they were frequently used to boost sales of re-issued pulp writers from the 1940s, such as the *Lensman* series of E.E. 'Doc' Smith and the profile of other subgenres, such as the long running *Perry Rhodan* franchise, which featured hack work by various writers and both series of paperbacks seem to have been the occasion for some of Foss's most meticulously painted and well composed work. In a very short period of time, as demand for his work soared, Foss's work spawned imitators, which continued throughout the decade until the decline in the popularity of science fiction novels at the end of the 1980s.

Considering Foss's work and its disjuncture with the novel it purportedly illustrates (but signally does not) raises a number of questions, not least of which is that of 'why?' The disjuncture seems so pronounced that arguably it is not sufficient simply to regard the choice of Foss's imagery as answerable in general terms of its commercial popularity, even if this was, on the face of it, the principal factor. In considering the odd pairing of Foss's cover with J.T. McIntosh's story, the question remains as to why this particular image rather than others should be deemed appropriate by the picture editor: after all, sexual imagery also sells and McIntosh's story – a tale of bifurcated human evolution preoccupied with the presence or lack of body hair – contains enough libidinous material to warrant a suggestive image. In response I want to suggest that Foss's extraordinary images offered another form of *jouissance*, albeit one in which the libidinal component was sublimated – namely, that of an unbridled embrace of accelerated technology torn free of human control. If the *mise-en-scène* of Kubrick's *2001: A Space Odyssey* – which Foss was urged to see on its release in 1968 by a sympathetic publisher – presents us with a signal 'triumph of man' then Foss's imagery emerges a few years later as a triumph of the machine: a montage comprising not a giant human foetus floating serenely in the amniotic fluid of the space time continuum as in the closing frames of *2001*, but rather tiny adult figures, dwarfed by monstrous starships resembling poisonous fishes, socked in by noxious atmospheres and polluted nebulae.

My extended description of its details above should, perhaps, serve to demonstrate the extent to which Foss's work bears some relation to montage in the manner described by Peter Bürger, in that it 'calls attention to the fact that it is made up of reality fragments' (1984: 72). In this respect, I want to consider the illustrations not only as pictures synthesizing various elements in the manner of the montage, but also as they appeared in public as a mass marketed object – as part of a paperback book. As has been noted, Foss's imagery resonates with fragments of real, extant structures of large size and mass: ships, earth movers and so on. Foss's images make manifest Jameson's 'piquant montages' as elements of recognizable mechanical technology, reconfigured as the future. However, Bürger goes on to suggest that the work of montage is one that breaks through the appearance (*Schein*) of totality (1984: 72). In Foss's covers, this might seem to find its expression in the rupture with the text itself: the seemingly random attribution of a meticulous cover illustration as *sign* that nevertheless fails to illustrate. There is a bifurcating gesture here: on the one hand, a querulousness in the face of feverish science fictional futurity in general (the cynical, misleading cover that sells, but does not deliver what it promises) and, on the other, a gesture towards a future history of random, rupturing violence that is, like Adorno's conception of the new, ineluctable. One element that so far I have not mentioned secures this reading: below the white 'Corgi Science Fiction' lettered masthead, below the '*Norman Conquest 2066*, J.T. McIntosh' inscribed in orange and white, the publisher's promotional blurb provides the flimsiest link between a story about car crashes, titillating disrobement and sexualized violence in a desolate English, post-World War II, new town called 'Sherburn' of the novel and the landscape, building and spaceships on the cover:

> The blueprint of man was being changed and a completely new race was going to inherit the Earth […]

> (McIntosh 1977)

McIntosh's story is not about spaceships, nor, for that matter, is it even set on an alien planet. As with much of the dystopian science fiction produced in Britain during the 1970s – work by Brian Aldiss, early stories by M. John Harrison and so on – the small world English landscapes of Wells and Wyndham, or, televisually, that of Nigel Kneale – lingers in an advancing state of decrepitude amidst increasing paranoia in a besieged middle class suburbia or furtive bedsit squalor. This is very much the case in J.T. McIntosh's new town. The absence of figures in Foss' image seems therefore inadvertently fortuitous: an image of *things* – machines, architecture, climate – forcing the tempo of change, rather than people.

Indeed, Foss's figure work seems at its very best when it is relatively small – like his hero J.M.W. Turner, his portraits rarely work – and here the clustered groups of figures seen at a distance are particularly effective.

The cover of *Norman Conquest 2066* being typical, Foss's landscapes are not only heavily polluted but also dusty – one of his recurrent techniques was to couch any action – mainly machinic, but when a brief called for it, also human or animal movement – in a nimbus of airbrushed dust thrown up by sudden lurches or impact.

The other example that I have chosen to focus on here, Foss's cover for *Earth Is Room Enough*, is for an anthology, first published in 1957. As with *Norman Conquest 2066*, Foss's picture fulfils no direct illustrational function in relation to any of the short stories in the book: rather, it signals an excess of visual desire that cannot be satisfied in Asimov's short stories. Indeed, there are two forms of disjuncture between text and image here. On the one hand, the paucity of imagism in Asimov's writing, characterized as it often is by a *lack* of descriptive detail, might evoke a desire for an impactful illustration as compensation, but, on the other hand, the image itself does not satisfy any requirement for fidelity to the written text that a normal illustration might either. This lack of satisfaction is signalled not in an inadequate sketch or cursory image, but in the dissonance between the author's honed writing and the obstinate labour of an artist painting an image that is detailed, well-crafted and captivating, but wholly inappropriate: Foss's image might have made a good illustration, but the story that it would illustrate is not in the book. Science fiction's often predictable obeisance to its own internal laws as a genre – that is to say, its histories and traditions as they are manifested in form – is a limitation, but it also provides moments when the *representative* function of those forms fail or are ruptured and something else is *presented*, as if the artificial eye suddenly malfunctions, but in so doing serendipitously reveals something hitherto hidden. I want to suggest that the 'something' thus revealed in Foss is a combination of *ennui* with extant tropes of the genre itself (as I have noted above, Foss did not read the science fiction books he was illustrating, claiming he found them boring) and the *jouissance* of surrender to the triumph of machinic power running amok (interview with author, 20 January 2016).

Unlike the *Norman Conquest 2066* image, *Earth Is Room Enough* does feature small human figures, amidst the dust and smoke rising from a crowded, half derelict shanty town encampment in the foreground, under an orange-pink sky, streaked with yellow stratus that ambiguously lie somewhere between natural clouds and aircraft vapour trails. There are no spacecraft visible this time, only a massive building with a precipitous over hang, seen below from an oblique angle. The building – vast, impregnable, but also showing the signs of age by way of streaks and clinging vegetation – might be a wall or gateway, perhaps some sort of toll gate. Whatever it is, the crowd of people, presumably denizens of the aforementioned encampment, stand on some delineated *outside* to it: this image is an evocation of power and violence embodied not in rampaging spaceships, but in the passive aggressive form of architecture. The encampment population seems to be milling around as if waiting for something – again, humanity portrayed as no longer the agent of its own destiny, but beholden to larger forces. Perhaps they await some signal or sign from the huge edifice:

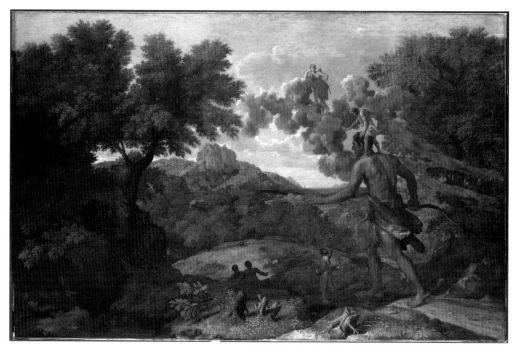

Figure 1: Nicolas Poussin, *Blind Orion Seeking the Sun,* 1658. Metropolitan Museum of Art, New York.

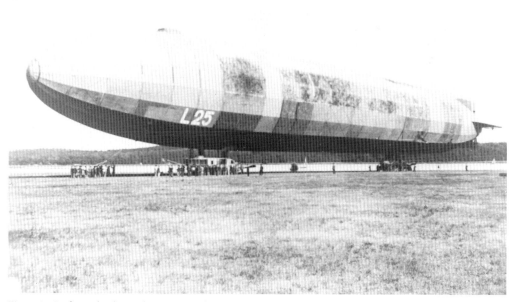

Figure 2: Airship in landscape, 'German Naval Airship L25' (Q58457). Imperial War Museum.

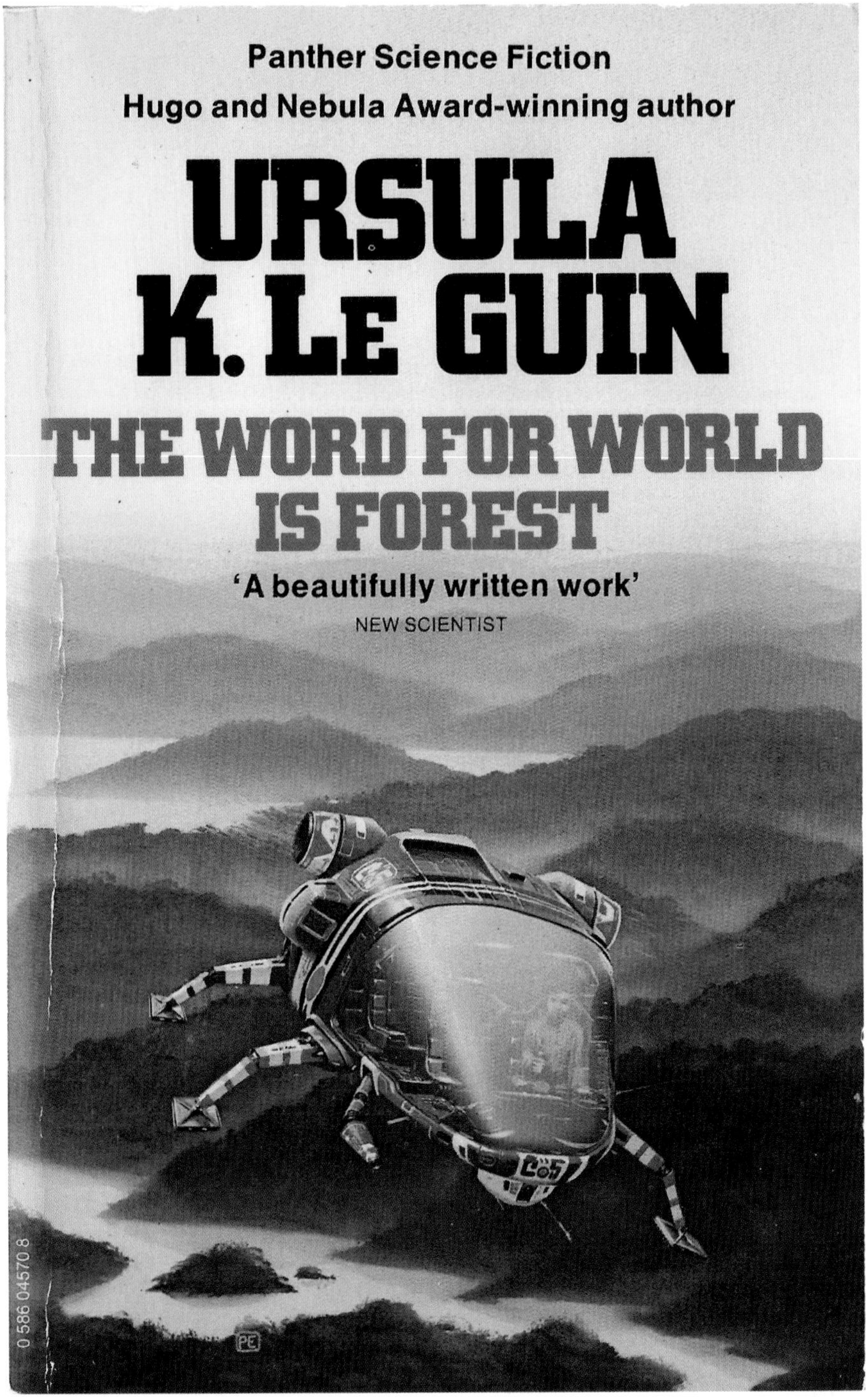

Figure 3: Cover of 1980 Panther Books edition of Ursula K. LeGuin's novella *The Word for World Is Forest*, 1973.

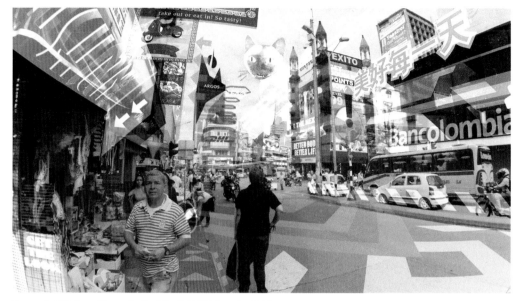

Figure 4: Still from *Hyper Reality*, Dir. Keiichi Matsuda, 2016.

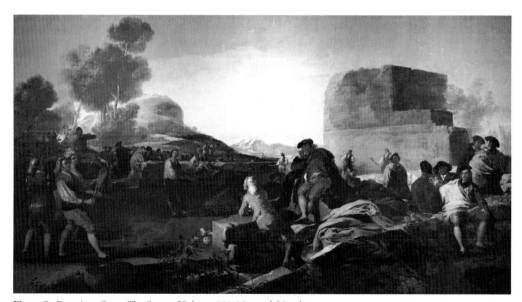

Figure 5: Francisco Goya, *The Game of Pelota*, 1779. Museo del Prado.

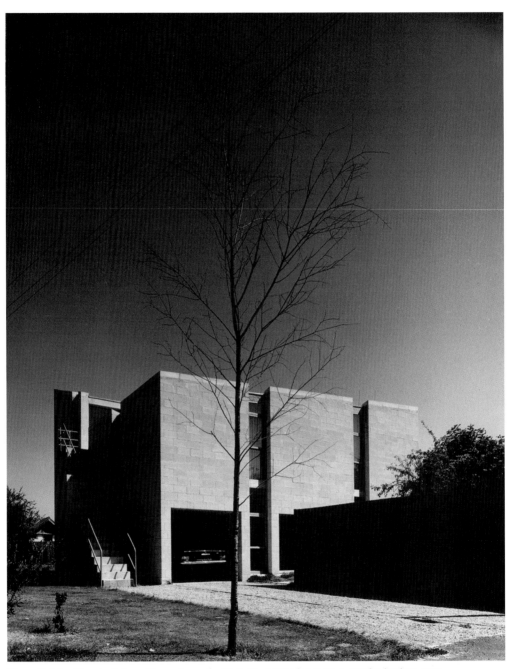

Figure 6: John Meunier & Barry Geeson house for Mr & Mrs J. Wendon, Barton, Cambridgeshire, 1965.

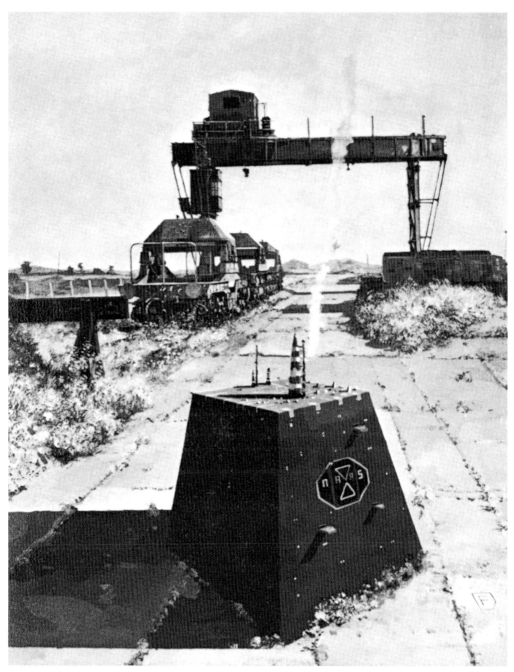

Figure 7: Chris Foss, *LYDD,* 1971.

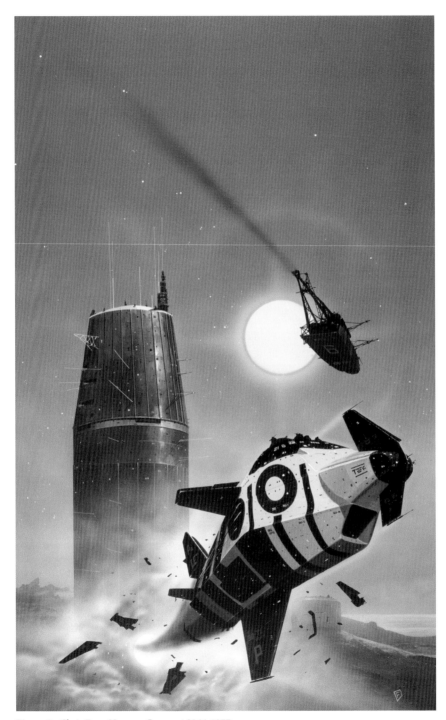

Figure 8: Chris Foss, *Norman Conquest 2066,* 1977.

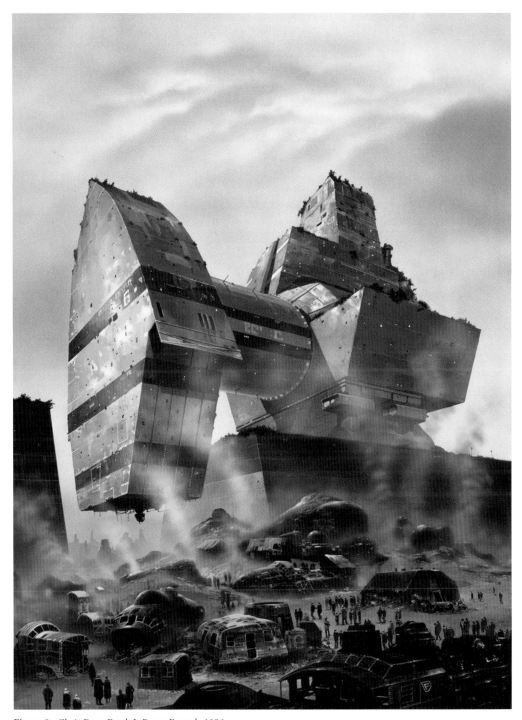

Figure 9: Chris Foss, *Earth Is Room Enough,* 1986.

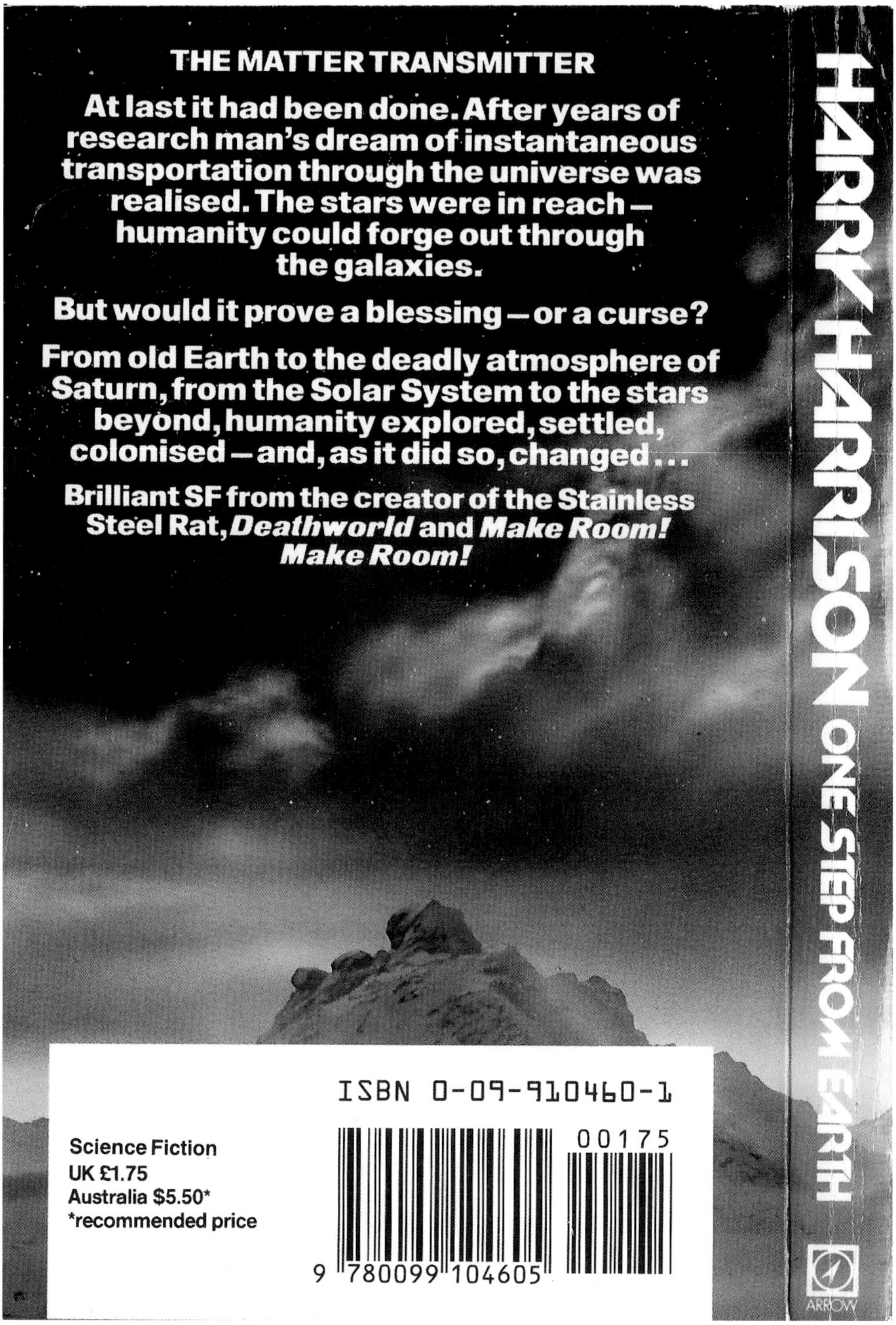

THE MATTER TRANSMITTER

At last it had been done. After years of research man's dream of instantaneous transportation through the universe was realised. The stars were in reach — humanity could forge out through the galaxies.

But would it prove a blessing — or a curse?

From old Earth to the deadly atmosphere of Saturn, from the Solar System to the stars beyond, humanity explored, settled, colonised — and, as it did so, changed...

Brilliant SF from the creator of the Stainless Steel Rat, *Deathworld* and *Make Room! Make Room!*

HARRY HARRISON · ONE STEP FROM EARTH

ISBN 0-09-910460-1 NBZI

00175

9 780099 104605

Science Fiction
UK £1.75
Australia $5.50*
*recommended price

ARROW

Figure 10: Back cover of Arrow Books edition of Harry Harrison's *One Step from Earth,* 1984.

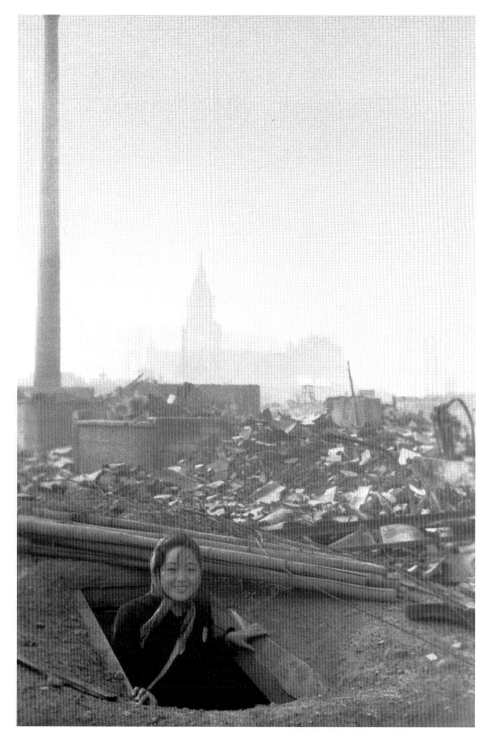

Figure 11: Yosuke Yamahata, *Nagasaki 10/8/1945*.

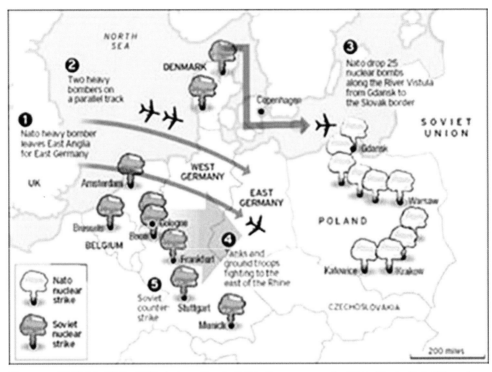

Figure 12: 'USSR World War III Map' released by the Polish Government and published in the *Daily Telegraph,* 26 November 2005. Used with permission.

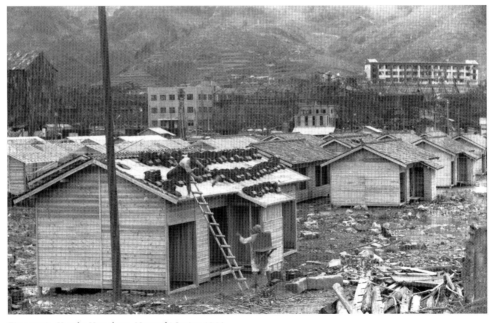

Figure 13: Yosuke Yamahata, *Nagasaki Spring 1946.*

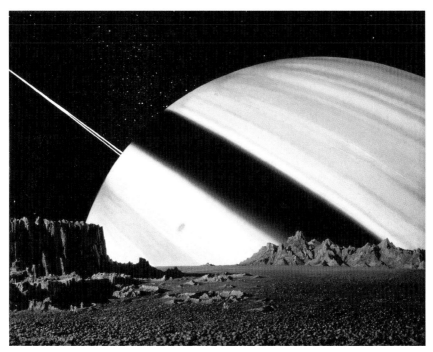

Figure 14: Chesley Bonestell, *Saturn Seen from Mimas,* 1944.

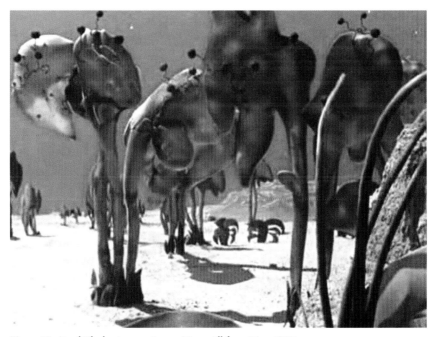

Figure 15: Pavel Klushantsev, spring on Mars, still from *Mars,* 1968.

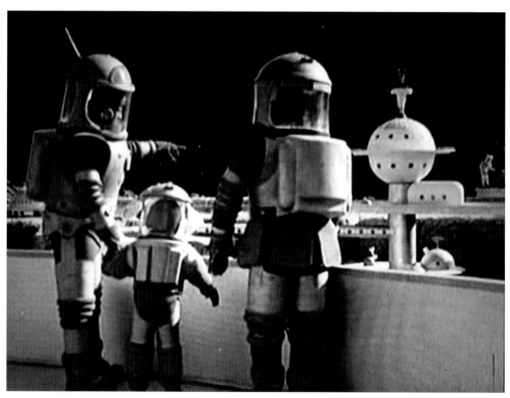

Figure 16: Pavel Klushantsev, still from *Moon,* 1965.

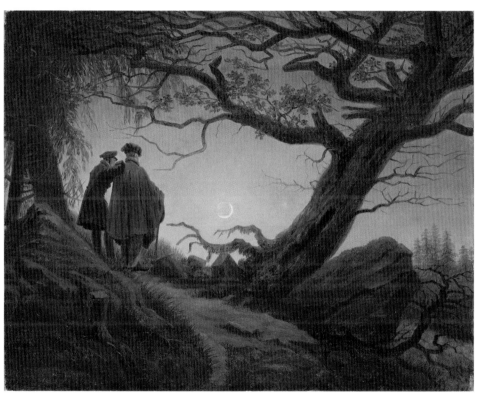

Figure 17: Caspar David Friedrich, *Two Men Contemplating the Moon,* 1825–30. Metropolitan Museum, New York.

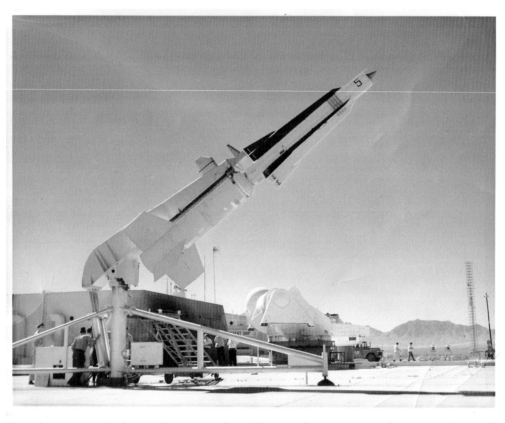

Figure 18: A two-stage Typhon missile consisting of a solid booster and a ramjet sustainer, being prepared for launch, White Sands Missile Base, Tularosa Basin, early 1960s. Digital copy of original C Print photograph.

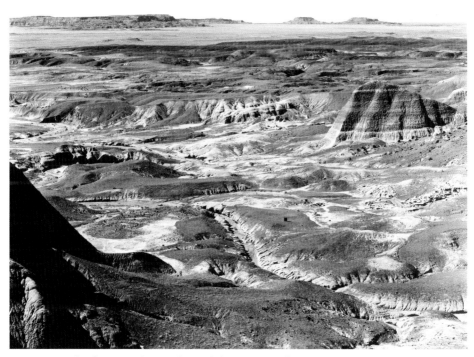

Figure 19: Frederick Sommer (1905–99), *Petrified Forest National Monument, Arizona*, 1940.

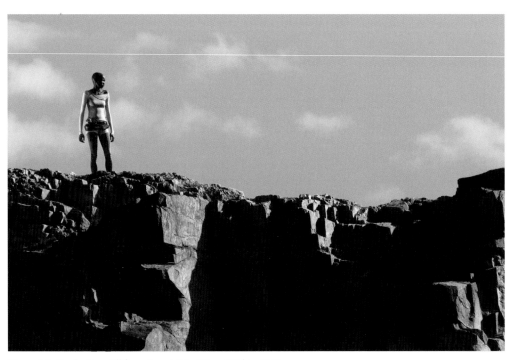

Figure 20: Production still from *Pumzi,* Dir. Wanuri Kahiu, 2009.

perhaps the egress of something or someone or alternatively to allow them access. However, the aging empty windows of the edifice suggest that if so, they wait in vain.

The even more dilapidated state of the foreground encampment, fashioned from a motley collection of immobilized rusting vehicle and aircraft hulks, delineated, like the occupants, by dull chiaroscuro glints and shadows, suggests dereliction in the social sphere as well as the architectural. Again, echoes of an abandoned mine or quarry, sparse, bare ground, with gorse-like plant life clinging on precariously.

The *Earth Is Room Enough* image in many ways summarizes Foss's architecture – fortified, impregnable, hostile. If architecture can be normatively imagined as a point of mediation between the body and the landscape – a place of shelter, of community or family, constructed from and within the environment in which it is placed – then Foss's buildings appear as emphatic rejection of such. The sense of looming imposition, of vast impenetrability, places itself as antithetical to any of the ethical claims of the domestic scale modernism of John Meunier and other architects whose work was prevalent at the time Foss was studying architecture (conversation with the author, 20 January 2016).

Whilst the montaging of twentieth-century machinic tropes into futuristic starships gives them an aesthetic poignancy, they are never so wrapped up in that to eschew the liberating euphoria that attends upon radical reconfiguration. Rigorously following the logics of such visual referents, Foss's visualizations sought to radically accelerate the visual possibilities of extant forms of machinic power: his huge robots, rovers and starships galumph, stumble, crash and soar as if perpetually on the precarious edge of capabilities that might be endowed with prodigious energy – an interesting fantasy in itself, given the 1970s oil crises – but are still structurally defined by metals and concrete. The diminution of figures within Foss's landscapes allows these machines to become agents themselves: as I have noted, in Foss's work, the active subject becomes the out-of-control technology or looming architecture rather than the human beings that are reduced to onlookers.

Describing Foss thus intimates a sense of accelerationism in his work generally: a sense of surrender to what is perceived as the inevitable rise of machinic power, wherein human bodies are deployed compositionally only to indicate gigantism. Therein lies a sense of history – 'this is unavoidable, so must be not only embraced, but intensified or speeded up' – and that is why I have chosen to describe this impulse as accelerationist in the context of Foss's images. The writer Benjamin Noys has described the generation of 'accelerationists' that emerged in the latter half of the twentieth century, contemporaneous to Foss, in the following terms:

> On the one hand, they try to stay faithful to the libertarian effects of May'68 that involved the breaking up of pre-existent moral and social constraints, especially in education, sexuality and gender relations; on the other hand, they also try to find a liberating dynamic in the 'unleashing' of capital flows due to the withdrawal of the post-war regulative mechanisms in the 1970s. They at once accept this situation and then try to "direct" it, we could even say "surf" it, to libertarian ends.
>
> (2010: 7)

Whilst Noys is specifically describing elements within a generation of political activists, I would suggest that analogous characteristics can be discerned within the popular culture of the same generation: rock musicians, paperback writers and artists. Foss famously illustrated the anarchist Alex Comfort's *The Joy of Sex*, which even taken alone would distinguish him as a leading and active participant in the 'breaking up of pre-existent moral and social constraints, particularly in education, sexuality and gender relations' of his time, but moreover, the starships and the blasted landscapes seem to embody the very same 'unleashing' of 'unregulated' flow. Whilst Noys's critique focuses on the problematic of accelerationism as a putative radical political strategy, Steven Shaviro (2010) argues that accelerationism is a 'useful, productive and even necessary aesthetic strategy' since it involves a 'project of cognitive and affective mapping […] to explore the contours of the prison we find ourselves in' (2010: 137).

Although speaking of 'prisons' in this context might seem hyperbolic, if we take the contours of Foss's particular 'prison' to be the landscapes and libidinal energies of post-World War II Britain, then I would argue that his work is animated by just such an accelerationist impulse.

I would suggest that the relationship of Foss's 1970s machinic delirium to that of the humanist technocratic extrapolations of the 1950s and 1960s (typified in TV and cinema by *Star Trek* or *2001*, or in illustration by the work of Mel Hunter or Robert T. McCall) is in some senses analogous to the relationship that Suvin (1979) suggests of J.G. Ballard's work in relation to 'hard' science fiction literature (Arthur C. Clarke, Fred Hoyle; some of Poul Anderson's work) in that it presents us with an ideological inversion (1979: 67). Alongside its disavowal of the determinist futurological function such as Kubrick and Clarke had reasserted in science fiction through *2001*, the appeal in Foss's work lies in its mischievous evocation and inversion of the superman plotting of science fiction pulp (in which the pre-determined character of the hero simply overcomes all obstacles, rather than being enriched or shaped by them): in Foss, it is machines that force their effects upon the landscape, not people. In terms of content this pulp resonance is found in the works' disregard for astronomical accuracy (except in specially commissioned works, Foss's images generally made no attempt to reflect extant scientific planetary knowledge) and, formally, it is seen in Foss's revival of bold background colours – red or green skies, yellow clouds and so on – not seen since the work of 1930s pulp illustrators such as Frank R. Paul (1884–1963).

Foss's work presents us with improbable concoctions that nevertheless function as *nova* visually in terms of what Suvin suggests is cognitively 'sufficient':

> Thus, if the novum is the necessary condition of SF (differentiating it from naturalistic fiction) the validation of the novelty by scientifically methodical cognition into which the reader is inexorably led is the *sufficient* condition for SF.
>
> (1979: 65, original emphasis)

In Foss's rocketships, what is 'sufficient' for the viewer's cognition of mechanical functionality is the outward paraphernalia of recognizable twentieth-century machinic tropes, regardless of the practicalities of coping with the three basic forces acting on the rocket: gravity, thrust and aerodynamic drag. It is perhaps not peripheral to the reception of these images that regard for such forces seems to have been so easily cast aside: in the context of the energy crises of the early 1970s and the end of the post-World War II economic boom in the Atlantic countries during the same period, Foss's rocketships seem to gesture towards a time when prodigious energy is once more in such abundance that it can be expended wantonly. To describe it thus is to acknowledge the erotics of Foss's machinery: indeed, in their complexity, intricacies, asymmetries and excesses, as in their gestures of desire, there is much in Foss's machines and landscapes that bears comparison to the rococo.

The Erotics of Paperback Landscapes

In the manner they were distributed and consumed – in the rapidly expanding paperback market of the 1970s – Foss's book covers competed with a wide variety of imagery designed to secure sales through attention grabbing titillation and promissory promotional texts designed to secure the sale once the book had been noticed. A significant proportion of the paperback covers produced by Chris Foss are therefore markedly asymmetrical in composition to accommodate these texts. The principal object/figure in the image and the action portrayed is concentrated in the right half of a picture with a typically 4:3 aspect ratio. This convention was to allow the image to be used as a wraparound image for a book cover, so that the title and author's name, perhaps with a brief quote, would be placed over the image on the front, whilst a more lengthy text, and the price, could be printed on the back. In Foss's work, what is noticeable about this convention is the frequent occurrence of a 'quiet' area of landscape on the back cover of the book, devoid of starships or imposing buildings (Figure 10). Typically, this portion of landscape is partly obscured by promotional quotes from favourable reviews or a teaser synopsis of the story: a backdrop of distant hills or dunes; a vast expanse of alien sky or towering airbrushed storm clouds; a nearby star or planet. As with the starships, such landscapes are often rendered in lurid colours. Blues, yellows and oranges tend to predominate rather than greens or browns. Foss maintains that the landscapes are 'of nowhere in particular' (interview with author 20 January 2016).

Nevertheless, the geological structures appear oddly familiar: the moorlands and tors of Devon and Cornwall, the crumbling Jurassic coastlines of Dorset and the Cambrian igneous rocks of the Channel Islands, the lowering clouds and heights of the moors around Macclesfield. In Foss's landscapes, the rocks appear quarried or mined. Coulises rise over collapsing slopes of scree and spoil: cliff faces appear as dynamited cuttings. Foss also affirms that the images did represent the world as he might like it to be (2016). In this context, the landscape on the reverse of the book cover is presented as peripheral but loaded with potentialities of empirical reality, filtered through estranging colouration: the action on the front cover hidden, we are left with an empty uncanny landscape overwritten with text, in which strange or wondrous things are about to happen. Foss's landscapes in and of themselves present therefore as charged environments, comprising shapes and forms drawn from the experiences of childhood, overlaid with estranging colours that suggest an alternate reality in the manner suggested by Suvin (1979). As such, the novum in Foss's landscapes is one constituted in that

> [...] oscillating feedback with the author's reality because it is, as a whole, an analogy to that empirical reality [...] although SF is not orthodox allegory, it transmits aesthetic information in direct proportion to its relevance and aesthetic quality.
>
> (1979: 75)

In these sections of Foss's landscapes, distance becomes key. Doubtless to make space for the publisher's promotional text, but also as if gesturing back to a formative landscape of both memory and desire, the rear cover landscape tends to sweep away from the action in the right hand portion to a vast distance. This can be seen as a sense of *genius loci*, in which the formative landscape of Foss's childhood re-emerges, rendered distant, clouded or veiled, as a sign of loss or abandonment. In his essay 'The Representation of Wish-Landscapes in Painting, Opera and Poetry', first published in 1949, Bloch (1988) discusses the trope of both erotics and distances in the landscapes of the rococo artist Jean-Antoine Watteau (1684–1721). It might seem that the rococo landscapes of Watteau had a certain resonance within British fantasy and science fiction of the 1970s – the science fiction writer Brian Aldiss had referenced the painter in his short story *The Day We Embarked for Cythera* (1970). Arguably, this element of rococo represents another facet of the ideological inversion of 'hard' science fiction that Suvin ascribes to the writings of J.G. Ballard (1979: 67): the move away from the extrapolative technologically determined manifest destiny of humanist optimism embodied by *2001* that I detailed above. Incidentally, Foss's work was used on editions of both J.G. Ballard (the Panther editions of *Crash*, in 1975 and *High-Rise* in 1977) and later Aldiss (Triad Granada's edition of *The Eighty Minute Hour*, 1985). In Foss, the motif of distance correlates with that described by Bloch: 'veiled in unrestfulness: it is a world that binds that searching look and attracts people because it is *veiled*' (1988: 281, original emphasis). Of course, Bloch's sense of '*veiling*' stretched beyond that of the literal overlay of text we see on the reverse of books; nevertheless, I would suggest that that is a sense in which both this literal sense of veiling, and the more figural sense, are equally pertinent here. 'Veiling' here becomes a compelling figure of tantalized scopophilia. For Bloch, writing of Rococo landscape,

> [a] distant mountain sits in the dusk, invisible, but the night of the island makes the movement and the anticipation of desire appear to be immanent in the picture.
>
> (1988: 282)

Desire, of course, is rooted in the experience of lack in a veiled past, and in that respect I want to suggest here certain similarities between Foss's approach and that of Piranesi, whose work I mentioned in Chapter 1. Both Foss and Piranesi utilize visual references drawn from the past – in Piranesi's work, the outsize or incongruous ruins of classical Rome, 'veiled' by time and loss, are juxtaposed against his visualizations of his own time; in Foss's case, the worn out signs of nineteenth- and twentieth-century industrialization linger in belching smoke, dysfunction and desolation. Both create senses of estrangement, but I think it is important here to distinguish their particular forms of estrangement from that of, say, strategies such as *ostranenie* (making the everyday world strange and new) of twentieth-century avant-gardes such as Soviet Constructivism of the 1910s and 1920s or the New Objectivity of Weimar era German photography. As Simon Watney notes in his 1982 essay 'Making Strange: The Shattered Mirror' the photographs of Moholy-Nagy, Man Ray and André Kertesz had a strong influence on the English painter Paul Nash (1888–1946) (1982: 154–55), who in turn influenced Foss (conversation with author, 2016). Yet in both these cases, avant-garde artists sought to rid themselves of the burdens of past forms – in the case of photography, for example, to erase the legacies and tropes of history which had sought to identify what was seen as virtuous in photography in reference to certain traditional forms of European oil painting. By contrast, in Foss, as in Piranesi, there is a different project of making the future curiously familiar with recourse to the reassembling of dismal remnants, imbued with new life in the form of a fantastical framing. Arguably, this echoes the engagements with history in literary science fiction expounded by Suvin and Jameson that I have referenced elsewhere in the present book. But in the case of the visual science fiction such as that of Foss or the 'proto-science fiction' *vedute* of Piranesi, there is the acknowledgement, as per Steiner's opening to his 1971 essay 'The Great Ennui' (1974) that 'it is not the literal past that rules us, save, possibly, in a biological sense. It is images of the past'. There are at least two ways of interpreting Steiner's phrase 'images of the past' as he uses it here: on the one hand, there is the immediate sense of the social impact of 'famous pictures' – that social-psychological nexus in which particular images become the focus for collective neurosis epitomized, perhaps, by the work of Andy Warhol; and, on the other, there is the *eikon*/*eidon* dialectic of imagistic thinking that I discussed in my introduction to this book via the work of David F. Marks and Gérard Klein, wherein lies the possibility of liberating moments of creative imagination. Steiner's implication seems closer to the second of these two – he writes of 'images and symbolic constructs of the past' and of 'a symbolic structure that presses, with the insistence of active mythology, on our current condition of feeling' (1974: 13–14).

For Steiner it might seem, beyond the Real of genetically determined bodily characteristics, strengths or vulnerabilities, history is not a fable agreed upon as much as an *accrochage* of semblances, and his use of the word 'rule' suggests that images dominate or oppress us. Steiner uses his assertion to open a discussion on what he terms a period of post-Revolutionary *ennui* afflicting European society, lasting one hundred years or more, from the defeat of Napoleon at Waterloo to the outbreak of World War I. Steiner insists upon preserving the French term 'ennui' rather the English 'boredom' because he sees the period as dominated by 'manifold processes of frustration' and a 'cumulative *désoeuvrement*' (aimlessness)

(1974: 17) that is ill served by the normative English rendering. Steiner also suggests that such a period is characterized by a collective, societal malaise – 'the kinship, the simultaneity of exasperated, vague waiting – but for what?' (1974: 17) a 'perverse longing, an itch for chaos' epitomized in a quote he takes from the writer Théophile Gautier's cry '*plutôt la barbarie que l'ennui*' ('rather barbarism rather than boredom/frustration') (1974: 18). Steiner's thesis is that such a 'great boredom' – the 'brutal deceleration of time and radical expectation' of the European bourgeois epoch that followed the end of the preceding revolutionary period 1789–1815 resulted from 'a reservoir of unused, turbulent energies' (1974: 22). One might easily suggest something similar in relation to an artist such as Foss, emerging after what Paul Nash referred to as the 'War of the Machines' of 1939–45 (Boyd Haycock 2002: 65) and the orthodoxies of extrapolative illustration that followed. Foss's images might seem to reflect *ennui* with the tropes and assertions of the genre at the point of his encounter with them. Foss's science fiction machinic violence is chaotic and explosive, although it rarely appears as war – more often, it seems to be the result of malfunction or haplessness. This also would suggest perhaps, in the gathering sense of crises of the early 1970s, a querulous sense of boredom, the exasperated sense of waiting for something undetermined. What I want to suggest is significant here, drawing upon both Steiner and Bloch, it is the manner in which, during the 1970s, 'the future was seen with those signs' (Bloch 1988: 288) in such a way that the starships and their settings become a 'wish landscape *ante rem*' (Bloch 1988: 282). The imagining of industrial scale pollution, the profligate expenditure of prodigious power, gargantuan architecture and extreme velocities are torn from the preserve of rational technocratic extrapolation and become the object of popular desires. Those of us who grew up in industrial and post-industrial landscapes sense a 'spirit of place' not in the conventional picturesque, but rather in that less secure space of polluted desolation we know to be wrong, ethically and ecologically, but which remains formative, evoking a perverse nostalgia through its displaced familiarities. In this context, the gaps, elisions and occlusions I have mentioned above in the paperback form itself – between cover and content or between image and occluding text – seem apposite: they return the viewer to a space of repetitive compulsion, in which elements resonate but are never resolved and closure remains elusive. Therein, perhaps, lies their lasting appeal.

Chapter 4

An Unforgiveable Composure: The Apocalyptic Imaginary Since Yosuke Yamahata's *Nagasaki*

Figures on the Threshold: The Apocalyptic and Utopian Subject

Amongst the tropes of depiction, that of 'Figure in Landscape', is something of an old saw, rather like 'Nude' or 'Cloud Study'. One might describe the depiction of the Apocalypse as a subgenre to that of the figure depicted moving through a landscape, because the presence of survivors in such a landscape might seem, at a cursory glance, to be inevitable: in cinema and literature, character drives plot and the dead have no personality.

Landscapes of the Apocalypse traditionally become those in which the dyad of figure/ground and its associate tropes is played out *in extremis*. In their emphasis upon the lone survivor, such as that typified by John Martin's oil painting *The Last Man* (1849), they present the figure-in-landscape *reductio ad absurdum*. The last survivor, as the only human consciousness left able to perceive the world, cannot but fail to perceive the magnitude of his/her isolation, neither is s/he perceived by another. As such, in the face of such absolute isolation, the survivor's sense of self cannot be sustained by social coping mechanisms – interactions with others – and must instead depend on previously established memories and habits: attempts to establish meaning. The evolution of dissociative and maladaptive coping mechanisms in the form of messianism or megalomania would seem inevitable. The apocalyptic and utopian imaginaries are closely aligned by virtue of simultaneous senses of megalomania and insignificance: if one believes that the world will end tomorrow, one's sense of importance is either inflated by virtue of being the culmination of human history or utterly liberated by being freed of any consequence. Whether outwardly self-important and inwardly devastated, or vice versa, the apocalyptic/utopian imaginary is simultaneously everyone and no-one.

It is thus in the contemplation of the apocalypse that its dyadic reverse – Utopia – might be perceived as a product of the fevered mind: the Utopia/Apocalypse antinomy is all-or-nothing, and the apocalyptic/utopian imaginary can only be simultaneously inflated and deflated, unable to locate itself as a stable mediating agent between the trauma of the Real and the imperatives of the Symbolic. Science fiction's landscapes of the Apocalypse typically focus on survival, both in terms of expediency – the need for a story about the living in which the dead present one dimensionally as ciphers of horror – but also because, in apocalyptic science fiction, the lone human survivor-subject becomes the location of ideality (in contrast to other sub-genres where this location might be found in technology, or new planets).

In her essay entitled 'Feminism and the Psychic' (2005) the Feminist critic and thinker Jacqueline Rose addressed the question of the unconscious and the future, specifically in relation to politics, and which, *mutatis mutandis*, I want to consider here in relation to the Apocalypse/Utopia dyad, which is arguably the antithesis of politics. The question Rose posed in her essay was what role, if any, the Unconscious could have in politics. Rose saw this as a matter of how studies of the mind embodied in psychoanalysis, ever since Freud, might relate to wider social issues and circumstances. In the course of discussing this, Rose observed that every time psychoanalysis's descriptions of the internal conflicts of the mind were considered in this way, they were swallowed up by that which they were placed alongside: contemporary social issues. The result of this, Rose argued, was that those discussing such a relation ended up not speaking about the Unconscious as one of a number of factors in the present shaping our lives, but as somehow a separate, ideal element, which in the future, would, in some unspecified way, allow escape from the complications of the present. Interestingly, Rose refers to the Unconscious not as an element, as I have just done, but rather as a *site*:

> [...] the unconscious shifts [...] from the site of a division into the vision of an ideal unity to come. As if the tension between the unconscious and the image to which we cling of ourselves were split off from each other, and the second were idealised and then projected forward into historical time.

(2005: 9)

Rose's explanation here is one that describes a regrettable shift from an actual place in the here and now, to a vision of an ideal delayed to some hazy, unspecified future time. The conscious 'image to which we cling of ourselves' is, as Rose understands, an incomplete and inaccurate one, precisely because it does not include those aspects which are unconscious. Moreover, I would suggest that the syndrome Rose describes tells us something about our conscious visions of the future, the ideals of science fiction and the pitfalls of such. For if the future habitually becomes the *site* of an ideal, unified subjectivity, expunged of the Unconscious (a utopian moment), then the future also becomes, simultaneously, the site of an *objective* disunity-to-come – the (dystopian) Apocalypse. This is because the utopian ideal of wholeness, purity and resolution of all conflict within any given individual – if such a thing were either possible or desirable – could only be constituted on the dissolution of all social life and interaction. Indeed, it is not unusual for these two fantasies to go hand in hand, as many science fiction films predicated on the 'last true surviving man' make clear. The archetype is seen in Jean-Baptiste Cousin de Grainville's *Le Dernier Homme* (1805) and Mary Shelley's *The Last Man* (1826). Shelley's extinction narrative was inspired by the volcanic winter that followed the eruption of Mount Tambora 10 years earlier. The trope is perpetuated in later twentieth century Hollywood by Charlton Heston in films such as *Planet of the Apes* (1968) or *The Omega Man* (1971) and, latterly, by actors such as Will Smith in *I Am Legend* (2007) or Tom Cruise in *Oblivion* (2013). The perpetual deferral of desires to some future ideal moment, when everyone and everything is united, and, also, when objective circumstances are ripe, is a common enough trope in the collective aspirations of certain schemas of millenarian ideologies, whether of the Left or the Right, just as it is common place in certain forms of religion. Contrary to this chiasmus, Rose argues, effectively, that the task at hand is to recognize the impossibility of such splits and 'projections' and, instead, to deal with the radically conflated present moment. In such a way, Rose suggests, the Unconscious and self-image are not idealized as separate entities, but understood together, so that the problematic but ultimately dialectically fruitful tension is maintained within that present moment.

The extrapolation of Rose's argument I have proposed here is one of a particular figure/ground relation constituted upon a ground that is historical/temporal (a future time) and spatial (the apocalyptic wasteland). I would suggest that there is also an interesting correlation in that to the argument advanced by Jameson in his book *The Political Unconscious*. Indeed, Jameson suggests that Walter Benjamin's famous assertion that the document of civilization is simultaneously a document of barbarism can be extended to 'the proposition that the effectively ideological is also, necessarily, Utopian' (2002: 276). Jameson's description of the historical inability to synthesize this antinomy of positive-good and negative-evil (described in *The Political Unconscious*) hinges to some future point in human history where dialectic can retrospectively be seen as an anticipation of 'a [collective] logic that has yet to come into being' (2002: 277).

However, I want to suggest here that through unpacking the dialectical relationship of utopianism and the apocalyptic as it is mediated through Jameson's yet-to-be constituted collective subject, we can also ascertain something about the relationship between Realism and Romanticism in relation to the depiction of landscape. The two are commonly regarded as antinomic and, indeed, the history of European image making in the course of the nineteenth century can be seen as a struggle between the two in the form of photography (Realism) on the one hand and painting (Romanticism) on the other. In Romanticism, the apocalyptic moment in which the 'dissolution of all social life and interaction' occurs is one that is endlessly deferred, just as much as the utopian moment of complete self-realization is – hence Romanticism's insistence upon the fragment, the unresolved, the crescendo that falls away. In Kant, this sublime moment can only be resolved internally through recourse to Reason, but that is no resolution as such, only the submission to the rationale that, 'it must be so' to the point at which objects in nature are represented in a way 'that determines the mind to regard the elevation of nature beyond our reach as equivalent to a presentation of ideas' (2007: 98). Shorn of this rationale, however, Romanticism can be construed as a reflection of the world founded upon such apocalyptic/utopian antimony, sustaining an unresolved, unending scream in response to the dualities of certain sufferings and possible pleasures around it, but also haunted by the persistent sense that a future that offers a better life can only be accessed through a journey 'through' annihilation. The impossibility of passing through something which annihilates produces a blockage, and that blockage is constituted as the paralysing split between the apocalyptic and the utopian.

I would suggest this splitting of the utopian *via* the apocalyptic is intimated in Derrida's discussion of *aporia* – in this sense – the 'impossible passage'. Again, it might seem that the analogue here is that of the figure traversing the landscape I introduced at the start of this chapter. Derrida cites the final chorus of Sophocles's *Oedipus Rex* in which the audience is advised to not pass judgement on whether a man has been happy until after his death. Derrida's gloss – 'I cannot consider myself happy, or even believe myself to have been happy, before having crossed, passed, and surpassed the last instant of my own life' (1993: 7–8). Derrida's discussion focuses upon the commonplace trope wherein death is seen as crossing (a threshold), passage or transit – *sic transit gloria mundi* – for example – but that such a border is seen as ultimate. Derrida parses this paradox of such *aporia* thus:

> [...] the impossible passage, the refused, denied, or prohibited passage, indeed the nonpassage, which can in fact be something else, the event of a coming or of a future advent, which no longer has the form of the movement that consists in passing, traversing, or transiting.
>
> (1993: 8)

A crossing or transit that cannot be regarded as such must be the one in which the transiting subject is no longer who s/he was, but rather, is obliterated and superseded by something completely new. The nexus established by conceptions of obliteration and complete newness is, of course, that of the apocalyptic/utopian. Derrida explicitly links the phrase *aporia*, within which he locates a sense of 'not knowing where to go' with that place 'where there is no longer any problem' (1993: 12). Etymologically tracing its Greek root, Derrida's sense of 'problem' here as 'that which one throws in front of oneself [...] so as to hide something unavowable' (1993: 11).

The nineteenth-century construction of the Apocalypse was, as John Martin's work proposes, frame-filling, in which all are equally damned. As such, it is a discourse of totalities and absolutes that is predicated upon such a separation or the hiding of something unavowable: the world-as-was and (another) world-to-come. In the twentieth century, post-Nagasaki, it is constituted as the zoning of concentric circles of reduction and destruction. However, in both cases, the apocalyptic landscape – that point at which the landscape appears as the all-encompassing, unsurvivable end – is constituted as 'that which one throws in front of oneself'.

A cultural corollary of this might be found in that which lies buried *in* the landscape, rather than on it, particularly during the nuclear era – bunkers, repositories, time capsules, designed to survive the fire. William E. Jarvis (2003) has posited the period 1935–1982 as the golden age of 'grand time capsules' – that is to say, those with trans millennial objectives, which tended to have an encyclopaedic quality, as opposed to, say small keepsakes or collections of heirlooms stored for 50–100 year period (2003: 138–174). Jarvis notes a proliferation of commemorative, curio and atomic landmark time capsules during the

1945–1990 period (2003: 229) and remarks that the atomic bunker and missile tunnels of the Cold War 'can be seen as Millennial votive offerings, futuristic dystopias frozen in time' (2003: 228).

Jarvis suggests that time capsules need not be regarded as 'surrogate survivalist offerings' and that 'The oblivion of today's culture will most likely occur naturally, even gradually, just as our languages become dead, transformed tongues' (2003: 231). Jarvis also suggests that the idea of the 'senders' of time capsules being at some sort of midpoint in human development was central to the reasoning behind the four most large-scale and ambitious time capsule projects of the twentieth century (2003: 146), in such a way that one might think of time capsule burial outside the parerga of imminent apocalypse. Nevertheless, it is worth thinking through how such a prospect of gradualism becomes supplanted, compressed or contracted into a putative future apocalyptic moment, as if considering the far future must involve an impossible, unavowable transition, that prospect of a moment of annihilation 'thrown in front of' contemporary civilization. Drawing on contemporary news reports, Jarvis describes how even two pre-nuclear age time capsule projects, the Oglethorpe University *Crypt of Civilization* (1940, target date 8113) and the *New York World's Fair Westinghouse Time Capsule of Cupaloy* (1938, target date 6939) were buried with great ceremonial solemnity involving speeches, removed hats, tolling of gongs and predictions of the end of contemporary society. Speeches at the Oglethorpe event, which coincided with the Nazi invasion of France, commented upon how 'The world is now engaged in burying our civilisation forever and here in this Crypt we leave it to you' (2003: 148), whilst at the New York World's Fair event, the leader of the project 'condemned despotism' (2003: 150). Both repositories reflected the preoccupations and vocations of the men who conceived them: the *Crypt* was a vault constructed of granite, steel and vitreous enamel sealed behind stainless steel doors measuring 20 feet x 10 feet x 10 feet, built by a team led by a scholar and Presbyterian minister; the Cupaloy Capsule project built a seven-and-a-half foot long, eight-and-three-quarter inch diameter hermetically self-sealing torpedo shaped device constructed of copper-silver-chromium alloy and heat strengthened glass and was headed by a rocketry enthusiast and science fiction writer (2003: 173).

In his history of the 2000 year time capsule buried by the British Broadcasting Corporation at Castle Howard, Yorkshire in November 1982 (target date 3982), Anthony Moncrieff includes messages to the future composed by some of the various corporate and public dignitaries who served as members of the project's managing committee and responded to the suggestion that they compose such messages. Five explicitly mention the 'possibility of nuclear destruction' (1984: 119), 'nuclear holocaust' (1984: 17), 'worldwide nuclear war' (1984: 41), the destruction of 'all we have by blast and fire in the course of one day' (1984: 116) or the threat of 'weapons of mass destruction' (1984: 16).

Such time capsules would seem to have been 'thrown out in front of oneself', into the landscape, as markers to the potentiality of nuclear war, now unseen, but persisting within the field of vision.

'The Worse Case of Our Common Future'

The landscapes of science fiction's nuclear apocalypses typically draw upon a hybrid conflation of two ur-images. On the one hand, the religious apocalyptic landscapes in the manner of the nineteenth-century painter John Martin remain – one might posit films such as Jonathon Mostow's *Terminator 3: Rise of the Machines* (2003) or Roland Emerich's *The Day After Tomorrow* (2004) as heirs to this tradition. As Julie Milne evidences in her catalogue essay 'The Abyss that Abides' for the major survey of John Martin's work curated by Martin Myrone at Tate Britain, London, in 2011, Martin's large-scale canvases *The Day of His Judgement* and *The Destruction of Herculaneum* have had long lasting impact on, amongst other things, twentieth-century disaster movie cinema, science fiction illustration and Heavy Metal album artwork (2011: 54–55).

On the other hand, Yosuke Yamahata's photographs of the destruction caused at Nagasaki, photographed less than 24 hours after the bomb had exploded, clearly stand apart from other images as a shocking rupture with the preceding cultural tropes of total destruction and constituted a new understanding of what might be understood as apocalyptic. I would suggest that the fundamental rupture that Yamahata's work presents is not that of the reality of city-wide destruction per se: photographic documentation of events such as the 1906 San Francisco Earthquake and Fire or the 1923 Great Kantō Earthquake had already been documented extensively. The key element I want to suggest here is that firstly, Yamahata's work horrifically posits the 'figure in the landscape' – the carbonized or calcinated body as residue, and secondly, it documents the destruction not as act of gods or nature, but of human design. As such, the terrain of Yamahata's work is that of a topos 're-landscaped' in accordance with military objectives.

The destruction of Nagasaki occurred at 11.02 am, on Thursday, 9 August 1945, when the American B-29 bomber *Bock's Car* released a 22 kiloton yield plutonium bomb over the city. To note the precise power of the bomb at this point is not merely a techno-porn indulgence: but rather to note its comparative small scale compared to the weapons subsequently developed: at the height of the Cold War, for example, NATO held in its arsenal a mass produced warhead, the W-53, with a 9 megaton yield over four hundred times more powerful than the Nagasaki bomb, and of course, one-off devices many times more powerful than that were tested up to the signing of the Nuclear Test Ban Treaty of 1963 – for example the Soviet *Tsar Bomba*, with a yield in the region of 52 megatons. Due to the topography of the city, the death and destruction caused at Nagasaki were initially less than that caused by a significantly less powerful nuclear bomb at Hiroshima, destroyed by the uranium-based Little Boy device three days earlier: the hills at Nagasaki confined the blast wave. However, the Nagasaki bomb, Fat Man, remains the most powerful single explosive device ever used against a city and its inhabitants, and its localized heat and blast effects were more severe. Various accounts and reports indicate that distant eyewitnesses to, and survivors of, the destruction of both cities assumed what had happened had nothing to do with the war between Japan and the United States: that rather it must be some freak natural calamity of the earth itself or a volcanic eruption. Either way, Richard Rhodes (1988: 715) writing at the height of the Cold War, mindful of a possible future nuclear exchange between the United States and the Soviet Union, makes a salutary point: the landscapes of Hiroshima and Nagasaki in August 1945 are not landscapes of survivors but landscapes of the dead:

> […] remember them. They were nearer the centre of the event; they died because they were members of a different polity and their killing did not count officially as murder; their experience most accurately models the worst case of our common future. They numbered in the majority in Hiroshima that day. […] 70,000 died in Nagasaki by the end of 1945 and 140,000 altogether across the next five years, a death rate like Hiroshima's of 54 per cent.
>
> (1988: 715–742)

Of course, the dying continued in the decades after that. In terms of military instrumentalization, this is the unique killing capability of nuclear weapons: a very high 'Standardized Casualty Rate' – six and a half thousand times more efficient, in fact, than conventional explosives (1988: 734). The combination of extreme heat, blast and radiation of nuclear weapons enables abstract schematics – concentric circles imposed over targets – guaranteeing what will happen to all living organisms and material things at specific distances from ground zero.

Yamahata, who was enlisted as a photographer in the Japanese Army, recalled later that he arrived in the ruins of Nagasaki 'at around three in the morning' with the writer Jun Higashi and the painter Eiji Yamada, 'directed to photograph the situation in Nagasaki so as to be useful as possible for military propaganda. At the same time I was concerned to discover the means for one's survival in the midst of this tragedy' (1995: 44–45). Along with two other men who remain unidentified, the party determined that they would attempt to walk, in as straight line as possible, from the damaged but still functioning train station Michino-o, on the northern fringes where they had disembarked, through the remains of the city, crossing the hypocentre (the area of ground directly under the point where the bomb had exploded, 500 metres overhead) and out again, towards the opposite fringes of the city, documenting what they saw. On arrival, Yamahata recalled noticing that the destroyed city, which 'differed from other bomb sites' he had hitherto seen, lay under a beautiful starry sky. He recalled later that he waited until the sun rose on what proved to be a hot, cloudless day and then commenced photographing until around three in the afternoon.

'It is perhaps unforgiveable' he later wrote, 'but in fact at the time I was completely calm and composed. In other words, perhaps it was just too much, too enormous to absorb' (1995: 94).

Yamahata's work presages a range of documentary approaches found in the post-World War II photographic canon – humanist, evidential, topographical – to show the horror he encountered. Viewing the photographs, one sees how that very calmness he retrospectively felt so guilty about enabled him, compositionally, to describe the actions and effects of the explosion as it instantaneously sundered and incinerated the city beneath it: amidst fragments and ashes, a scattered assortment of flat panels and upholstered benches, stanchions like ribs and twisted burned corpses tell the story of a tram car, shattered and burned, accelerated along its tracks until, derailed, it spewed its passengers into a drainage ditch; a nursing mother and her baby, their eyeless faces seared black, lying amidst broken tiles and rubble; unknowable of indeterminate age or gender, carbonized to the point at which one can only say of them 'this was once a human being' (as such, this last category became, like the piles of corpses in the Nazi death camps, a powerful impulse behind Humanism in the post-World War II polity).

Yet Yamahata's 'unforgiveable composure' allowed him to demarcate the incinerated city as a geographical zone: the simple, almost reductive act of 'walking a line' (again prescient of the thinking behind much later works of art, such as Western land-art of the 1960s and 1970s) demarcated Nagasaki itself as a *zone* of destruction rather than a collection of *scenes* in the manner of John Martin and his heirs.

The most effective and authoritative commentary on Yamahata's photographs written in recent years is surely an essay by Mark Silver, entitled 'Framing the Ruins', which was published in 2010. Framed within the context of comparative historiography, a humane historicity and a nuanced reading of Barthes, Silver decodes the semiotic construction of Yamahata's photographs and recollections whilst not losing sight of the truth of the historical tragedy of Japan's 'forgotten' atomic bombing, so often subsumed into the epoch defining monad of Hiroshima.

As Silver points out, there is a discrepancy to be read between Yamahata's recall of events and the rationale behind his actions as he related them during the years of the post-war political settlement and those views and intentions he expressed during the war in his own writings (2010: 236). This discrepancy effectively throws into relief the shift of perception in the purpose of the photographs: by the time of the Nagasaki bombing, Yamahata had considerable experience constructing effective propaganda images through his assignments as a photographer for the Japanese military's News and Information Bureau. As would be expected, he demonstrated considerable skill in photographic composition, framing and the construction of effective photographic signifiers to that end (2010: 240–42). By his own account, Yamahata arrived in Nagasaki to make photographs 'as useful as possible for military propaganda' and to 'discover the means for one's survival'.

Yamahata's initial propagandistic intent was experienced by some of the traumatized and burned survivors in the destroyed city itself: in addition to the professional compositional efficacy the photographs evidenced in terms of positioning, framing and lighting, Silver notes the extent to which survivors recalled, years later, being actually instructed in how to pose by Yamahata – a woman wearing a headscarf, pictured emerging from a bombshelter unscathed remembered later being told to smile by Yamahata, even though she was terrified and found it difficult to do so (Figure 11); likewise, Jenkins in *Nagasaki Journey* (1995) reports that a young man carrying his dying brother remembered being 'ordered' to stop in order to be photographed, leaving him 'disturbed for years'

(1995: 17). Notably, in his discussion, Silver ignores outstanding further evidence of such intervention by Yamahata, where, in a particularly famous sequence of pictures of the wounded and the dying, sheltering by a broken down pickup truck, in which a girl in a heavily soiled and bloodied singlet lies prone and listless whilst another of a similar age, possibly younger, dressed in a stained calico blouse and trousers is shown sitting up, drinking from a water bottle: in the most reproduced image of this sequence of four images, the last one shows an older man, in rags and bare footed, suddenly perched on the corner of the quilt the girls are sitting on, whereas in the previous shots made moments earlier, the man is nowhere in the vicinity. More generally, outside the frame and deep within Yamahata's formative influences, Silver also analyses the powerful influence in Yamahata's photographs of a nexus of *Ur-images*: Christian iconography – the mother and child, the skull (death) and the young woman (maiden) – and Japanese landscape. The composition of Yamahata's landscape panoramics, comprising two or more adjoining negatives, shows formal similarities to those of pre-war Japanese landscape photography. Likewise, as Silver demonstrates, Yamahata's framing repeatedly uses the tangled and fallen cables of the ruined Nagasaki to obtrude into the frame in a manner redolent of blossoming or leaf laden tree branches that features as a traditional trope in Japanese depictions of landscape.

Of course, to note such discrepancies and the influences of such ur-images is in no way to undermine the moral impact of the works as records of unimaginable suffering or even decrease their validity as documentation (this amorphous category, is perhaps best summarized by John Grierson's definition as 'the creative treatment of actuality' fits Yamahata's work, as it does any number of other photographers) but merely to be cognizant of Yamahata's 'comprehensively applied strategy of representation' that leaves in the pictures 'subtle reminders that [the photographs] are abstractions of the reality they denote rather than complete and seamless analogs for it' (2010: 245).

This is the historical fact (that is to say, a recording of actuality, transmitted to us through the historical process): Yamahata plied his craft as a professional photographer amongst unimaginable pain and suffering, and nothing in the photographs detracts from communicating that fact. For the few able to listen to his instructions and respond as 'ordered', others present were, clearly, beyond caring. In the image of the girls on the quilt, for example, there are two women immediately behind them, whose faces, hands and chests are flash-burned beyond recognition. They must have lain there in agony, prone and indifferent to any instructions by passing propagandists.

Silver notes what he terms the 'Atomic Difference' of the landscape. Discussing 'rubble as a [inevitable, but nevertheless repeated] motif' in Yamahata's photographs, he goes on to note that the ruins of Nagasaki were not composed of sudden alien elements, but rather 'constituted of everyday things' and it is the character of rubble to present a 'combination of uniformity and particularity' (2010: 249).

This is an important point of differentiation to the 'generic' rubble of endless fictive backdrops and imagined landscapes. In the Apocalypses of John Martin and most fictions of mass destruction, suffering is depicted across sundered landscapes that seem as alienated to their occupants as to the viewer. With notable exceptions – the BBC TV dramatization *Threads* (1984) is a particularly strong example – this trope is often present in novels and cinema alike. In Cormac McCarthy's moving 2006 novel *The Road* and its less successful 2009 film adaptation, for example, the unnamed father and son move through a post-apocalyptic landscape that is strange to them not only because of the destruction and horror they witness, but because they are travelling into areas they have never been to before in which such horrors are encountered. Contrastingly, the reality attested by survivors of Hiroshima and Nagasaki is that of the destruction and horror visited upon them in their regular haunts and domiciles. Survivors were not transported somewhere else, but rather continued to orientate themselves towards familiar locations – work, school, home, river and so on – under and over the new topography of wreckage, ash and corpses: two young brothers go to meet their father at his factory, to find the factory a blackened twisted shell and their father's partially carbonized corpse amongst many, many others. Debating whether to take his remains back to their shattered and burned home, they eventually decide to cremate what parts of his body remain unburned at the factory site, only to find while attempting to lift the body that his carbonized skull crumbles open and his half broiled brain falls out (Nagasaki Atomic Bomb Museum archives).

Just as photography's twentieth-century Modernist moments – *ostranenie*, Neue Sachlichkeit, Edward Steichen's post war humanism – all reflect the re-presentation of the familiar as different – Silver notes the manner in which Yamahata's photographs emphasize the bomb's capacity to present 'something familiar altered by a disturbing difference' and the nightmarish 'overlapping of the known and the unknown, the familiar and the uncanny' in the resulting photographs (2010: 245–47). Uncanny perhaps, but 'unknown' is surely wrong here: survivors know the actual rubble of their cities is made up of familiar objects reduced to a deracinated and broken state, but it is not a wilderness.

Silver's discussion points to an important differentiation to be made between the fictive depiction of atomic destruction and its lived reality: in films and other depictions the nuclear landscape contains only occasional, isolate familiar elements that serve as flashes of poignancy or pathos for the audience/viewer. Ruins in fictive renderings are, mostly, generic and alien. However, the Nagasaki survivors found themselves, not in a suddenly alien environment, but in the same place they had been before surrounded on all sides by familiar things, albeit smashed, burned or melted. Insofar as one can speak of the 'viewership' of the survivor – or those who, at least, as Richard Rhodes remarks 'still have eyes to see' this is a question of ocularity: the viewer of the fictive rendering or the photographic documentation continues to view rubble and ruin in terms of figure/ground relations. On the other hand, the traumatized view of the survivor is the point at which the dyads of figure/ground that obtain in the cinematic or rendered landscape are collapsed into an immersive *field*. Only the actual survivor can truly perceive the *generalized* aspect of this *particularity*; the viewer of the photograph may recognize this or that particular form amidst the generalized tangle, but not recognize everything.

Prior to the twentieth century, the apocalypse was envisaged in terms of *scenes* regarded from afar – philosophically, that of Edmund Burke, regarding the Terror of the French Revolution from the other side of the English Channel or artistically, Caspar David Friedrich's lone wandering *Rückenfigur*. This division between by scene and onlooker is replicated in modes of viewing and detachment. In the apocalyptic imaginings of the nineteenth-century painters such as John Martin and Francis Danby et al., crowds of anonymous sinners are tossed into Hells that are destinations. Hell does not come to them, but they are transported towards it.

What Yamahata photographed on 10 August 1945 can be read as one of many moments in the course of the tortured history of the twentieth century where the dyadic relations of the nineteenth-century paradigm described above are collapsed, and horror is not destination, but is visited upon the domicile. In the twentieth century, 'scenes' – typified as horizon-filling, frame-filling, but no more than that – become *zones*, where the division between landscape and human is as separate as body (or rather bodies) burned and torn open: this is what it is to be burned, seared, rendered and eviscerated. Yet the argot of nuclear war includes a category beyond destruction, namely that of *reduction*, taken from chemistry, wherein organic compounds are broken down to their base residues of carbon and calcium. Bodies are not tossed whole into hellfire: they are melted, calcified, carbonized, burned or scorched according to their precise relationship to radii: where they sit, stand or walk. This leaves behind, accordingly, zones of indexical traces. Yamahata's act of walking through the city – through the destruction, through the reduction and back out through destruction – simultaneously realized and bisected the concentric abstractions of post-strike aerial bombing surveys with the concrete particulars of horrific suffering.

Zones in the post-nuclear landscape are thus determined by heat and radiation: although Silver's emphasis on Nagasaki's rubble is persuasive and useful, it is, arguably, not the form of destruction which becomes the normative trope of the imagined post-nuclear landscape in the latter half of the twentieth century. Rather, the normative trope is the melted and irradiated landscape. *Gadget,* the 18 kiloton precursor to the Nagasaki *Fat Man*, test exploded at Alamogordo in July 1945, left an area of sand fused into a translucent green glass: as Richard Rhodes relates, later in the hours after the pre-dawn Trinity test scientists entered this new landscape in lead lined tanks to collect samples using rocket launched cups (1986: 677). Firestorms were not unique to nuclear bombing, nor are they inevitable: one occurred at Hiroshima, but not at Nagasaki. As World War II reached its climax, conventional bombing raids caused firestorms – for example, Dresden, Hamburg and Tokyo. Nevertheless, it is the relationship to radiation – thermal or isotopic – that becomes the differentiating factor between post-nuclear landscapes and those of other forms of destruction, in which rubble can be seen as a ubiquitous commonality rather than an exclusive defining point.

The action of melting was noted at Hiroshima – roof tiles, metal – but the same action on the actual organs of human vision were more clearly noted at Nagasaki. In the Cold War visual imaginary, the obscenity of melted eyeballs, witnessed in bomb victims at Nagasaki (and related in Watkins' *The War Game*) is transposed onto the landscape and the environment:

into lakes of melted glass that were once cities in Walter J. Miller's novel *A Canticle for Leibowitz*; into the high pitched whine of a melting hotline telephone in Moscow in Sidney Lumet's 1964 film *Failsafe*; into the melted Venusian cityscape of Kurt Maetzig's 1960 DDR film *The Silent Star* (*Der Schweigende Stern*) discovered by a Soviet mission as the remaining trace of a civilization unable to control either nuclear weaponry or its predilection for waging war. Indeed, both *Canticle* and *The Silent Star* date from the same period in which the terrible power of thermonuclear fusion based weaponry was being demonstrated repeatedly in the frenzied atmospheric testing that preceded the Limited Test Ban Treaty of 1963. *Failsafe's* chilling evocation of landscape of immolation by means of nothing more than a monotone sound transmitted thousands of miles away (anticipated by a brief, matter-of-fact explanation in the dialogue) reflects the dominant Cold War trope of pseudo-documentary: millions of deaths flatly delivered by voice-over as statistic rather than tragedy.

In Cold War period science fiction themes of melted, irradiated zones produce recurring landscapes of both *sterility* and *periphery*. As evinced by the figure of the time capsule, this post nuclear landscape is also divided between the horror above ground and putative safety below it or beyond it. One of Yamahata's posed images, again, proved prescient in relation to this dichotomy: that of the clean faced, smiling woman mentioned above, directed to smile as she apparently emerged unscathed from a cellar bunker. This germinal image of division between a clean/'sterile' environment located underground, and poisoned radioactive surface posits another survivor-subject. Post-nuclear fantasy landscapes in these decades feature pristine, sterile containment underground or behind sealed domes – architecturally or spatially – as seen in Mordecai Roshwald's 1959 novel *Level 7*, or temporally (Ted Post's *Beneath the Planet of the Apes*, 1970) or both, for example, the sealed computer controlled environments of Michael Anderson's 1976 film *Logan's Run* or George Lucas's 1971 *THX1138*. This hygienic obviation or suppression of the actuality of the Nagasaki trauma can be seen as the dyadic opposite to the pseudo-documentary mode. In the more ridiculous escapist mode, it allows the possibility of recourse to heroic epic fantasy – the 1960s *Planet of the Apes* films and the 1980s *Mad Max* films being prime examples. Such films use the zoning of nuclear landscapes to elevate that which was peripheral or disregarded to positions of centrality (in landscape, desert or shorelines) or in the case of characters, the socially marginalized find themselves elevated to positions of power: as Aunty Entity, the matriarch-queen played by Tina Turner in *Mad Max: Beyond Thunderdome* (1985) remarks, before the thermonuclear apocalypse, she was no-one.

The Transposition of Nagasaki: The Landscapes of Western Cold War Drama-Documentary and Nuclear Melancholy

Whilst the name Hiroshima, more than that of Nagasaki, became the byword for nuclear bombing in the years that followed the two attacks, it was, arguably, the experience of Nagasaki that cast a longer shadow on the world in several ways. The Uranium bomb

Little Boy used to attack Hiroshima was something of a technical cul-de-sac, giving rise to very few technical descendants, *Fat Man* became the basis for many, many more complex and powerful nuclear weapons designs in the years that followed. Variations on the Nagasaki bomb's basic configuration became the entry point design for all subsequent emergent nuclear powers. As Richard Rhodes (1995) relates, after the bombings of Hiroshima and Nagasaki, the US atomic bomb laboratory at Los Alamos had prepared another plutonium core to be transported to the bomber base on Tinian Island, to be mated with a bomb assembly, and dropped on a third Japanese city. President Harry Truman ordered that this process be stopped and the third bomb not be used, since he regarded 'wiping out another 100,000 people too horrible' (1995: 205). A year later, before the test explosions at Bikini Atoll in July 1946, the United States had just three viable nuclear bomb cores in its arsenal, two of which were then used in those tests. The Soviet Union had no bombs until its *First Lightning* test in 1949.

Nevertheless, despite this initial reluctance on the part of Truman, after Bikini, in August 1946, the United States built nine more bombs. William Liscum Borden, a former bomber pilot, published a book in the same year about a new world war fought with rockets and atomic bombs called *There Will Be No Time*. Lobbying for the United States to pressure the then non-nuclear Soviet Union into submission, Liscum Borden rose to become executive director of the Congressional Committee overseeing the US arsenal of atomic bombs (Rhodes 1995: 357–58). Two years later, following the successful Operation Sandstone – a series of tests of more advanced, powerful bomb designs – the Atomic Energy Commission reported to the Joint Chiefs of Staff that the United States would have 400 atomic bombs for use by January 1951 (Rhodes 1995: 261–361). The Joint Chiefs of Staff assigned ten atomic capable bombers and crew and up to twenty atomic bombs from its arsenal for use in the Korean War (1950–53), in full expectation of using them (Rhodes 1995: 445–46).

Whilst amateur photographic documentation of the events at both cities continues to emerge – as recently as 9 January 2013, the London *Daily Telegraph* reported the discovery of another image of the Hiroshima cloud taken on the ground about six miles away from the epicentre – the decades following the Nagasaki bombing saw Yamahata's photographs of 10 August 1945 become iconic images in a range of diverse contexts, extending through Edward Steichen's 1955 *The Family of Man* exhibition to the literature and posters of anti-nuclear campaigns. As Spencer R. Weart noted, writing in the later stages of the Cold War, the censoring of images of the effects of both bombs on human bodies by the US Government in the immediate years after the attacks on Japan meant that the predominant images of nuclear war in the public imaginary at the time were 'vast landscapes of rubble, empty of victims' (1988: 236). As Weart also points out, in US publications of that period, illustrations of nuclear attacks – such as those by Chesley Bonestell, better known for his astronomical landscapes discussed in the next chapter – tended towards views composed as if from the safety of great altitude. This distancing was in line with official released photographs of the *Crossroads* and *Sandstone* test detonations (using *Fat Man* and *Fat Man* derivations) at Bikini Atoll in 1946 and 1948. It also points to a psychological difference between the construction of depopulated landscapes of rubble on the one hand and melted, irradiated landscapes on the other: in both, the body is the object of denial; but in the former, the body and the terrible effects of nuclear weapons on it is the subject of foreclosure, whereas in the latter, the melted body is transposed onto the landscape and merged with it.

It is in this context that the incidents and sights documented by Yamahata, Yamada and Higashi during their journey through the ashes of Nagasaki presented a visual account that re-populated that emptied landscape with actual human suffering in subsequent decades. Images derived from the bombings at Hiroshima and Nagasaki found their way, in subsequent years, into the fictions and visual culture of the Cold War as persistent, macabre motifs: a burning hand projecting from a pile of rubble, its extended five digits each ending in separate flames like candles, witnessed at Hiroshima, appears in the smouldering ruins of 1980s Sheffield in Mick Jackson and Barry Hines's *Threads* (1984); likewise, the vacant, bereft stare of traumatized Tanaka Kiyo, the nursing mother whom Yamahata photographed attempting to breastfeed her dying baby Yoshiro, becomes a touchstone motif in a Kent destroyed by thermonuclear missiles in *The War Game*, and in the aftermath of the nuclear attack on Sheffield, South Yorkshire in *Threads*; Yamahata's photograph of an unidentified crawling woman in black rags, struggling on hands and knees across a flat middle ground surrounded by ruins is, likewise, referenced in the firestorm sequence in Peter Watkins's *The War Game* (1965) and again in Hines and Jackson's *Threads*.

Peter Watkins's film, which imagines nuclear war occurring as an escalation of the contemporaneous conflict in Vietnam, originally commissioned by the BBC, was never screened on British television due to pressure from the British government and within the BBC itself. Although taking the form of a dramatized fictional account of thermonuclear attacks on the towns of Canterbury and Rochester, one of the key features of *The War Game* is its documentary style: as if imitating Yamahata at Nagasaki, characters, in some cases introduced to the audience by the officious voice-over, are accosted on camera and asked to respond to questions emanating out of frame. However, this use of actors in speaking roles is modulated to the contrivances of drama-documentary: for example, repeatedly, an emphatic freeze-frame accompanied by continuing voice-over serves to reduce characters to that of indicative examples of mass behaviour or condition (e.g. preparation, panic or suffering in the various stages of the diegesis) rather than fully rounded characters.

Like the later *Threads*, from the very start, *The War Game* establishes a sharp division between those still orientated through power structures (armed police, soldiers, film crew) and those disorientated by both the pre- and post-attack crisis. Echoing the unbridgeable gap between Yamahata and the Nagasaki survivors, *The War Game* is played out through the antimonies of the directed and the directionless. Both play out the futility of preparation, but in sharply contrasting ways, far more than their US counterpart *The Day After*. In the early stages of the film, a point of view camera shot establishes the viewer as if riding pillion on a military dispatch rider's motorcycle, speeding through London streets to ministerial offices, where, once inside, meetings are in progress and announcements made; a Black woman is then seen on a bus being evacuated, whilst a voice-over informs us of the various logistical and social problems that mass evacuation would have on both hosts and evacuees. Tannoys mounted on police vans and officious hands knocking doors, followed by shots of argumentative residents of Kent towns disputing the number of evacuees they are compelled to take, create a mounting sense of urban tension and confusion before a cut to another tailing shot of a lone serviceman, shown accosted and questioned by the out-of-frame voice with the words 'Excuse me, what are you doing, exactly?'

Despite its broadcast ban by the BBC, *The War Game* was available for hire during the 1970s and 1980s in film reel format, and Watkins's film was screened in the United Kingdom at public meetings organized by activist groups such as CND (Campaign for Nuclear Disarmament) during the 1970s and 1980s: the present author first saw a somewhat worn print at a screening attended by approximately 50 people in a public meeting room at his local library in 1981, in his early teens. As such, the torched landscape of Rochester-as-Nagasaki, with its exhausted injured medics and whimpering survivors subjected to mercy killings by armed police constables, won the film a notoriety for its demonic inverted discourse on the logics of the British Welfare State in a landscape where, to use the famous phrase attributed to Nikita Kruschev, 'the living would envy the dead'.

Threads, made nineteen years later, continued this theme in more diverse forms – the doleful fate of council officials in town hall bunkers, amputations without anaesthesia in wrecked hospitals – but more significantly, perhaps, included a lengthy epilogue set thirteen years later showing the longer term environmental calamities of nuclear winter and ozone depletion. In a stunted, brutalized society where an intellectually and culturally impoverished population work for food under martial law, the burned cities have been abandoned except for scavenging forays and subsistence farming has become the normative mode of production. *Threads* was unique in this longer perspective, effectively locating not only the nuclear attack itself but modern technocratic society as a brief moment within a far longer continuum of agrarian subsistence. Moreover, through its vivid fictionalization of the nuclear winter hypothesis – the catastrophic darkening and cooling of the Earth by millions of tons of soot from burning cities – *Threads* presaged post-Cold War existential pre-occupations such as climate change and ecological deterioration.

Landscapes of Repressed Guilt

The twenty year period which saw the release of films such as *The War Game*, *Threads* and *The Day After* was one that saw the possibility of nuclear war veer at times towards probability. The rapid de-escalation of the nuclear standoff seen in the period after the end of the Cold War makes it easy to forget the widespread sense of foreboding that afflicted many across Europe, the United States and the USSR, with the steady build-up of nuclear weapons under successive regimes and administrations on both sides. In Britain, the notion of the 'four minute warning' (the estimated time between the detection of inbound Soviet missiles by the NORAD early warning system and detonation over their target) entered common parlance and the jokes and games of school children. Nuclear war was often posited as something that inevitably screened off the future from the present – as in the *Star Trek* mythos or the Japanese anime *Akira*, as a sort of rite of passage that humanity would have to endure before it could reach for the stars.

Throughout the Cold War, the Soviet Union maintained a declared policy of 'no first use' of nuclear weaponry in any future escalation of conflict with the West. Following US Secretary of Defense Robert McNamara's formulation of a Flexible Response posture for NATO during the 1960s, no such parallel undertaking was made by the United States and its allies. Part of the strategy of Flexible Response was the deployment of increasing numbers of both strategic missiles and bombers, but also so-called Intermediate Range and 'Theatre Weapons' putatively designed with the intention of fighting nuclear wars in localized regions of the globe – for example, Europe. Whilst subsequently published NATO and Soviet plans seem to demonstrate that the military on both sides believed this would be possible, most fictions and depictions of nuclear war supposed that any 'theatre conflict' would rapidly escalate to global level and that any conflict in Europe between Warsaw Pact and NATO forces would at most last around ten days before escalating to an all-out exchange of strategic nuclear missiles that would be launched to kill tens of millions of non-combatants on the opposing side.

As with the actual destruction of Hiroshima and Nagasaki, the responsibility for the *intent* to murder millions cannot simply be laid at the door of military generals or political leaders, however bellicose and reckless many of the time were, as Richard Rhodes notes in his 1995 *Dark Sun*, Curtis Le May, the US Strategic Air Command General, demanded 'a weapon that could kill a nation' (1995: 345).

Just as no scientist, political leader or serviceman stood trial or investigation for the burning of Japanese civilians, no Cold War era commander or politician was ever brought to trial for the stated intention to 'kill a nation'. It was, arguably, the realization of the shared responsibility in the wider population for this murderous mentality that inspired anti-nuclear peace movements throughout the period of the Cold War, from the first protest marches to the Atomic Weapons Research Establishment at Aldermaston in the United Kingdom in the late 1950s, through to occupations, sit-ins and mass demonstrations of hundreds of thousands during the 1980s demanding disarmament and de-escalation. Although successive Strategic Arms Limitations Talks (SALT) and Strategic Arms Reduction Talks (StART) between the two sides during the 1970s and 1980s and the end of the Cold War in 1991 did bring a sharp reduction in the number of nuclear weapons kept primed for immediate launch, outside the peace movement there was never any formal public acknowledgement of this intention to commit mass murder.

Whilst in a telling section of *The War Game*, Watkins asks passers-by whether they would condone or support mass nuclear retaliation that would entail the incineration of enemy civilians (the majority answer yes). The end of the Cold War merely brought with it denial, disavowal and repression: the military secrecy of weapons research paralleled by a cryptic secrecy of unacknowledged guilt. Fantasies of nuclear destruction – of torched and decimated landscapes, of carbonized corpses and melted glass – live on as a nexus of anxieties for the lost certainties of the Cold War, as a perverse nostalgia for something that cannot be grieved because it cannot be acknowledged.

The oppressive tension of the Cold War – preparations for the replication of Nagasaki thousands and thousands of times over, carried out in what would have most likely been no more than a total of a few hours – left behind it the paradox of a memory of a war that never actually occurred. A remark attributed to Richard Nixon, the US president from 1969–74, 'I can walk into my office, pick up the phone and within 25 minutes 70 million people will be dead', underlines the immediacy and totality of a war fought with intercontinental ballistic missiles. As such, terrible alternate histories of the period – ones in which the war happened – remain visible as cultural tropes but cannot be mourned as actual memories or experience. This, I would suggest, is analogous to the syndrome of what Stephen Frosh has described as

> […] an encrypted thing that acts as a hole in history; something imagined and felt as absent, but denied being, a never-having-been that continues to haunt the present.
>
> (2013: 54)

Frosh here is writing about postcolonial melancholia – the psychic legacy of colonial oppression which denies the histories of those it oppresses, but I would maintain there are parallels with what I would call here 'nuclear melancholia', which haunts the undestroyed glittering cityscapes and financial centres of the hegemonic West and is acted out in disaster movies *ad nauseam*.

Moreover – and herein lies a key difference between nuclear and postcolonial melancholies – I would suggest that the undefined, unresolved legacy of the Cold War cannot be resolved by the retelling in a similar way that historians of colonial oppression can begin the process of historical restitution by challenging the accounts of the colonizers and uncovering accounts of actual suffering from those who were oppressed. Therein lies the crucial difference – the sense that the unresolved leads to repeated, morbid cultural apparitions of World War III in spectral form.

Nuclear War as False Memory: 'An Arena of Burning Ruin for My Thoughts to Roam Uneasily'

In her 2005 book *The Past Within Us: Media, Memory, History*, Tessa Morris-Suzuki records how Yamahata's photographs were incorporated into a 1995 website project organized by the Exploratorium, a San Francisco museum, alongside a separate section entitled 'Atomic Memories', in which visitors to the website were encouraged to record their own recollections of first learning about the atomic bomb and its effects. As Morris-Suzuki notes, Yamahata's images tend to provoke a very wide range of divergent responses. However, a common characteristic emerges: many of these visitors' responses focus less on the actuality of historical suffering but rather on the imagined trauma of transposing that historical experience of others on to the self – *'This could be/could have been me'*. As one visitor states '[I]t could have been us, or our siblings or our cousins – and in a sense it was' (2005: 208) whilst another states,

> '[i]t's easy to pity these victims, it's easy to mourn or feel sorry. I'm more interested in the thorny questions of relative justice, distortions or omissions of history, interested in what mix of feelings these images bring out in me'. This visitor goes on to thank the organizers of the exhibition for providing 'an arena of burning ruin as it is [sic] for my thoughts to roam uneasily'.
>
> (2005: 209)

An iatrogenic disorder is that which arises as a negative, unwanted result from a medical treatment or therapy. In psychotherapy, an iatrogenic disorder such as False Memory Syndrome allows the patient to see him/herself as victim. During the 1990s, a number of cases were studied involving apparent memories of physical or sexual abuse that may inadvertently be suggested to the person undergoing therapy by an ill-trained or inexperienced therapist. As Mollon (2005) has pointed out, the terms of the debate were contentious to say the least: '[the] purported syndrome has not been validated, is not listed in official diagnostic texts and no clinical case studies outlining its features have been published in any medical or scientific journal' (2000: 5). Whilst scientific research on the issue was subsequently produced, Mollon's observation was that the debate's intensity – and the attack on Freud – emerged as it were from elsewhere than clinical evidence. However, as Mollon also points out (2005: 5), the heated character of the debate which erupted in the 1990s around False Memory Syndrome goes to the heart of the act of remembering itself – which, (according to Mollon) as current scientific understanding tends to argue, is not a process of accessing recorded data filed away in the brain, but rather a reconstructive process, hostage to the deceptive plasticity of memory in circumstances of suggestion, or pressure from either therapist or peers. My concern here, however, is to seek an analogy between those iatrogenic disorders generated by 'bad therapy' and those arising from the extended period of cultural, political and social conditioning of the Cold War. My contention is that there is a useful analogy in thinking through how the self-inflicted experience of the arms race, international tensions and crises of the Cold War period allows the West to imagine itself as a victim or sufferer: in other words, the construction of 'False Memory' of a martyred and destroyed Europe, constructed from the actual destruction of Japanese cities a generation earlier, juxtaposed with the real but evaded risk of nuclear annihilation faced at the height of the Cold War.

I should stress that what I am proposing here is not an etiology. What I present here is an analogy, which rests upon the understanding that all remembering is reconstructive, and that the complex combination of fantasy, the deferred action of trauma and suggestion from authoritative voices can result in the construction of collective as well as individually subjective narratives, the effects of which may, in and of themselves, have real consequences. As is well documented, the immediate response of the US Command structure on the day of the 11 September 2001 attacks bore strong similarities to that which would have been initiated in the event of attack by Soviet nuclear missiles during the Cold War. By the time of the 9/11 attacks, of course, the Cold War had been over for over a decade. However, in the United States, the four airborne command aircraft, the so-called 'Doomsday planes', designed to oversee a nuclear missile retaliation, were dispatched and the steel doors of various strategic command centres in the American Mid-West, designed to withstand a nuclear attack by the USSR, were closed for the first time, along with various other measures, including the mobilization and deployment of National Guard.

The conflation of the terrorist hijackings and subsequent mass murder of 9/11 with nuclear war was not limited to the immediate response on the day. Notably, in the decade since the attacks, I have noticed various cases where the actual 9/11 attacks have become conflated with the false memory of the nuclear war that was *not* fought sometime between 1949 and 1991. Examples of this might include the titling of Peter Taylor's series of programmes for the BBC, *al-Qaeda: The Third World War*; David Levi Strauss's collection of essays *Between the Eyes* (2004), wherein he likens the 9/11 fireballs at the World Trade Center to those of nuclear weapons; more anecdotally, having personally witnessed the attacks in New York on 9/11, I recall Manhattan residents comparing the events to that of the Hiroshima bomb, even though even a comparison of the respective death tolls for these events reveals huge, magnitudinal differences.

Such responses can be regarded as symptomatic of a wider iatrogenic disorder in that culture defined by NATO during the period of the Cold War. The logic of strategic military planning, of course, involves considerable and repeated attempts to *imagine oneself under the type of assault one intends to inflict upon one's enemy*. Such visualization of nuclear war scenarios reached a particular peak in the cinematic, televisual and literary culture of the North Atlantic during those periods of greatest tension. It is in the context of that culture and psychology that I wish to draw certain analogies between Cold War culture and iatrogenic disorders. One might start with the general culture of paranoia engendered by armed stand-off and espionage – Richard Ofshe and Ethan Watters, for example, remark in *Making Monsters: False Memories, Psychotherapy and Sexual Hysteria* (1994): therapy techniques which (1994: 16–44) re-interpret the mundane remarks as sinister derogation. Iatrogenic disorders of this nature often result in false accusations of abuse against not only the alleged perpetrator, but significantly, supposed or alleged neglect by another guardian or parent. Studies of false memory syndrome highlight the manner in which a parent or guardian *not* alleged to have perpetrated the abuse can be made the central object of anger and resentment, for their alleged inaction, neglect or indifference to the analysand's suffering revealed through constructed memory.

The publication in 2005 by the Polish government of Soviet war maps, containing details of which European cities would be attacked in the event of a nuclear exchange with NATO

(Figure 12), was presented in the context of an outcry against Russia, Poland's former Warsaw Pact ally and Russia's preparedness to 'sacrifice' Poland, even though the maps made clear that the destruction that would have been visited upon Polish territory would actually have come from NATO bombers, laying down a barrage of 25 thermonuclear bombs extending from Gdansk to the Polish-Slovak border rather than the then Soviet Union. Indeed, during the 1960s and 1970s, British Vulcan nuclear bomber crews were trained to fly with a patch covering one eye. The logic of this rationing of eyesight was simple: as such crew would be flying through that barrage along the Vistula, they faced a strong risk of being blinded by the flashes. The patch ensured that once they lost the sight in one eye, the crew could uncover the saved eye, and continue flying. Between them, the pilot and co-pilot could thus afford to have three eyes blinded and still be able to reach their targets. Such a blinkering might seem historically poignant (Channel 4, 24 April 2005).

I want to suggest that, along with the 9/11 examples, there is a tendency here, analogous to the responses to Yamahata that I cite from Morris-Suzuki's work above, to again position oneself as a victim. This is the analogy that I wish to draw with the phenomenon of False Memory Syndrome.

Of course, the posturing behind the Polish government's outcry can be seen as part of a wider repositioning by a conservative government, seeking to align itself with the United States – which was spared any criticism – and blame the Cold War on Russia. This might seem to be analogous to what psychotherapists term 'Reconstructive Retrieval' (Brainerd and Reyna 2005), wherein the subject begins with general concepts ('Russia has never been an ally of Poland, the West was never an enemy') and generates events by constructively processing that concept (e.g. Poland's nuclear annihilation through a presumed betrayal by Russia, not by NATO bombs). As the work of E.F. Loftus has shown (quoted in Brainerd and Reyna 2005: 383) reconstructive retrieval would seem to be a consistent feature of patients with iatrogenic false memories.

In the immediate aftermath of 9/11, a further spectral fragment of the nuclear war that never happened re-emerged. In March 2002, two American magazines, the left leaning *The Nation* and the more conservative *Newsweek* both reported that Soviet made 'suitcase bombs' were possibly in circulation, and that in the immediate aftermath of 9/11, the US security services had been acting on credible evidence that such a bomb was somewhere in Manhattan. At the same time, fears were raised around the possibility of a nuclear device being concealed in one of the thousands of shipping containers being delivered to New York every day. This fear of a bomb carried in a cargo ship resurrected earlier anxieties entertained by the British government half a century earlier in the 1950s. Indeed, as Brian Cathcart (1994) relates, Britain's first nuclear test, *Hurricane* in 1952, involved a bomb detonated in the hold of a ship moored in the Bunsen Channel, a stretch of water off North West Australia chosen for its similarities in depth and mud content to the River Thames and the Port of London. The British government feared such a bomb vaporizing river water and spreading a deadly radioactive mist over southern England. This fear arose not from a demonstration of such intent by its enemy (the Soviet Union, which at the time of the British commencement of its own bomb project had no such capability) but from *Bikini Baker*, a nuclear test conducted in 1946 by its ally, the United States.

Again, as in all the examples cited, there is the lingering sense that the nuclear war that did *not* occur sometime between 1949 and 1989 remains a touchstone, but also a possible threat projected on to, and emanating from the Other: nuclear war as a constructed recollection of a traumatic experience from which belief and motivation can be drawn and via which any challenges to one's self-positioning can be assiduously avoided.

The City Rises: Neo-Tokyo versus Nagasaki without the Bomb

I began this chapter with Jacqueline Rose's remarks regarding splitting and projection. I suggested that the inverse corollary of that which Rose describes is to be found in the 'last man' lone survivor, often figured in Hollywood films. Yet whilst the abiding trope of landscapes of desolation might seem to be that lone survivor amidst the ashes, Yamahata's last photographs of Nagasaki testify not to individual survival, but evidence of collective reconstruction of the cityscape itself, whilst individual death continued unabated: Yamahata's photographs show new temporary wooden houses, made from fresh timber (Figure 13).

Nagasaki, like it sister Hiroshima, became a thriving city once more with astonishing rapidity. An article by Justin McCurry in the British newspaper *The Guardian* (18 April 2016) reported how, in Hiroshima, electric light had been restored in some less damaged areas by 7 August and around Hiroshima railway station a day later. Some telephony had been re-established eight days after the bombing, and by the end of November 1945, all the homes that had not been damaged by fire had had power restored. To date, the extant chronicle of nuclear destruction leads not to one of mass extinction but, despite unimaginable suffering, to that of reconstruction. Indeed, one of the salutary lessons to be drawn from the destroyed cityscapes of the twentieth century as a whole might be that reconstruction seems inevitable: it actually requires a determined museological impulse of memorialization to maintain any site, let alone a city, in its destroyed state. The village of Oradour-sur-Glane, whose inhabitants were mass-murdered by the Nazis in 1944 and was thus preserved by the French authorities, might be an example of this. In sharp contrast, the photographs of civilian Yoshita Kishimoto, from October 1945 onwards, now held in the Hiroshima Peace Memorial Museum, evidence the remarkable regeneration of the scorched city, seen from the same location at regular intervals.

It is therefore not surprising that whilst in the West, the science fiction imaginary has duly 'preserved' destroyed cities as either sublime ruins (Caprica in the 2004–09 *Battlestar Galactica* or the crumbling towers and Harbour Bridge of Sydney seen at the end of *Mad Max: Beyond Thunderdome*) or abandoned zones, in *Akira* (Katsushiro Otomo, 1988), the pace of reconstruction and repopulation suggests an almost inevitable pulsation of perpetual development, as the new technologically advanced cosmopolis rises over the ashes of the old one. Whilst the destruction in *Akira* is ostensibly 'psychic' rather than nuclear, it initiates

World War III. Indeed, the superbly detailed hand-rendered cityscapes of Neo Tokyo in *Akira* can be read as reflecting the human labour of rebuilding the burned cities of post-war Japan: every window replaced, every scrap of rubble cleared.

Since the end of the Cold War, the depiction of desolated cities has more commonly become a sign of ecological collapse rather than of nuclear destruction. Curiously, however, the forms of the trope remain more or less the same: ashes, rubble and ruin; Nagasaki re-staged, but without the Bomb. The growth of the so-called 'Prepper' movement in the United States, predicated not on the aftermath of an expected nuclear war as earlier survivalist movements were, but upon more diffuse causes of apocalyptic societal collapse, points to a continuation of the individual survivor versus hostile desolation. The science fiction writer Bruce Sterling suggests that since the end of the Cold War, whilst the Bomb itself no longer occupies its former position in the popular imaginary as the prime threat to human existence, the Bomb's progenitor, human intelligence itself, remains the 'explosion' threatening life. As Sterling points out, in geological timescales, the statistical human norm is that of the illiterate hunter-gatherer, whilst the explosion of potentially planet destroying technology of whatever form is a relatively sudden, alarming turn. However, while a nuclear bomb lets a great deal of energy loose all at once, fossil fuels slowly spread their pall of wasted energy throughout the whole planet. In both ecological collapse and nuclear holocaust however, as with *Battlestar Galactica*, '[I]t is self-indulgent laziness' Stirling castigates teleologically, 'to predict that the clock will stop ticking – just because it happens to be our watch' (2003: 264). Stirling's pun on 'watch' raises once more a well-established device of science fiction since Wells: that which delineates and differentiates not only human historical time from that of the planet's ecology, but also its ends.

The regeneration of Nagasaki established not simply a 'before and after' dyad, nor simply the possibilities of repetition of the catastrophe and its aftermath elsewhere in germane to the 'survivability' rhetoric of the Cold War, but rather in the science fiction imaginary, narrativizations of geological time through which rhythms or pulses of birth and extinctions cascade. 'Sometimes a Great Notion', Episode 13 of Season 4 of the 2004–09 *Battlestar Galactica* re-make, portrays the competing Humans and Cylons arriving at their long sought destination of Earth only to find the entire planet has been destroyed by nuclear war 2000 years earlier. One of the lead characters, Admiral William Adama (Edward James Olmos), arrives on a windswept beach of a grey sea, only to kneel and sift black grains of ash through his fingers, whilst in the distance across the bay – or perhaps the 'long cape' from which Nagasaki takes its name – half lost in the sea haze and spray, the scorched ruins of tower blocks stand like tombstones. What is significant in this particular iteration of the Nagasaki trope is its visualization within the wider cyclical theme which permeates the series as whole: 'All this will happen again'. Indeed, the diegesis subsequently reveals that this particular iteration of humanoid civilisation was Cylon, not *homo sapiens*. As *Battlestar Galactica* reaches its *finale* there appears to be more than one Earth, there is more than one species of humanoid, more than one set of humanoid robot Cylon antagonists, stretching in all directions across the galaxy and spanning the ages through rhythms of destruction and rebirth. Landscapes of Nagasaki, then, become momentary windows.

Either way, the trope of the individual survivor in the perpetually burned, never-to-be-reconstructed cityscape speaks to individual survival, and the depiction of such appeals and thrills whilst perpetuating both the mythologized projections of individualism I referred to via Rose and the individual's fear of death. Nevertheless, the trope hides a greater truth that was ultimately revealed by Yamahata's pictures and confirmed by his own untimely death – namely that individual survivors ultimately succumb, whilst on the other hand, collectivities reform, regroup, repopulate and reconstruct, re-landscaping as they do so.

Chapter 5

'Suppositional Realism' and the Fictions of Science:
The Astronomical Landscapes of Pavel Klushantsev
and Chesley Bonestell

With the passage of time, both the groundbreaking planetary landscapes of Chesley Bonestell (1888–1986, Figure 14) and the stunning cinematic sets, backdrops and special effects of Pavel Klushantsev (1910–99, Figures 15, 16) can be seen to have shed their respective potencies as portents to become signifiers of a past future that never materialized and of landscapes that do not exist. As such, both bodies of work have become the opposite of what they were intended to be, not only in content, but also in form: Bonestell's paintings are collected and displayed as works of Fine Art, perhaps as signs of the faded technological optimism of *Pax Americana* and as symbols of 'golden age' science fiction. Similarly, Klushantsev's imagery is presented as symbolic of the failed dream of Soviet Communism. This affective shift in the mode of reception is not merely ironic: it effectively robs the work of agency, eroding the ontological claims of the content, which it replaces with a maudlin preoccupation with style. This generally can be seen as one of the corrosive cultural effects of nostalgia: the past's cultures and politics become estranged, the intentions of its protagonists obscure.

Arguably, with time, this process is exacerbated by the increasing opacity of the media used: the dyes of colour film age and fade at different rates, so photographic images lose their yellows and cyans, leaving images predominantly magenta; particular styles of illustrational rendering once so fashionably commonplace as to be unremarkably transparent, become opaque; materials once regarded as obvious choices to build the technology of the future become quaint. People no longer trust a proposed space shuttle made of rolled steel and hot rivets, nor a high key rendering of a jagged moonscape in casein colours. In time, these aspects of an image come to dominate its phenomenological reception.

For obvious reasons, it is hard to imagine – perhaps at times almost *impossible* to see – science fiction itself and the fictions of science (of which I will write more below) except through the lens of the contemporary capitalist culture within which, for the most part, it remains embedded. Contemporary culture thrives on retelling – and reselling – the past. Indeed, arguably, capitalist visual culture of the early twenty-first century is little more than the retelling and reselling of the past, to the extent that we are bombarded with remake and 're-imaginings' – for example in Hollywood cinema – or with pastiches of 'design classics' in fashion and architecture, to name but a few. Apparently unable to sufficiently manage economic development to meet what some might see as the pressing ecological need to recycle and re-use, capitalist culture nevertheless appears supremely efficient at recycling styles from earlier epochs or even those from scant decades earlier.

Recent discoveries by robotic space probes – for example the incredible amount of stunning information and images received from the surface of Mars and in its orbit – extend far beyond what was known about that planet in the time of Klushantsev and Bonestell. It is a commonplace that the technology that has gathered such data is far superior to that of their era. Yet the *cultural* tendency of our present age is to view the aspirations indicated by such science – namely, exploring the planets – as one belonging to the past. This tendency is diametrically opposed to that which prevailed when Klushantsev and Bonestell were making their landscapes of other planets, basing their constructions on informed supposition and creative guesswork. This contemporary tendency to consign the hopes and possibilities of science to the past represents a crisis within contemporary capitalist culture. It extends to include a maudlin view of the future generally. *The Economist* therefore saw the end of the US Space Shuttle programme in 2011 as the end of human exploration of space *tout court* and, by inference, any further developments as not only an already redundant and retrograde endeavour, but as a sort of nostalgic coda or epilogue to a narrative already played out. It is in this context that these articles in *The Economist* make for interesting reading, indicative of they are of a wider trend within contemporary culture: the horizon becomes a signifier of limitation, rather than possibility. For whilst ostensibly decrying continued human space exploration, both on rationalized cost analysis grounds, the essays reference the past of space travel with the most misty eyed nostalgia:

> But the heroic phase of space exploration, with chiselled-jawed astronauts venturing where no man has gone before, inspiring schoolchildren and defending democracy (or socialism), is now a thing of the past.
>
> (*The Economist* 30 June 2011)

Arguably the tendency represented by *The Economist* article flows directly from the tendency towards short-term investment inherent within capitalism as a whole. From this flows a sense of atomization – away from viewing innovations such as space travel as indicative of the possibilities of a positive future, towards seeing them in a doubtful or maudlin fashion as passing spectacle or fading dreams. Noticeably, both articles speak of the Apollo era of the 1960s as long ago. In terms of a single human life, this is perhaps so; but in terms of the scales, distances and evolutionary leaps that human space flight represents, several decades is momentary. In free market capitalism, it is extremely difficult for private individuals or corporations to invest substantially in any project that would incur serious losses for many years before substantial returns could be garnered.

The landscapes of Bonestell and Klushantsev were made in an era of huge investment by government and state agencies in pursuit of human space flight. Moreover, whilst it may now be their epistemological features – the style and execution of their imagery – that stands out, it was the ontological claims their work made which had such widespread cultural impact: namely, the implication of a *longue durée* of human history implicit in space exploration that would transcend short-term economic and political issues. Therefore my interest in writing a chapter about the landscapes of Bonestell and Klushantsev is determined in part by the possibility of thinking about landscape and the science fiction imaginary in a context that was radically different from our present, and, in so doing, tracing those supercessionary elements of both artists' legacy which are, nevertheless, to be found in contemporary culture.

As a citizen of the Soviet Union, Klushantsev's professional life was lived out outside of the capitalist polity I have just outlined above. For his part, Bonestell's long life made him a citizen of a very different phase of capitalist development to that in which the present book is written. What might now seem to be the works' *iconic* resemblance to the signifiers of a particular era of science fiction can, in some cases, be seen as the outcome of a dialectical relation between its particular forms of realism and shifting paradigms of reception. In short, the work of both men has accrued the patina of successive re-framings and appropriations: in this, one can trace the effects of various forms of ideological, cultural and political pressure. This might seem obvious in the case of Klushantsev's work, which is now framed as part of a wider nostalgic story of the technological ascendancy of Kruschev's USSR and as such, in a capitalist world, too easily dismissed as a comical fiction. Klushantsev's complex relationship with science fiction as a genre can be seen as directly determined by the Stalin-Kruschev era polity in which he worked and under which, as I detail below, science fiction as a genre was at times suppressed. However, different but substantial pressures can be seen to act on the work of Bonestell, whose relationship to science fiction was problematized, not least by what would seem to have been cognitive dissonance on the part of the artist himself. Whilst free from such overt state policing as suffered by Klushantsev, Bonestell's landscapes also bear evidence of cultural and ideological pressures, whether 'internally' imposed by the artist himself or 'externally' in terms of editorships or perhaps a combination of both, in terms of the artist's attempts to place himself in relation to certain discourses he regarded as authoritative and legitimating and at a distance from others he regarded as degraded.

Prosopography is the study of an historical group, sometimes through the imagining of a typical subject. At face value, Bonestell and Klushantsev might seem an odd pairing for any prosopographic project – there might seem to be few grounds on which to establish commonality and far more for differentiation. A cursory glance at their respective biographies clearly indicates the two men did not live 'parallel lives', they never met, nor can they be said to offer much symmetry, beyond the wider oppositions afforded by the hegemonic competition between their respective nations which grew to define the global polity between 1945 and 1991. Nevertheless, beyond identifiable similarities in visual tropes common to their respective forms of extrapolative visualizations, their engagements with mixed media and their respective relationship with (of which of course I will say more), I would suggest there are further parallels both in their engagement with the extant scientific knowledge of their day and through that, their respective relationships with scientific authority.

Working with supposition and extrapolation, the work of both Bonestell and Klushantsev can be described as intimately bound up with the *fictions of science*, rather than science fiction per se. To frame it thus is in no way to resort to the pejorative: the century in which these two artists worked was one in which such fictions were not only politically necessitated but aspired to hold immense cultural sway. It would be a mistake for contemporary readers to sneer at this, since, as I will discuss later in this chapter, our own era's efforts at visualizations are constructed upon ideological conceits that may be distinct but nonetheless analogous and, in time, no doubt appear just as quaint.

Bonestell's aversion to science fiction as a genre resulted from personal choice as opposed to pressure from any direct state edict or political censorship – science fiction, after all, thrived in the mid-twentieth century US. Nevertheless, a certain amount of cultural pressure seems to have been felt by Bonestell also, namely from those scientific authorities whose favour he sought out, leading him to make various pronouncements that would appear as attempts to differentiate his astronomical landscape work from the landscapes of science fiction per se. According to Bonestell's biographer Ron Miller (2001: 78), Bonestell appears to have adopted the pragmatic – if not mercenary – approach of the jobbing illustrator to science fiction magazines. The appearance of Bonestell's work in science fiction magazines drew criticism from technical and astronomical specialists he worked with, and Bonestell expressed a strong dislike to being associated with the term 'science fiction' as much as he felt uncomfortable with the term 'artist' – he preferred the term 'illustrator' (2001: 105) and in his relations with scientific authorities he professed a disdain for science fiction (2001: 78).

In the context of the concerted effort amongst scientists and technicians in the 1950s to raise spaceflight as a serious and imminent technical possibility, such an aversion might seem understandable. So, in addition to the pressures delineated above, the pressure of an aspiration to work within parameters delineated by the empiricist claims of science must be added to any assessment of Bonestell. Even though, as I discuss below, there were occasions when he clearly departed from these parameters, such occasions were determined by other powerful ideological impulses, rather than mere whim, flowing from a pressure to acknowledge the social and practical implications of what was being depicted. This is the realm of ideology, and I will suggest that Bonestell's work intimates this in particular ways, albeit more subtle and benign than the pressures of bureaucratized ideological bullying suffered by Klushantsev.

If we take Louis Althusser's well-known definition of ideology as the 'imaginary relationship of individuals to their real conditions of existence' and, as such, accept that ideology constitutes the relationship between illusion and allusion (1992: 932), we must also accept that ideology asserts itself as much in Bonestell's work as Klushantsev. Althusser's definition proposes a distinction between ideology and science insofar as the former is located within social and practical realms, rather than knowledge gained from empirical research. This can be seen in Bonestell's paintings of lunar mountains.

As Miller (Schuetz 1999: xvii) records, Bonestell's decision to paint the mountains of both the Earth's moon and other satellites in his characteristically craggy, precipitous style was a conscious choice on the part of Bonestell: in sharp contrast, earlier formative influences, such as the French painter Lucien Rudeaux (1874–1947) had already determined, through careful observation, that the Moon's mountains were smooth and undulating.

Bonestell's mountains, undeniably more exciting, conform to tropes of precipitousness and precariousness, as if the confident certainties of astronautical extrapolation are to be undermined by a backdrop of geological forms indicative of risk, danger and attendant dramas. As such, the craggy mountains of Bonestell, I would suggest, act as visual metaphors for the social and practical challenges and dangers attendant upon space flight, looming in the background. Ron Miller (Schuetz 1999) frames the issue of Bonestell's mountains in relation to the ostensible 'photographic' realism of his works by pointing out that even most scientists of the time did not raise any open criticism of their inaccuracy, but also suggesting that

[…] there is considerable argument in favor of the idea that we would not have been half so anxious to land on the Moon if we had known it looked as boring as it does – that Bonestell's romanticised landscapes helped encourage the development of a lunar landing program.

(1999: xxv)

Miller's use of 'romanticized' here seems particularly poignant. For just as it is well understood that Photography's early claims to objective realism in the first instance have to be qualified by the acknowledgement of its incorporation of the subjective 'romantic' compositional, technical and cropping choices of the photographer (not to mention the subsequent receptive conditions of the viewer), one can even more readily discern analogous choices – composition, points of view, conventions of what might constitute a naturalistic realism which predetermine, if not over-determine, the claims to realism in Bonestell's work. Both these tropes of realism and, as I discuss below, the material forms with which they are expressed, have become more opaque with the passage of time. Therein, I suggest, lies the importance of seeing both Klushantsev and Bonestell not simply as emblematic of the century in which they lived, but as artists intimately bound up with attempts to visualize the objectives, methods and trajectories of science and technology, through rational supposition, whilst, in so doing, not being able to free themselves from the ideological preoccupations of their time. Fictions of science, perhaps, but ones that trace the outline of the Other to those fictions. As Alain Badiou (2007) asserts:

Nothing attests to the real, nothing that is, except that system of fictions wherein it plays the role of the real.

(2007: 52)

With this in mind, we might therefore consider the fictions of Klushantsev and Bonestell *via negativa* as much in relation to what they do not show as what they do. An example here would be a landscape by Bonestell from 1961, showing two Fujiyama-like volcanoes spewing yellow lava on the horizon, whilst a fall of molten lava plunges into the depths of a rocky chasm in the foreground. High above, a break in the dark brown and orange sky reveals huge bolts of fork lightning discharging towards the barren ground. This was Bonestell's depiction of the landscape of Jupiter – something the huge gas giant planet is utterly devoid of. As Miller and Durant (2001) remark, the picture depicts not only rocks and mountains, but what they term 'Bonestell's scientific conservatism […] despite the great advances in astronomical knowledge [Bonestell] was still depicting Jupiter as he had the 1940s' (2001: 232). However, as Miller and Dunant also record (2001: 232) in the same year, 1961, Bonestell also painted dust devils blowing across the sands of Mars, a phenomenon actually observed in later decades. Fictions of science, then, or science fiction? At a distance of decades, the two are seen intimately and complexly entwined.

Securing the Ground: Certain Kinds of Realism in Landscape

The particular 'systems of fictions' under scrutiny in the work of Klushantsev and Bonestell are those of *extrapolation* – that which Darko Suvin (1979) describes as 'a delusion of technocratic ideology' which is 'no doubt extremely important for the historical understanding of a given period, but theoretically untenable' (1979: 73).

Nowhere, it would seem, is the ideology of visualizing planetary landscapes more clearly delineated than here, for this is the visualization of expansion and territorialization, the incorporation or sundering of times and spaces in the form of possible futures acknowledged and incorporated or elided and erased: in short, the securing of ground. Both artists made extensive use of a particular type of vantage point that accompanies the advent of military air-power. Repeatedly in the landscapes of Bonestell, and later Klushantsev, we see landscape as a topography, obliquely laid out before us as if viewed from some altitude, or as an intricate architect's model on a table or plinth. This trope is found not only in Bonestell's astronomical images, but also, for example, in his paintings of contemporary cities such as Los Angeles or landscape features such as Mount Everest. This 'God's Eye' viewpoint elevates the viewer, but also leads to inhabitants in the picture being reduced in scale, sometimes to the threshold of invisibility. A somewhat schizoid position for the viewer is thus presented: one identifies with diminutive itinerants or explorers, whilst at the same time beholding all under an idealized, omniscient purview. Thus, as with the science of aeronautics, Bonestell and Klushantsev's imagery seems to offer us power through altitude: the viewer hovers, ascends or descends. This sense of aerial freedom is echoed by social freedom – both Bonestell and Klushantsev's landscapes suggest social freedom through planetary conquest: tiny space suited figures raise their arms in apparent jubilation and space suited families hold hands, sharing the wonders upon which they gaze.

In the case of Bonestell, there is a serpent in some of these gardens. Melvin Schuetz (1999) notes that alongside the depictions of planetary landscapes, moon landings, rockets and space stations, of the years 1953–54, we also find Bonestell's illustrations for magazine articles entitled 'How Hellish is the H-Bomb?' (1999: 30), 'The End of the World: A Scientific Inquiry' (1999: 30) and 'Seascape of a Half Dessicated Earth' (1999: 36), signalling an

126

underlying preoccupation with not simply national security but planetary extinction. Miller and Dunant's monograph *The Art of Chesley Bonestell* (2001) contains six depictions of cities under nuclear attack, mostly New York. If his landscapes are, mostly, idealized portraits of a conquering human species, then these works appear in the corpus as *memento morii*, the haunting doubt amidst the triumph.

It might be tempting to compare and contrast Bonestell and Klushantsev through historiographic equivalences and differentiations, but I will not attempt that here. Rather, what I would suggest is key here is the typical manner in which, in their professional work, both Kluschantsev and Bonestell cleave to the *instrumentalization of the image as schema*. As Jameson has it, schema is

[…] the use of visual materials not to represent the world, but to represent our thoughts about the world.

(2015)

Therefore I would suggest that both men worked to produce *schemas* rather than symbols, aiming to produce images that, as accurately as possible, reflected emerging scientific and technical ambitions, rather than the febrile imaginings of genre fiction. In this sense, their shared schema has endured. For whatever the differences between their conjectures about, say, the landscape of Mars and its actual character subsequently revealed by robotic exploration and so on, our contemporary notions concerning the possibilities of travelling to and living on the Red Planet still owe their *schematic* character to the visualizations of Bonestell and Klushantsev.

There are also parallels in relation to the visual sources and references around which their respective visualizing of that schema were constructed, even prior to that period of direct confrontation and competition in which their respective national polities were locked. That is to say, just as there are parallels between the two men's techniques – Bonestell constructed plaster models of his landscapes to make reference photographs from which he could then paint or paint directly on to, whilst Klushantsev built film sets – there are also parallels to the painting of landscape which each inherited, both in Russia and the United States, stretching back to the middle of the nineteenth century. Both cultures saw brotherhoods of realist painters exhorting the natural wilderness, and an idealist fiction of agrarian lives that found freedom in great plains and wild forests – the *peredvizhniki* (Itinerants or Wanderers) in the Russian Empire, and the Hudson River School in the United States.

Both the *peredvizhniki* and the Hudson River School, in their respective and distinct ways, equated landscape with ideologies of nationhood and individual liberty: each saw veracity – and therefore realism – to be located in replication of detail and naturalistic effect. Both schools combined Realist and Romantic elements and Influential *peredvizhniki* painters such as Vasily Vereshchagin (1842–1904) combined an expansive, large canvas realism with implicit critiques of war and colonial brutality (e.g., *The Road of the War Prisoners*, 1879 and *Suppression of the Indian Revolt by the English*, 1884), whilst Frederic

Edwin Church (1826–1900) sought elements of allegory and symbolism in depictions of the western territories as the Union's manifest destiny: Church's *Our Banner in the Sky* (1861) depicts stratus clouds flushed red by the rising sun juxtaposed against paler backlit cumulus, whilst a few bright stars set against a bluish night sky are arranged to complete a supposedly naturally occurring image of the United States flag fluttering over the landscape.

Beyond any claim to disinterested realist fidelity, I would suggest such contrivances point to how oil painting's capacity for realist representations becomes bound up not only with the visualization of territorial and political claims on both time (history) and in space (territory), but an ideologically charged illustrative function that positions itself as an alternative to the indexical realisms of photographic documentation.

Both the Hudson River and Itinerant schools pursued an intimate competition with – rather than submission to – the emergent new technology of photography: *peredvizhnik* painter Rafail Sergeevich Levitsky (1847–1940), like his father Sergei Lvovich Levitsky (1819–98), was an established photographer, whilst Frederic Edwin Church on occasion painted directly onto and over photographic prints. Like many painters of the period, photography skills were developed, maintained and retained as a supplementary form or facilitating adjunct to the culturally elevated aspirations of painting. The photographic document becomes a verified source to secure a subsequent painting's visual authoritativeness. In the period covered by Bonestell's long life, this use of the photograph as document evolves into model and set building, not only for cinematic special effects but also within the artist's studio, to be used both to verify and expedite particular forms of verisimilitude.

Mixed Media, Detail, Science and the Instrumentalization of Painting: Realism and 'Astronomical Art'

In thinking through the competing verisimilitudes arising from the cultures that Klushantsev and Bonestell were born into, I want to suggest that such a relationship between photography and painting practices – initially oil in the case of fine art, but also later, casein and acrylic in twentieth-century illustration for reprographic purposes – is founded upon the expediencies of a particular form of realistic rendering and as such is one that goes beyond any perceived duty or virtuosity ascribed to purity of medium. Moreover, the terms of this particular painterly realism's relationship with that of nineteenth-century photography is one of differentiation – for example, it is not one of emulation or mimesis as in the case of what, in the later part of the twentieth century, becomes known as Photo-realism. Painting directly onto photographs or painting *around* photography (that is to say, competing with Photography's ability to capture detail) in the manner of these nineteenth-century schools is not the same as mimicking the ocular effects of photography's means of capturing an image that we see in Photo-realism. This is an important distinction to make when we consider the forms of realistic representation in twentieth-century astronomical landscape illustration and subsequent changes in the conditions of its reception. Church's painting over of photographs – it is, incidentally found in other painters of his time, for example, the English painter John Atkinson Grimshaw (1836–93) – is also found in the work of Chesley Bonestell and, I would suggest, is echoed indirectly in the mixed media: painted backdrops, tricks of camera special effects and constructed landscapes that made Klushantsev's work so magical.

As such, I want to suggest that the work of realistic visualization under examination here is a hybrid form of grandiose realist pictorialism that can be traced from this encounter between landscape painting and early photography, through to the twentieth century, where it is constituted as instructive illustration in the form that becomes known in the West as 'Astronomical Art'.

The ambition of this particular form of illustrative realism might seem, therefore, to *rival* that of photography rather than replicate it, insofar as its aim was to picture, accurately and in detail, a space that was not yet 'photographable' – Outer Space itself. Astronomical Art aimed – and still aims – to achieve this by its close attendance upon the latest understandings of scientific research. Like science itself, this was not without ideological inflection. Astronomical Art in the twentieth century might be seen as an enterprise that is heavily inflected by Positivist philosophy and which cleaves to relationships with both realism and photography firmly rooted – and seemingly unchanged – since the middle of the nineteenth century. However, I want to suggest that Bonestell and Klushantsev's combined legacy is one of a distinct form of realism – what I describe below as a 'suppositional realism' which whilst today might be seen to present the viewer with more opacities, errors and lacunae than transparencies, nevertheless rewards careful consideration in terms of its historical trajectory and comparisons with other forms of realism seen as completely transparent today. This is because the landscapes of Bonestell and Klushantsev arose from an imminent sense of the possibility of travel to other planets. I would suggest that this sense is reflected in the depiction of recognizable everyday tropes of Earthbound landscape that I have discussed above.

By the mid-twentieth century, the scientific feasibility of space travel had been established in both the United States and the Soviet Union. Through test flights of captured, modified and improved Nazi V-2 rockets teams of scientists in both the United States and the Soviet Union had established that rocket propelled travel in space was possible, thereby confirming the earlier predictions of the Russian Konstantin Tsiolkovsky (1857–1935) and Robert Goddard (1882–1945) in the United States. As a result, the sense that space travel was a *realistic* proposition, rather than a romantic fantasy, was established publicly during this period. The work of popularizing this endeavour, both in its propagandist value as predictive claims of technological capacity over national rivals and educating a motivated workforce at home, can be seen as a moment in which science fiction is eschewed in favour of various 'fictions of science', tied to the economic boom of post-World War II reconstruction and an extreme optimism that the new technologies that might not destroy the world, but open up new ones.

The extent to which the landscapes of Bonestell and Klushantsev were shaped by such fictions is cause to reflect upon parallels in the respective modes of production and reception that both artists encountered. Illustration for books, magazines and painted backdrops for the cinema are, for the greater part of the twentieth century, perhaps the most obvious form in which painting was instrumentalized. On the one hand, whilst the artist produces as an individual, nevertheless s/he is subject to only a qualified valuation as such; that is to say, the illustrator is commissioned to be creative within certain parameters established by another, autonomous logocentric discourse – 'the text' – to which the illustration is ancillary. To say this is not to demean the competences or virtuosity of the illustration, but it is to recognize the extent to which the painting as illustration does not allow itself to have a representational function in ways other to those ascribed by Peter Bürger (b. 1936) to fine art, which is, of course, subject to other forms of hegemonic instrumentalization. It is therefore interesting at this point, following the Sacral/Courtly/Bourgeois historical typology of Peter Bürger to think through aspects of Soviet painting and, indeed, other forms of visual representation such as cinema and photography at during the decades prior to, and during, Klushantsev's era. Bürger's typology proposes 'Sacral' as those conditions in which art functions as cult object. Bürger further proposes that, in the Sacral mode, all art 'is wholly integrated in the social institution "religion"'. The modes of both production and reception are collective – the production is therefore in craft form, indistinguishable from any separate category of 'fine art' (1984: 47–48). Both the artist's employment schemes of Roosevelt's New Deal in the United States of the 1930s and Stalin's USSR saw examples of such instrumentalization.

Gleb Prokhorov (1995: 70–72) has suggested that the so-called gala painting of 1930s period of Stalin's Terror – monstrously sycophantic large-scale oil paintings, the perspective and lighting of which always contrived to highlight Stalin's wise beneficence – are sacral works. However, I would suggest that titles such as Grigory Shegal's *The Leader, Teacher, and Comrade* (1937) or *The Great Oath* (1950–51) painted by Gerasmov, Dyruchin, Zenkova, Papikyan and Podlyasky, in their glorification of Stalin and his attendant functionaries, bears closer comparison with Bürger's typification of 'Courtly', serving

[t]he glory of the prince and the self-portrayal of courtly society [...] the artist produces as an individual and develops a consciousness of the uniqueness of his activity. Reception, on the other hand, remains collective. But the content of the collective performance is no longer sacral, it is sociability.

(1984: 47)

Both Klushantsev's work, and that of Bonestell in its own way, were subject to the pressures of 'Courtly' approval. Whilst this instrumentalization of illustration might seem most clearly felt *in extremis* in the form of dictatorship and terror, I would suggest there are parallels also for our understanding of the mode of address and reception pertaining to both Klushantsev and Bonestell. To look at the work of either Klushantsev in the Soviet Union or Bonestell in the United States is to remember that instrumentalizations of figurative painting in the Twentieth Century – commercial advertising, political propaganda and so on – were in effect produced in environments more courtly than sacral, insofar as they were produced as *craft* forms, seeking validation and approval received through socialized institutional channels such as education or instruction in widely available publications or filmed mass media. As such, their production and distribution were institutionalized ideologically as secularized articles of faith – namely national narratives of technological progress and scientific and cultural pre-eminence.

Sergei Kapterev has suggested a differentiation here between the instrumentalizations to be found in Bonestell and those of Klushantsev: Kapterev (2011) suggests that Soviet logocentrism meant that the text came first and illustrations were ancillary, whereas with Bonestell the primacy lay with the picture. However, as I have suggested above, both Bonestell and Klushantsev's work can be regarded as equally open to this charge: as Bonestell's biographer Ron Miller has observed, Bonestell's work was accompanied by authoritative extended textual commentaries by leading experts of the time, evidencing the reasons behind the pictorial choices of colouration and form (1999: xiii–xxviii). Miller has also pointed out that astronauts and spaceships only began to appear in Bonestell's astronomical landscapes once Bonestell had met and conversed with the rocket scientist Willy Ley, at the time one of the leading experts in the field and author of the influential scientific study *Rockets: The Future of Travel Beyond the Stratosphere.* Ley and Bonestell subsequently collaborated on the highly influential illustrated book *The Conquest of Space*, with Ley writing the text and Bonestell producing the images.

In his succinct schematic of the Communist bloc experience as a Platonic government of philosophers, Boris Groys (2009) persuasively suggests that the notion of Soviet logocentrism was, and remains, as much about the West's attempts at monopolizing claims to sensuous luxury and the irrationalism of desire and, *via negativa*, alluding to its own rationalizing, logocentric tendencies. As such, Groys argues that allegations of logocentricity reflect more the preoccupations of those outside of the USSR as it was than any such privileging within. Certainly, as Groys notes, science fiction as a genre is replete with such implicit differentiations – Zamyatin's *We*, Orwell's *1984*, all place the individualist irrational desires of sexual freedom as the undoing of what Groys terms the 'linguistification of society' (2009: 1–37).

Whilst Bonestell is typically remembered as a magazine illustrator and Klushantsev as a film producer, the truth is that both men worked with similar range of materials and media, and the difference between them can be seen to be variations of quantity, rather than any fundamental qualitative difference: as Ron Miller has recorded, Bonestell worked in an architect's office, as a cinematic matte painter as well as model builder, and frequently used not only photographic material, but also equipment to produce his images, building models of landscapes to photograph and then transcribe or even paint directly over. Both Bonestell and Klushantsev can therefore be seen in the tradition of the *monteur* (the etymological root of 'montage') – in other words, 'image technicians' – producing images as 'conceptualizations' whose claims to value were contingent upon extant data and understanding within the natural sciences. As Ron Miller notes, Willy Ley's introduction to *The Conquest of Space* insisted that Bonestell's scenes should not be considered 'artist's conceptions in the customary sense' but rather what one would expect to get 'from a very good camera with a perfectly true color film [...] manned by a good photographer' (Miller and Durant 2001: 57).

The particular notion of a kind of 'photographic realism' revealed by Ley's remark here seems to be one in which the photograph is a legitimizing comparator. Moreover, Ley seems to suggest a certainty in Bonestell's painting that could only be chanced at, but not *guaranteed* by photography: he is at pains to account for the material and subjective fallibilities of photography that can only be guarded against by means of 'a perfectly true color film [...] a good photographer', suggesting a certainty only to be found in the work of a skilled painter informed by scientific deduction.

As Ley's quote reveals, the form of painting we see in Bonestell (and, through its effects and backdrops, in the visualizations of Klushantsev) did not stake its claims to veracity in the conscious replication of photographic *effect*, nor in a simplistic replication of the Itinerants, but in an underlying obeisance to scientifically based supposition. This scientism – in some sense in spite of Ley's quote, but also because of it – leads the realism of Bonestell's work into direct competition with the claims of photography, finding as it does its object in those places and spaces where photography cannot possibly satisfy the desire to visualize – speculations on the future, Outer Space and the suppositions of natural science that extend beyond the correlations of human experience.

I choose to term this 'Suppositional Realism' since I suggest the forms of painting rested upon that which Quentin Meillassoux (2008: 12) terms the 'ancestral event' (that is to say, an event that the scientific deduction has determined must have occurred before humans existed, or in some way separated by space and time that is completely independent of human correlation). Meillassoux suggests that,

> [...] every theory advanced by empirical science is by right revisable: it can be falsified and supplanted by one that is more elegant, or that exhibits greater empirical accuracy. But this will not prevent the scientist from considering that it makes sense to suppose that her statement is true: that things could actually have happened the way that she has described them and that so long as her description has not been supplanted by another theory, it is legitimate to assume the existence of the event such as she has reconstructed it. And, in any case, even if her theory is falsified, this can only be by another theory which will also be about ancestral events, and which will also be supposed to be true.
>
> (2008: 12)

The 'Suppositional Realism' reading of Bonestell and Klushantsev that I am proposing here, thus registers those aspects of their work that now seem opaque or erroneous not as merely quaint, but as evidence of their essayistic character, bound up with those wider errors contained within the unfolding of those scientific projects still in progress and shaped by the ur-forms predicated by sociopolitical, ideological and historical pressures. An example of this can be seen in both artists' respective treatments of the landscape of Mars.

Miller (2001: 79) relates how the deep blue sky in a Martian landscape by Bonestell for a book co-authored with Willy Ley and Wernher von Braun entitled *The Exploration of Mars* caused problems with deadlines because advice from the eminent scientist Gerard Kuiper suggested the sky of Mars was in fact grey. Further telephone conversations exposed a schism in opinion between experts, based on differing telemetric measurements, as to whether the sky of Mars would indeed appear grey or blue. In the end, Bonestell kept his sky blue, in line with the majority of scientific thinking on the subject. Of course, neither opinion proved correct – in daytime, the sky of Mars would appear a rusty pink-orange to human eyes.

Klushantsev's *Mars*, made more than a decade later in 1968, bears both similarities and departures from the renderings of Bonestell. Whereas Bonestell's Mars draws upon some superficial iconic similarities between the colouration of Mars and that of the barren, sun baked deserts of Arizona, Klushantsev is able to use his cinematography to create a Martian landscape of cycles and seasons, seen over time. Speculation around different colouration is illustrated with effects to simulate pyroclastic flow of tephra and volcanic ash across the Martian landscape or the spread of vegetation: in other words, nature.

As with Bonestell, Klushantsev's Martian landscape is subjected to the purview – we see the topos spread out below us as if flying alongside (but not aboard) a silver space plane; comically, from the viewpoint of a spacesuit wearing dog and, finally, from the viewpoint of a Friedrichian *Rückenfigur* gazing from a hillside across a valley towards the shining towers of a prosperous colonial outpost. As with Bonestell, the mode of presentation here is that of peer reviewed and substantiated scientific extrapolation, rather than merely that of individual fantasy. Klushantsev also counterposes these Bonestellian macroscopic vistas – and comedic intervals – with detailed close-ups of imaginary plant forms blooming in the relative warmth of a Martian spring, of meltwater in the steppes and a focus on geological and ecological *processes*, rather than merely momentary appearance.

Klushantsev's detailing of seasonal shifts and natural cycles carries poignant resonances, both in its recollection of the tradition of annular seasons and changes in weather found in Russian landscape painting and its attendant 'reading in' of political or social metaphors. There is a rich tradition of 'reading in' of symbolism in Russian landscape, of visual signs of things unsaid. Even before the Soviet epoch, works such as S.A. Vinogradov's *Spring* (1911), M.F. Larionov's *Lilac Bush in Flower* (1905), M.V. Nestorov's *Autumn Landscape* (1906) or *September Snow* (1903) by I.E. Grabar all tend to have lent themselves to a particular politicized ocularity, registering hope or aspirations, defeat or despair. The five years immediately preceding the production of Klushantsev's *Mars* had seen dramatic power struggles between rival intra-Party cliques in the USSR. Nikita Kruschev, widely credited with having removed Stalin and initiating a period of political reform combined with economic and technological successes commonly referred to as 'The Thaw' (Sidorov 1992: 30–40) had in turn been removed from power by the faction around Leonid Brezhnev in the Autumn of 1964.

Whilst Kruschev was seen as a relative cultural and political liberal (his time in office saw the rise of the so-called 'Severe School' of formally more expressive Modernist figuration), his own attacks on artistic experimentation – Sidorov points to an outburst at the Thirtieth Anniversary exhibition of the Moscow Artist's Union in 1962 (1992: 36) – tend to suggest a lack of political will to pursue the excessive prohibitions of Stalin based on expediency, rather than any clear long-term committal to artistic radicality.

The Soviet intervention in, and crushing of, the Hungarian Uprising in October and November 1956 demonstrated a continued intolerance in the Kremlin of political pluralism. This brutal enforcement of strict limitations in political life was echoed in the Arts. As Sidorov (1992: 38) notes, a plenum of the Russian Artist's Union, held year and a half before Kruschev's fall, in April 1963, had seen a speech by Vladimir Serov, the President of the Academy of Arts, reassert neo-Stalinist principles and censure artists who were seen to be replacing 'realistic truth' with 'the ugliness of artificial formal experiments'. It is difficult therefore not to read Klushantsev's portrayal of Spring on Mars as poignantly aspirant, through its reassertion of the possibility of renewals and awakenings on another planet.

The golden age of early Soviet science fiction films as such had been drawn to a sharp close by the time Pavel Klushantsev commenced work in the Soviet state film industry in the 1930s. Darko Suvin (1979) relates that the Stalin regime had inherited a strong and diverse tradition of Russian language science fiction that the Lenin era (1917–24) had seen continued from the pre-Revolution period and, indeed, expanded. Under Lenin, leading Bolsheviks such as Alexander Bogdanov (1873–1928) and Anatoly Lunacharsky (1875–1933) had authored novels and film adaptations. Planetary exploration, rapid scientific, medical and technological progress and far-reaching speculation upon the development of human society were popular themes. Suvin (1979) records that an average of 25 new science fiction books were published in the 1920s – peaking with 47 separate new titles in 1927. By 1931, publication had fallen to just four (1979: 264). Similarly, the extraordinary outpouring of early Soviet science fiction silent films which had followed the October Revolution – the most famous of which is Yakov Protozanov's *Aelita* (1924) – likewise came to an abrupt end. Bogdanov died in suspicious circumstances ostensibly from an experiment in blood transfusion which went wrong and Lunacharsky, purged from his role as Commissar for Enlightenment, posthumously joined the thousands of other intellectuals and creatives whose names were erased and writings banned by a largely new careerist generation of Communist Party bureaucrats in the course of the 1930s.

As Sergei Kapterev (2011) has pointed out, Stalinism had a paranoid fear of genre or 'structured fantasy', as much as it was paranoid about most things. Suvin (1979) dates the start of the Stalinist attack upon science fiction to 1929–30 (1979: 260). This was a crucial period in terms of the history power struggle within the Soviet Communist Party between different factions on the Centre, Right and Left: Leon Trotsky, the leading figure within the Party's Left Opposition that had blamed the Stalin faction for the failure of Communist-led revolutionary movements in German and China in the previous decade, and likewise been heavily critical of domestic economic policy, was stripped of Soviet Citizenship and exiled from the Soviet Union in 1929. The leading theorist and intellectual on the Right of the Party, Nikolai Bukharin, who in the years 1926–29 had enjoyed an uneasy alliance with Stalin in their shared antagonism towards the Trotskyist Opposition, was likewise pushed out of power in the same year, leaving Stalin and his supporters supreme.

The cultivation of particular forms of collective cultural acts – brigade painting, instructional films and so on – post-1917 is one in which art is seen to be reflective of the reorganization of Soviet society. As Susan Weissman's biography of Victor Serge (2013) relates, the aftermath of the depredations of the Civil War and the Volga famine, the crushing of revolutionary movements in other countries that might otherwise have established sympathetic international alliances for the Soviet Union, and the failure of the Bolshevik leadership to establish an open pluralist polity based on consensus support for the socialized economy, meant that the bureaucratic command structure within the economy generally inevitably found particular political expression within the only structure available – the Party itself. The rise of 'Stalinism' in the late 1920s and early 1930s was the nominal expression of this process. Therein, an experienced and pragmatic party operator with little ontological investment in political theory per se but who, fortuitously for him, occupied the middle ground between the Party's Right and Left, utilized the skills he learned as a provincial operator to become its titular head, and oversaw the liquidation of millions (including practically all the leading Bolsheviks of the pre-1917 period), in the bloodbath and paranoid reaction of the Purges.

This political and societal shift had a dramatic effect on what was speculated upon and what in turn was visualized. That which had seemed, in the revolutionary dawn, as infinite possibility became stultified and fettered.

In his *The Revolution Betrayed: What Is the Soviet Union and Where Is It Going?* first published in the West in 1937, the exiled and soon to be assassinated former Bolshevik leader, Leon Trotsky, who saw the Soviet Union as 'a contradictory society, halfway between capitalism and socialism' but which, nevertheless, remained composed of 'dynamic social formations, that have had no precedent and have no analogies' (1983: 255) noted:

> While the dictatorship (of the Proletariat) had a seething mass-basis and a prospect of world revolution, it had no fear of experiments, searchings, the struggle of schools, for it understood that only in this way could a new cultural epoch be prepared […] All the best youthful forces of art were touched to the quick. […] To the same times belong, it is worth remarking, the creation of those excellent Soviet films which, in spite of a poverty of technical means, caught the imagination of the whole world with the freshness and vigour of their approach to reality […] Such prescriptions as, 'portray the construction of the future', 'indicate the road to socialism' 'make over mankind' give little more to the creative imagination than does the price list of a hardware store, or a railroad timetable.
>
> (1983: 185)

Henceforth, the logics of his dictatorship over the Party and the state apparatus meant that only Stalin himself could be seen to have foresight: speculative fiction, art and film were suspect. Suvin (1979) records that the Leningrad Section for Science Fiction was completely purged in 1935, a year before the first Show Trial. All its members were either jailed or shot. Science fiction was denounced as a harmful genre, then damned with faint praise in the form of a partial rehabilitation as a juvenile and marginalized form. The aim of Stalinist policy was to expunge remaining Soviet science fiction culture of any long-term prognoses or anticipation. Speculative fiction thereafter was to focus on solving practical short-term technical problems. As Suvin remarks, the least boring of these were novels about exploration (1979: 264). As Sonja Vesterholt and Mads Baastrup's 2002 biographical documentary *The Star Dreamer* shows, Pavel Klushantsev's early work as a cameraman included films documenting deep sea diving in such a vein.

Practical scientific research into actual space travel suffered as badly as science fiction in the period of the purges. Building on the groundbreaking Tsarist-era theorizations of Konstantin Tsiolkovsky, rocketry research in the Soviet Union had reached a milestone in August 1933 when the Group for the Study of Reactive Motion (GIRD) had successfully launched an experimental liquid fuelled rocket, and this had led to the foundation of a Reactive Scientific Research Institute (RNII) in the following months. Shortly after the third Show Trial in March 1938, all the members of RNII were arrested and accused of subversion. Amongst those rounded up was the deputy leader and former chief of GIRD who had been working on the technical problems of human space flight, Sergei Korolev, who was charged with 'being an active participant in an anti-Soviet Trotskyist wrecking organisation' and sentenced to ten years hard labour in the gulag (Millard 2014: 81–82). Having written personally to Stalin about his rocketry work, Korolev was eventually moved to a prison factory as the first step in rehabilitation. In his lifetime Korolev remained largely anonymous, allowed only to publish under a pseudonym. However, paradoxically, this obscurity only highlighted Korolev's importance to a paranoid dictatorship. In 1957, the same year that Klushantsev's groundbreaking film *The Road to the Stars* was released, Korolev was the chief engineer responsible for the successful launch of Sputnik; in 1961, he bade farewell to Yuri Gagarin before his first orbit of the Earth.

Korolev met Pavel Klushantsev during the 1960s: in Vesterholt and Baastrup's film, a witness recalls that whilst Gagarin had criticisms of details in Klushantsev's work, but Korolev commended him warmly. Indeed, Oleysa Turkina (2014) relates that Klushantsev's speculative imagery proved so prescient that Korolev had to intervene on his behalf to allay suspicions from the authorities that Klushantsev was spying (2014: 12).

Although the Kruschev years saw a tentative re-birth of science fiction in the Soviet Union, Klushantsev's work always remained under the watchful eye of bureaucrats who might prohibit or censure his films on one occasion only to demand more of his work shortly afterwards when the Party line changed. As a colleague of Klushantsev relates in *The Star Dreamer* (2002), filmmakers were still often asked why they were not concentrating on 'making films about growing better beetroot'. In this context, the scientific endorsement of Klushantsev's work by Korolev obviously bears parallels to the endorsement of Chesley Bonestell by Willy Ley, but carries with it a greater political impact, and greater political risk. 'Making *The Road to the Stars* was the right thing to do. One must envisage the future, people should be able to see that life can be changed radically', a witness filmed in *The Star Dreamer* quotes Klushantsev as saying.

Formative events in Klushantsev's life – a childhood of war, abandonment and deprivation, an adulthood scarred by the Nazi Siege of Leningrad (1941–42) and a career working under ever watchful state tyranny – meant that he worked privately and conscientiously in '[f]ear, eternal fear' haunted by a sense of loneliness: 'We are all lonely, all of us who live on this Earth – billions of people all locked in their own prison cells' he recorded in his diary (diary excerpts quoted in Vesterholt and Baastrup 2002).

Loneliness as a theme is present in Soviet revolutionary writing – the Bolshevik leader Alexandra Kollontai suggested a mounting crisis of loneliness in her essay 'Sexual Relations and the Class Struggle' of 1921, suggesting '[p]eople have perhaps never in any age felt spiritual loneliness as deeply and persistently as at the present time' (1977: 240) and pointing to a millenarian resolution: 'It could hardly be otherwise. The darkness never seems so black as when there is a light shining just ahead' (1977: 240). For Klushantsev, who, as his colleagues said, kept his distance from friends, a similar escape from contemporary social isolation seemed possible via the emerging technology of spaceflight: 'I want to create a utopia – a dream of a future, friendlier society about a new race of people' (diary, quoted in *The Star Dreamer*, 2002).

What Suvin describes as 'Utopian anthropology' detailing the development of new ethical relationships arising from space travel (1979: 226–27) was a prominent feature of the revived interest in creative scientific speculation tolerated by the Soviet state bureaucracy with the advent of Sputnik and Gagarin which saw the publication of Ivan Yefremov's *Andromeda* (also 1957). After *The Road to the Stars* (1957) and *Planet of Storms* (1961), Klushantsev planned another feature film, *Moonstone*, about three separate lunar missions from the rival US, the USSR and Germany, which, when crisis occurs, have to cooperate to survive: it was rejected for funding.

In old age, Klushantsev told the Hollywood special effects producer Robert Skotak that he had produced 'three hundred different constructions, all done to help with the creation of illusion' (*The Star Dreamer*, 2002) and it is hard not to hear the tinge of bitterness and regret in his choice of description. Skotak, who went on to work on the special effects for James Cameron's *Aliens* (1986) and *Terminator 2* (1991), recounts seeing a clip of *The Road to the Stars* broadcast on Walter Kronkite's news magazine programme *The Twentieth Century* that had a profound and lasting influence on his own work. Skotak credits Klushantsev with key innovations in a number of ingenious predigital special effects.

The planetary landscapes of Klushantsev and Bonestell are presented as landscapes of successive initial encounters with another nature: the first probe, the first human landing, the first colony and so on. As such, we view the planet first from afar, then from orbit, then from the upper atmosphere, until the 'flags and footprints' moment of human landing. Klushantsev's *Moon* (1965) moves from a discussion about cratering illustrated with spectacular studio pyrotechnics (the extent to which the Moon's craters were the result of bolide impact or, on the other hand, past volcanic activity was still at issue at the time) to an animation speculating on how far a human foot might sink into the lunar surface, and the possible hazards that different surfaces might present. Klushantsev works with a wide chromatic scale: the lunar surface is lit with pale pinks, pastel blues and purple shadows. Notably, in contrast to Bonestell, viewership in Klushantsev is reported as gendered – Klushantsev's *Moon*, different actor's voices – including that of a 'girl cosmonaut' speak of their imagined experiences of their sojourn on the lunar surface. Bonestell's inclusion of only tiny figures in his planetary landscapes makes gender indeterminate: Klushantsev's depiction of gender is more explicit, but not unproblematic. *Planet of Storms* (1962), his only feature, was criticized at its premiere by Yekaterina Furtseva (1910–74), the then Soviet Minister of Culture, who criticized the assigned gender roles within the *mise-en-scène*, in which the exploration party landing on eponymous planet were shown to be all male, whilst the sole female member of the crew was left in orbit, having been assigned a relatively passive role and is shown to be prone to emotional outbursts. Furtseva also said she thought it inappropriate that a female Cosmonaut should be shown crying. Furtseva's criticism seems well founded in terms of both its general opposition to sexist stereotyping but also the specifics of the time: the Soviet Union had already committed to sending the first woman into space the previous year, shortly after Yuri Gagarin's first flight, and by the time *Planet of Storms* was released, five women, including Valentina Tereshkova, who became the first woman in space, were undertaking cosmonaut training.

Nevertheless, in the work of both Klushantsev and Bonestell, the planetary landscape *qua* terrene landscape – that is to say, that moment at which the surface is seen for the first time not as point of light, nor globe, nor topos viewed from the air or during descent, but rather when it is seen as ground and sky, delineated by horizon – is posited as the end in itself: the moment of fulfilment, *jouissance* even.

Perhaps, partly for personal reasons cited above (his sustained sense of loneliness, the wish to create a vision of a new society and so on), in Klushantsev's oeuvre, there is a repeated staging of the gazing figure or figures in the extraterrestrial landscape. Sometimes from the back, sometimes from other angles, we see a space suited wanderer and his comically space suited dog, or a family of two adults and a child, enter the frame. In both *Moon* and *Mars*, this is the moment when music of the soundtrack swells in an aural sign of emotional excess – wonderment and joy. Biographical details already cited might suggest Klushantsev's repeated staging of this device – the depiction of families as well as individuals looking on into the picture – had a personal poignancy. Historically, the contrivance of the figure with his or her back turned into the picture, simultaneously doubling as an idealization of the viewer, and in some cases partially obscuring the precise object of the gaze, is associated with the remarkable sequence paintings of *Rückenfiguren* (back turned figures) of Caspar David Friedrich (1774–1840, Figure 17).

As such, William Vaughan (1994) suggests, 'Friedrich painted precisely the paradox [the earlier Romantic] Runge wished to resolve: man's yearning for the infinite and his perpetual separation from it' (1994: 142). As I have already noted, in both Klushantsev and Bonestell, this Friedrichian moment is both culmination and closure.

Arguably, a discursive line is traceable between Friedrich's *Rückenfiguren*, produced in the early decades of the nineteenth century, through the philosophical debates of the nineteenth century between Ludwig Feuerbach and Karl Marx and onwards, to the ideology of Soviet Russia of Klushantsev. This discursive line, I would suggest, is centred on the question of 'species being'.

In Ludwig Feuerbach's *Essence of Christianity*, first translated into English by the novelist George Eliot, the fundamental difference between man and brute was not merely consciousness implied by the feeling of self as an individual, but rather the conception of consciousness as 'in the strictest sense is present only in being to whom his species, his essential nature, is an object of thought' (Feuerbach 2008: 1). The logic of Feuerbach's position was that God existed only as a perfected ideal of that thought: Christianity, in anthropomorphizing that ideal thought in the figure of Christ, had successfully obviated any obstruction between identifying the individual with the species. Karl Marx's subsequent critique of Feuerbach, which argued that what was actually happening was the reverse to the ideal posited by Feuerbach, hinged on the problematizing element of alienated labour that not only estranged individuals in the course of work from their creativity but, moreover, established a cleavage between individual life and the life of the species as an integral part of nature, reducing the aim of collective experience to that of the idealized individual:

> First it estranges the life of the species and individual life, and secondly, it makes individual life in its abstract form *the purpose* of the life of the species, likewise in its abstract and estranged form […].
>
> (1970: 112, my emphasis)

We can see landscape as the dialectical corollary of species being in relation to an ontology of nature: landscape, as a conflation of spatial and temporal perception, and as a presence of that which is 'non-human', is a condition of the lived relationship with that contradiction.

Klushantsev's '*Rückenfiguren*' seem to resonate with this. They reference Friedrich's imagery, but have transcended that sense of 'perpetual separation' that Vaughan describes – Klushantsev's figures stand *on* the Moon, pointing at human achievements in sustaining life there. As such, they resonate with Friedrich, but are posited not as a vision of something unattainable (the moon as a distant mystery) but at a moment when interplanetary travel and human colonization of space are understood as potentially imminent, and with it, as Klushantsev suggested in the diary quote I cited above, the possibility of a 'new human race' cognizant of its changed collective relationship with the cosmos and with it, a transformed understanding of what it is to be part of the human species.

In contrast to Klushantsev, Bonestell avoids large-scale renditions of human figures in his paintings. In part, Klushantsev's focus on cinematic effects and set building meant that certain shots required close-ups of human actors to enable characterization and narrative development. In the more predominantly illustrational mode that characterized his oeuvre, Bonestell's human figures remain tiny, dwarfed by their surroundings. Yet in Bonestell's work too, I would suggest, we find a sense of a renewed quest to understand humanity's relationship with the Universe. Small scale becomes an indicator of both courage and humility, on the part of the imagined explorers no doubt, but also a visual *merging*: the sense that the viewer can look at the planetary landscape and not immediately notice the tiny astronauts evokes a precipitous sense of the momentary nature of human presence in the universe, and with it, the sense that these landscapes are understood to have existed long before the human visitation, and will exist long after. I would suggest this aspect of Bonestell's work also reflects an underlying concern with species being.

Planets Pictured Like Earth and 'Earthlike Planets'

I want to suggest that it is in the doubt evoked by the question of species being that we see the drive to find Earthlike planets. For obvious reasons, both Bonestell and Klushantsev painted and constructed landscapes that drew upon Earth bound elements as source material and inspiration. In some cases, particularly Mars, picturing planets with reference to Earth's features proved a reasonably accurate model. In other cases, such as Jupiter (Bonestell) or Venus (Klushantsev) this analogizing proved very wide of the mark indeed. Nevertheless, the thought of similarities between Earth and other planetary landscapes retains a comforting appeal to the science fiction imaginary: that is to say, that chain of signifiers across which plays the effect of landscape within the imaginary, formed through its ecologizing of Earth's topography and biosphere, is used to attribute meaning to rock, gas and ice formations seen on other planets by virtue of their iconicity.

David Harvey, in his book *Spaces of Hope* (2000), lists a basic repertoire of elements of 'Species Being' that he posits as 'derived from evolutionary experience'. Amongst them, alongside 'the production of hierarchy', 'adaptation and diversification' and 'collaboration, cooperation and mutual aid' he lists 'a humanized nature broadly in accord – though with frequent unintended consequences – with human requirements' (2000: 209).

The Bonestell-Klushantsevian construction of planetary landscape evokes a sense of landscape-as-end (in the sense of 'end' as final objective) and the *landscaping of ends* (that is to say, the shaping of final objectives, both topographical and ideological). These elements arise out of the 'production of hierarchy and homogeneity' as well as the 'adaptation and diversification' we find in Harvey's list, but obviously entail that '*humanized nature*' Harvey posits in terms of human requirements. I would suggest this lies at the heart of the construction of 'Earthlike' which we find commonplace in the extrapolative picturing of Klushantsev-Bonestellian constructions, as well as the imaging of today, where we find the sobriquet 'Earthlike' frequently applied in the growing study of exoplanets (planets outside our own solar system). That is not, of course, to say that most exoplanets revealed by technologies such as the Kepler space telescope are believed to be like the Earth at all. Since the earliest possible exoplanet candidate, HD114762b, was detected in 1989, the development of satellite telescopy specifically focused on the search for more planets has seen a huge increase in the number of stars known to have planets circling them. In particular, the remarkable results yielded by the orbiting Kepler telescope suggests that our galaxy is rich in planetary bodies circling various types of star (or in some cases binary stars – a particularly vivid moment for a generations of film goers familiar with the famous double sun set viewed by a bored and wistful Luke Skywalker from his home planet of Tatooine). The discovery of Kepler-186f, an Earthlike planet orbiting a red dwarf star, the most stable and common form of star in the Milky Way galaxy, suggests that Earthlike planets – rocky, with atmospheres not too deep, hot or cold, orbiting at a distance where water would exist in liquid state – may indeed be common.

One might immediately ask why an Earthlike planet should be more engaging here than one that presents as fantastically strange – and of course, on one level there is absolutely no logical reason why this should not be so. It is easy to frame this emphasis on the Earthlike as a sort of cosmic mirror stage, and this is certainly the thesis presented in a number of science fictions: before it, any sense of self as a planetary species, where it exists at all, is fragmented, inchoate. In this schema, repetitive, unarticulated drives result in random acts of violence on each other and the ecology of our world. The developmental milestone of recognizing another planet like our own would bring some sense of place and narrative – cohesion – to Earth. Jonathan Frakes's *Star Trek: First Contact* (1996) presents just such a thesis. Earth in the 2060s is still recovering from World War III. A small, diverse survivalist community is shown living amongst pines in rural hills, seeking out an existence re-booting and adapting inherited technology from an earlier age. One character, Lily (Alfre Woodard), refers to 'factions' suggesting that the rugged mountainside existence is the setting for violent competition between warring bands with various allegiances.

It is in this context that a drunken eccentric, Zefram Cochrane, invents a faster than light warp drive which, opening the gates to the famous 'new worlds, new civilizations' of the *Star Trek* sagas, creates the foundational event that unites the human race by giving it new purpose. In the same film, when questioned by Lily, the starship captain Jean-Luc Picard (Patrick Stewart) states that it is precisely the challenge of star-flight that has eradicated monetary wealth acquisition as a human motivation. Arguably, the precise character of the psychological impact of contact with another 'Earthlike' planet would, of course, depend on whether it was inhabited, and by whom. An uninhabited world, say, for example, one old enough to support intelligent life but bereft of it, would slowly fuel suspicion and doubt just as surely as contact with a world inhabited by intelligent life would instantaneously transform our image of self. Either eventuality would, however, provide a profound proof of the possibility of existence and survival far beyond any current speculations based upon surmising and supposition, not to mention those elements of dread arising from our past and current projections on our closest planetary neighbours within the solar system, Venus and Mars.

Both Venus and Mars represent in concrete terms what it means to claim that a planet has 'Earthlike' qualities, not only to the extent to which they might be said to have defined such a typology – rocky spheres with gaseous, relatively shallow atmospheres – but also to the extent their respective landscapes have presented case studies of the catastrophic variations possible in that which is 'Earthlike'. Just as Mars and Venus respectively present as the polar opposites in their relative extremes – the thin cold zephyrs of Mars versus the boiling density of the Venusian greenhouse effect run riot – so in fantasy and projection the two planets have been imagined 'like Earth'.

The potential fallacies of the 'Earthlike' paradigm are highlighted in contemporary scientific debates around respective supporters of a human return to the Moon or, alternatively, a human landing on Mars. In many ways, the 'Earthlike' appearance of the Martian landscape – its dry river beds, dusty mountains and deserts, along with its russet sky – belies the many ways in which Mars remains prohibitively hostile and distant to any sustained human presence. Whilst a human landing on Mars could feasibly be achieved with existing technology, a sustainable long-term colony remains, for the moment, financially and technically very difficult, and any economic benefits – for example, the mining of mineral or metal resources – would only be attainable after many, many years. A human mission to Mars at the present historical juncture would likely result in a so-called 'flags and footprints' spectacle, but little else. The Moon, on the other hand, is close enough to Earth to present a realistic possibility for a small scale permanent presence along the lines of the Antarctic survey or International Space Station, and eventually, possible mining of minerals or rare-isotopes such as Helium-3 or deuterium: space craft or barges permanently in cislunar orbit, such as the Lunar Cycler proposed by Edwin 'Buzz' Aldrin could provide an effective and relatively cheap Earth-Moon-Earth conveyance. Yet the Moon presents, visually, as positively non-Earthlike, in a manner that Mars, deceptively, does not.

However, in acknowledging 'Earthlike' as a point of reference – an important 'milestone' in DARPA's lexicon – we are drawn emphatically back to both the frames of reference set by this book – the question of landscape and the extent to which the new is unknowable. Yet the abiding fascination of identifying New Earths points to two enduring aspects of the whole enterprise – the search for that landscape that would, despite all its differences, be recognizable as a potential home and at the same time, ones that might not be a home for humans, but the home of someone else, perhaps occupied now, perhaps not. Whilst this carries with it the sense of the *unhomely home* - the haunted house of gothic fiction theorized by Anthony Vidler in his influential book *The Architectural Uncanny* (1994), there is also a sense of Ernst Bloch's concept of *Heimat* – the home that is sensed within the Utopian imaginary but has yet to be experientially known.

The doubts and uncertainties attendant upon any sense of Species Being are constitutive of human attempts to landscape any *topos* – to chance upon and claim a space as home is to acknowledge oneself as an interloper or intruder. This is also true of our claims to the veracity of our speculations, suppositions and visualizations.

As I have sought to demonstrate with reference to both Bonestell and Klushantsev, their landscapes occupied a precarious relationship with veracity because of the steady advance of both empirical knowledge and sudden changes within the prevailing technocratic or scientific paradigm under which the artists respectively laboured – one that placed their output contiguous to, and subsequently, with the passage of time, convergent with, strands or tendencies within science fiction as a genre. The obvious contemporary heirs to that strand or tendency today is to be found in the recent resurgence of science fiction cinema making claims to extrapolative realism – Alfonso Cuarón's *Gravity* (2013), Christopher Nolan's *Interstellar* (2014), Sebastián Cordero's *Europa Report* (2014) and Ridley Scott's *The Martian* (2015). Set in low Earth orbit (LEO) for the majority of its diegesis, Cuaron's film is devoid of any landscapes save for the last moments of the final scene; I deal with *Europa Report* in Chapter 6, so my focus here will be on Nolan's *Interstellar* and Scott's *The Martian*.

The Martian begins when Mark Watney, a botanist and mechanical engineer on the third human mission to Mars, is lost and left for dead by the other five crew members during a sand storm on Mars which forces the other crew members to leave the planet and return to Earth.

Scott's film was closely based upon an originally self-published novel of the same name by Andy Weir, which was subsequently published by Random House in 2014 and, significantly, promoted and marketed not as a science fiction, but in the general fiction sections of bookshops as a survival thriller, aiming no doubt to reach beyond the traditional readership of novels about space flight.

Both *The Martian* and *Interstellar* made claims to scientific accuracy. In the case of *Interstellar*, which I will discuss in more detail below, this principally took the form of the widely publicized involvement of the distinguished astrophysicist Kip Thorne in the production of the film. In the case of *The Martian*, scientific veracity was suggested by a first person explanatory voice-over by the protagonist, Mark Watney (Matt Damon) in which various processes and situations were explained and quantified. As in Andy Weir's original novel, with raw materials but rations insufficient to last the time until any rescue mission can reach him, Watney's survival depends on being able 'to science the shit out of this'. Weir's novel is replete with the arithmetic of survival, from the calorific value of growing of potatoes (fortuitously brought from Earth for Thanksgiving) fertilized with human waste in the abandoned habitat, to the escape, orbital insertion and rendezvous velocities of spacecraft. Notably, however, Whilst distances between key features on the surface of Mars are accurately portrayed, but the landscape of Mars itself (some sequences were on a constructed sound stage, whilst others were filmed in Wadi Rum, Jordan) is not mathematized in any comparable manner.

The film's principal departure from what was scientifically known about Mars at the time of production centres on the interaction between the Martian surface and its atmosphere – namely, the impossibility of a sandstorm occurring on Mars producing such catastrophic and near-fatal effects. Whilst Martian dust storms can cover the entire planet and last for months, the thin atmosphere of Mars would mean even the worst storms would seem as no more than light breezes to human explorers. Despite taking due account of the general climate, temperatures and aridity of Mars (subsequent discoveries by NASA's Mars Reconnaissance Orbiter of sporadic flowing water suggest the latter was exaggerated) both Weir's novel and Scott's film altered the actual weather of Mars sufficiently to allow a human drama to unfold. Such 'holes' in the plotting of *The Martian* admits of its status as fiction but also remind us how un-Earthlike Mars is in its actualities. There are, perhaps, analogies here with Bonestell's precipitous mountains: the weathering of turbulent atmospheres and storms as a cliché signifier of adversity in human affairs. Such plot holes reveal the projection – the human *landscaping* qua Mitchell (1994) – of these agglomerations and accretions of silicates and gases that bear an iconic resemblance but no human connection to the skies and hills of Earth in order to expedite human scale stories and possibilities. In this aspect, it is at the point where a drama other than large-scale schematic extrapolation entails *The Martian* placing a predetermined landscape around a figure, rather than placing a figure on a topos which, in due course, they see as a landscape.

The character of Watney is one marked by a humorous resilience in the face of crushing odds. Indeed, it might seem plausible that someone with such perky indefatigability would be best placed to survive such a situation, impossible sandstorms notwithstanding. In contrast to the seat-of-the-pants optimism of *The Martian*, Christopher Nolan's *Interstellar* (2014) for the most part strikes a sombre and melancholic tone. Like *The Martian*, or the works of Bonestell and Klushantsev seen in retrospect, the 'closer' the claims for scientific veracity, the greater the acuity of error or plot contrivance – space fantasies such as the *Star Wars* franchise or *Star Trek* would not expect nor attract the same sort of scrutiny. In the case of *Interstellar*, the temptation to read the diegesis as schematic parable is particularly strong, given the technical contradictions, which arguably begins with the possibility of a crop destroying blight that consumes nitrogen spreading across the entire Earth, and continues with anomalies such as the need to launch the crew on their mission using a huge rocket launcher from Earth's 1g gravity, yet the same crew only requiring a relatively small lander craft to escape the 1.3g tide locked oceanic planet orbiting a black hole. Nevertheless, the affecting melancholy of *Interstellar* lies in its attempts to consider the effect on human beings of the encounter with the terrible aspect of Meillassoux's *arche-fossil*: untold numbers of uninhabited planets spread across an incomprehensibly vast space-time continuum, the superficial similarities of which only serve to underline their huge differences to our own world.

For all its contrivances, through this effective staging of the paradoxes of both planetary landscape and of relativistic space travel, *Interstellar* succeeds in positing the question of species being through the antimony of the figure in a landscape in a manner which *The Martian* does not. However, in the end, of course, as Suvin (1979) might have suggested, the film's extrapolatory tendencies prevent the *mise-en-scène* from escaping the pull of ideology any more than the film's space craft *Endurance* can escape the gravity well of the black hole: the closing scene shows Amelia Brand (Anne Hathaway) returning to a homestead she has established on the plains of Edmond's Planet, over which flutters the US flag.

Planetary Landscapes, Correlatives and Opaque Realisms

In conclusion, I want to therefore suggest that the sense of the uncanny 'Earthlike' and Ernst Bloch's conception of *Heimat* that are evident in the extensive recourse to empirical tropes in the work of Bonestell, Klushantsev and their heirs, contain something unseen. If, as I have argued, within the visual signs of these images there is contained a perpetual oscillation between Earthlike and *Heimat*, then that oscillation is indicative of an invisible Other, namely a schematic cipher of astronomical time. As such, this schematic cipher is discernable *via negativa* much as that Real which can be attested to only in its relation a 'system of fictions' that Alain Badiou refers to in the quote I used earlier in this chapter. This schema occurs as an imagining beyond that presented by that which is Earthlike – the realization that the spaces and times of the Earthlike must be pertinent to only a tiny minority of possible worlds. I would suggest this realization is evident at the point at which the correlatives of Earthlike landscapes become impossible to sustain. As Raymond Brassier (2007) explains:

> It is strictly impossible to prolong the chain of experience from our contemporary perception of the radioactive isotope to the time of the accretion of the earth indexed by its radiation, because the totality of the temporal series coextensive with possible experience itself emerged out of that geological time wherein there simply was no perception. We cannot extend the chain of possible perceptions back prior to the emergence of nervous systems, which provide the material conditions for the possibility of perceptual experience.
>
> (2007: 52)

As I have noted above, human figures emerge only at certain specific points in the landscapes of both Klushantsev and Bonestell. Beyond those points, the landscape exists not as landscape per se – that is to say as a perceived composite of sky and ground, subject to human perceptions, but rather is shown without human presence. Whilst the absence of human figures in any landscape does not, in itself, negate the condition of being a landscape, in the case of Klushantsev and Bonestell, whose work, as we have seen above, was composed according to extant scientific knowledge, I would suggest the figureless landscape infers not only temporary desertion by human occupants – as, say, a painting of an empty farm yard or silent forest might – but the possibility that the planetary landscape is imagined at some point of time perhaps before humans existed, or long after human extinction.

What differentiates the figureless landscapes of Kushantsev and Bonestell from other figureless landscapes such as those of the Itinerants and the Hudson River School is their schematic inference of an absence of human time. This schematic inference of that which exists outside and beyond human correlation, and as such is only deduced from that which mathematizable – calculations of age, distance, luminosity, light wavelengths or refractive properties and so on – makes the work of both Bonestell and Klushantsev the site of a particular encounter for the viewer – one which intimates both species being and species extinction. This makes the errors of veracity in their landscapes – those mistakes that have subsequently emerged as data have been refined or revised – indexical of a realism compelled to acknowledge the mathematizable properties of the object physical laws that exist independently of human presence and are not established according to our physical existence. As Quentin Meillassoux (2008) has suggested in relation to the formation of the planets of the solar system:

> It makes no sense to say that 'it was hot then' or that the light was 'blinding' or to make any other subjective judgements of this type. Since we do not know of any observer who was there to experience the accretion of the earth – and since we do not even see how a living observer would have been able to survive had she experienced such heat – all that can be formulated about such an event is what the 'measurements', that is to say, the mathematical data, allow us to determine.
>
> (2008: 11–12)

Meillassoux's and Brassier's insistence upon the impossibility of correlation might seem implicit in some of Bonestell's landscapes, in particular his depictions of Saturn seen from its moons. In these paintings, the ringed gas giant is viewed from empty rocky deserts devoid of human explorers, and the interplay between familiar looking rock formations, the unfamiliar black sky, the looming disc of Saturn and scattered moons bisected by the ring plane evoke a disturbing interplay between cognition, iconicity, empirical experience and unsettling estrangement. In these particular works, I would suggest Bonestell's achievement lies in his marshalling of all the constituent elements of science fiction, but in such a way that the iconicity of the rocky mountains unexplored by humans implies an inversion of the empirical referents of 'Earthlike': no longer referencing back to Earth, as much as making them substantive in their own right, at which point cognition is sundered from historical correlatives, and the mountains of Earth become just one more momentary example amongst billions in the space time continuum.

Chapter 6

Beyond the Periphery: Desert and Darkness

Dust Clouds and Contrails

Paul Thomas Anderson's 2012 film *The Master* tells the fictional story of Freddie Quell, a demobilized and traumatized drifter who, in the years following World War II, becomes closely involved with the charismatic Lancaster Dodd, the fictional leader of a religious cult bearing distinct resemblance to Scientology, the religion founded by science fiction writer L. Ron Hubbard (1911–86). In one scene, a well-placed but unexpected jump cut places the viewer in a sun bleached desert salt flat where Dodd (Phillip Seymour Hoffman) and Quell (Joaquin Phoenix) attempt to resolve the accumulating psychological, ideological and interpersonal tensions in their relationship by recourse to speed trialing a motorcycle in a straight line across the flats, competitively pushing the machine and their own nerves in a somewhat forced but determined celebration of machinic and bodily resilience and masculine bonding. As the speed trial scene suggests, Dodd's philosophy, which the filmic diegesis grotesquely reveals he is making up as he goes along, offers his followers the directives of temporal and spatial mastery: like any common or garden variety of megalomaniac, Dodd aggressively claims the lead role in galactic grand narratives of 'trillions of years', suggestively intimates special knowledge of the frontiers of scientific research and rewards or punishes his disciples with accentuated or diminished bit parts in unfolding fictions of manichaeistic conflict. In short, Dodd's revelations endow his followers with the speed and scope to race over their featureless lives by imagining themselves part of something stupendously transcendent and, outside of the nothingness of space, the desert is the setting which allows the positing of this elevated sense of species being *in extremis*. Under the windswept blue sky of the hard salt flat, the combined testing of motorcycle speed and nerves necessitates a linear form that suggests purposeful direction, running counter to the directionless despair of William Morris's '*waste that has no way*' I referred to in the Introduction. Similarly, in the form of the man on the motorcycle, a speeding trail of dust *loosened* or *set free* (the etymological origin of the term 'absolute') from the strictures of road traffic regulation or concern for pedestrians or bystanders, the speed trial scene locates notions of personal freedom as the ability to avail oneself of the maximum power one has to hand.

Robbie the Robot first appears in Fred Wilcox's 1956 film *Forbidden Planet* as a speeding trail of dust, spotted by the visiting crew of the starship *C-57D* in the middle distance of the empty plains of Altair IV. For the technocratic world that the febrile megalomania Anderson's Lancaster Dodd seeks to emulate – and pretends to understand – the desert offers the safety of seclusion and sterility similarly prized by Robbie's master, Dr Morbius. This is a common enough trope of the desert test site: as such, back on Earth, the desert becomes the screen on to which is projected what the mathematician John von Neumann called 'this Buck Rogers universe' (quoted in Rhodes 1995: 362) – atomic America's confidence in its scientific paradigms and all the madcap potential it presumed to master through such, arguably beginning with the Wright Brothers at Kitty Hawk in 1903 to the testing of missiles and rockets at White Sands and elsewhere.

How speed and freedom might be conflated is partially articulated by Paul Virilio in his *Speed and Politics* (1977):

> [...] their ability to reduce geographic space to nothing or almost nothing [...] the essential object of any strategy consists in maintaining the non-place of a general delocalization of means that alone still allows us to gain fractions of seconds, which gain is indispensable to any freedom of action.
>
> (2006: 153)

Virilio's 'their' refers to missiles, not humans, although missile systems become cybernetic extensions as surely as does the motorcycle that Dodd and Quell take turns at riding. For Virilio, the rocket motor's transformative ability resides in its extreme collapsing of distance and time:

> Territory has lost its significance in favor of the projectile [...] with the supersonic vector (airplane, rocket, airwaves), penetration and destruction become one. The instantaneousness of action at a distance corresponds to the defeat of the unprepared adversary, but also, and especially, to the defeat of the world as a field, as distance, as matter.
>
> (2006: 149–50)

Virilio's differentiation was presaged by Curtis Le May, the US Air force General I mentioned in Chapter 5. Appointed head of the US Strategic Air Command in 1948, May observed that the United States emerged victorious from World War II because '[w]e had space between us and our enemies which could not be spanned by the then-existing weapons [...] this gave us time' (Rhodes 1995: 345). May understood that the advent of the Nazi V-2 supersonic ballistic missile in the latter stages of the war made clear that such distances would be strategically meaningless in the foreseeable future.

Notably, Virilio's excitement over the language of speed is at times almost as remarkable as the imprecisions of that usage: in *Speed and Politics*, he tells the reader that the growth of speed is such that it was measured in the 1940s *in knots*, by the 1960s *in machs* (sic 2007: 150). Of course, no such unit of measurement as 'machs' exists, and no scientist would refer to a vehicle's speed as '*x* machs': the division of local flow velocity by the speed of sound in any given medium (e.g. air) gives a quantity number *preceded* by the surname of the physicist Ernst Mach who first mathematized the observed phenomenon that sound velocity increases as the fluid velocity decreases. 'Mach's number' is therefore the speed of sound, which at sea level under normal Earthbound conditions is 340 metres per second or 760.9 miles per hour. Henceforth, with the advent of supersonic flight, Mach numbers – M 1, M 2 and so on, have been used to denote multiples of Mach's number. (Miles 1950: 17–18). Similarly, speed and velocity are not interchangeable in the manner Virilio seems to imply: speed, as with, say, length or temperature, is quantified in scalar terms and has only magnitude, whereas velocity, like acceleration is a vector, quantified by magnitude and direction. Nevertheless, the test makes the desert the site of the relation between time and distance which is mathematizable: $v = d/t$. Nevertheless, the grim reductivism of Virilio's theses on the implications of high-speed weapons echoes that of the military, and is instructive in thinking about the technocratic encounter with the desert landscape that occurs in the latter half of the twentieth century.

Although the first successful liquid fuel rocket was flown by Robert H. Goddard amidst snow and ice on farmland in his native Massachusetts in March 1926, by 1930, with financial support from Daniel Guggenheim, Goddard's team had moved to Roswell, New Mexico. After a two-year respite for non-flight experiments in Massachusetts from 1932–34, Goddard conducted tests there until 1941. Following Goddard's death in 1945 and the Allied victory work on rockets and high speed 'X planes' continued in and above the deserts of both California and New Mexico (Von Braun and Ordway 1975: 202–05).

Following Goddard, in the early 1940s US Army Ordnance chose White Sands in southern New Mexico for missile research (Figure 18). The area includes the Trinity Test Site at Alamogordo, where the first atomic bomb had been tested. An account of the White Sands desert missile base from 1953, *Sacrifice at White Sands* (1953), written by the journalist Jonathan Norton Leonard, gives a sense of both the missile base, its desert location and the traces of a buried pre-history and the attitude to the desert landscape. Leonard draws upon a range of exoticizing, antique and mystical analogies:

[…] an uninhibited wilderness presses from all sides upon this isolated outpost of technological man […] in front, for forty miles, sweeps the gray-green desert of the Tularosa Basin. Dust devils swirl across it like yellow tornadoes, and sometimes great sandstorms blot out the sun. But much of the time the air is as clear as a vacuum, showing a rim of distant mountains around the flat desert floor. A person standing in the centre beyond where the rockets fly can easily imagine himself in one of the moon's great craters with the jagged rampart circling around the horizon.

(2011: 370)

Leonard writes further:

on a steep mountain slope perches a massive concrete structure that has the soaring aloofness of a Tibetan monastery […] far out in the desert stands an even weirder structure – a peaked concrete igloo with walls and roof as solid as the stone of a pyramid [...] Near this modern donjon keep gather strange auxiliaries: tomblike underground storage places [...] lacy steelwork towers; a forest of poles and a spider web of wires [...] Radars sweep the sky with their pulsed electronic beams. The wide glassy stares of cameras and theodolites stare at the launching site. Far off on the mountain rim, great telescopes with forty-inch mirrors wait to follow the rockets on their flight into space.

(2011: 370)

All this, Leonard acknowledges, on the bones of earlier, vanished cultures:

There are ghosts in this desert too. The hollows between the mesquite hummocks close to the launching site are sprinkled with fragments of brilliantly painted pottery. Long ago, when the Tularosa Basin was a fertile valley, it supported a dense population of Indians, whose burial grounds and building foundations can still be traced among the thorny scrub. No one knows what happened to these ancient people [...] At any rate, they are gone. Perhaps the climate grew drier, They lacked the knowledge and resourcefulness to deal with such changes of environment. They left their dead and their poor, weak weapons [...] But their ghosts do not bother the rocket men, who live in a hard, taut world of the confident present'

(2011: 370–71)

In a similar vein, a short film, *Tularosa Frontier* (director unkown) commissioned by the US military in the 1950s, frames military activity at White Sands as one of pioneering regeneration, but sets this occurrence within a deeper perspective of both geological and historical time. *Tularosa Frontier* begins with the geological timescale of ancient inland seas and volcanic processes before describing the gradual erosion of fertile land and its transformation into desert. Following settlement by Europeans, '[g]reen farmlands dotted the Tularosa, livestock flourished' the voice-over declares before intoning, '[t]hen came tragedy. Improvident abuse of the soil brought its own retribution as drought struck the Tularosa [...] Nature, once bounteous, turned hostile'. Shots of tumble weed, deserted crumbling adobe huts and the bleached bones of long horn cattle create a sense of abandonment and desolation before declaring that in 1945 '[h]istory took a hand and a strange new band of pioneers' entered the basin to establish the Trinity atomic test site and subsequently, the White Sands Proving Grounds. Showing shots of motor traffic on the streets of developing desert towns, the voice-over declares, '[t]oday's civilian pioneer may work in the laboratories where missile components are tested'.

Whereas the visualization of speed in the deserts of the nineteenth century was one of arduous treks by camel or wagon train, in the second half of the twentieth century, it becomes that of the acceleration of rocket boosters or the mach stems of advancing nuclear shockwaves. The ocularity of such an undertaking engenders is bound up with the high speed photography of Harold Edgerton (1903–90), a professor of electrical engineering at MIT who developed very high speed camera shutter and filter technology capable of capturing the initial stages of nuclear fission explosions on film. The specialized and refined visualization of such atomic bomb detonations, enabling the peculiar shapes and interactions of expanding fronts of radiation and shockwaves in the millionths of seconds after detonation to be seen, was important for the development of so-called 'staged' thermonuclear weaponry, if such atomic bombs were to be used as 'primaries' (initiators) of the larger hydrogen bomb devices.

Sites such as White Sands, Bonneville Salt Flats, Woomera in South Australia and Hammaguir in the Sahara became the primary site of bodily encounters with speed in the form of the *test*: on the one hand, this would appear as the ontological claim of Virilio's 'Dromology': history developing at the speed of its weaponry technology; the *tabula rasa* of the desert periphery becoming the discursive centre of the cosmopolis, in perpetual anticipation of the cosmopolitan centres instantaneously becoming peripheralized deserts. One might think here of the United States' Sprint Anti-Ballistic Missile rocket tested at White Sands, capable of such speeds that aerodynamic heating raised its surface temperature during flight to greater than that of a an oxy-acetylene torch or the Soviet Gorgon ABM, capable of velocities seventeen times the speed of sound. Sprint's speed was to enable it to reach and destroy other missiles. In order to avoid being foiled by decoys deployed by such incoming enemy missiles, Sprint had to be launched in a very narrow window of time, once the missile it was aimed at was below a certain altitude, on its own final approach to the city it was heading to destroy (Von Braun and Ordway 1975: 146). Indeed, Virilio suggests the subsequent development of speeds in such rockets acted as a brake on their development due to the devolution of command and control necessary to facilitate the required response times:

> In the case of a surprise attack the supreme authority would have to risk abandoning his supremacy of decision by authorizing the lowest echelon of the defense system to immediately launch anti-missile missiles. The two political super powers have thus far preferred to avoid this situation through negotiations, renouncing anti-missile defense at the same time.
>
> (2006: 153)

Weapons development utilizes both areas of true desert such as the Salt flats of Nevada, but also other ecologically diverse areas of varying degrees of sparseness – bush-land such as the sacred sites of Maralinga in Australia, the steppes of Kazakhstan or salt marsh and shingle areas such as Orford Ness in England, and leaves them scarred and polluted.

This particular military-technocratic utilization – and visualization – of the desert of the mid-twentieth century draws upon and intersects with both its own technocratic mythos and that of precursory mysticisms centred on signs and wonders: the wanderings of the Book of Exodus, the tempting of Christ by Satan, the acetic delirium of John the Baptist, the distortions of heat, light and thirst, the enduring Native American Thunderbird mythos and urban myths around the activities at Roswell and UFO sightings: again, mythologized traces of things vanished or 'gone before'. John Beck (2014) has written persuasively of these test sites as the 'Purloined Landscape' hidden in plain sight in the manner of Edgar Allen Poe's short story 'The Purloined Letter', and the great photographer Richard Misrach has documented the residual effects in serial colour works showing polluted craters, upended military vehicles used as targets and animal corpses. The photographer Carole Gallagher (1993) has documented the human cost on the communities of 'down winders' – the inhabitants of deserted towns in the path of drifting radioactive fallout.

Fast moving dust clouds, lights in the sky, racing contrails, the distortions of heat and haze: as with the urban mythology around UFO sightings and restricted desert test sites such as 'Area 51', the question of the desert landscape in the science fiction imaginary is as much about what is *not* seen as what is. This is a perennial question in all deserts of course, but the deserts of the twentieth century become, through the oppositional politics of ecology, seen as something other than deserts after all. The legacy of testing in its various militarized form posits the desert as a wounded landscape – and thereafter a site of ecological reclamation. It calls into being the trenchant argument that these spaces were not deserts in any case – but rather finely balanced ecologies that those who thought of them as sterile spaces simply chose not to see or investigate. Fredric Brown's influential short story 'Arena', published in John W. Campbell's pulp magazine *Astounding Science Fiction* in 1944 as World War II progressed towards its climax, imagines a man from Earth named Carson awakening to temperatures of 'a hundred and thirty Fahrenheit, at a guess' in a desert of 'blue, bright blue' sand and scrub to find he is pitted in combat against an alien 'Outsider' (Aldiss 1964: 68–92).

Like Carson, the roller-shaped Outsider is required to fight to the death to secure the survival of its own civilization. Again, the desert is posited here as a landscape of reductive extremes in which things – in this case sentient beings – are tested to breaking point. Victory won at great physical and mental cost, Carson awakes once more on his spaceship realizing through his crew that little time has passed and that they are unaware of the mortal struggle he has just been through. In Brown's story, the desert is unreal (blue sand) but moreover, it is quarantined from clock time or history: either eternal or momentary, dissociated from time, it is merely 'space', so that what happens there is not subject to the normative ethical imperatives. Brown's story presages the attitude towards the desert of post-World War II tests of speed and power as merely space or *zone*, used at will without consequence: in Leonard's account quoted above, the scattered shards of others' history are denied agency through the erasing imposition of mystery and dismissed as objects of curiosity. To insist that the desert *is* landscape is, therefore, to acknowledge in small part its histories and its ecologies.

No Home but the Struggle: Desert Landscapes as Social and Ecological Test Sites

Ostensibly antithetical to the militarized test site mentality, the desert landscape as the site of ultimate tests nevertheless recurs in the ecologically concerned science fiction imaginary as one of reductive absolutes in which other experiments are conducted: extremes of survival, extremes of capability, extremes of threat. As in *Tularosa Frontier*, the desert, which spreads, appears or encroaches, is often presented as a sign of deep time, rather than necessarily being old itself: desertification as process, as incipient threat, but also as something to be preserved. Frank Herbert begins his baroque desert planet *Dune* cycle with a dedication offered across the globe and perhaps beyond:

> To the people whose labours go beyond ideas into the realm of 'real materials' – to the dry-land ecologists, wherever they may be, in whatever time they work, this effort at prediction is dedicated in humility and admiration.
>
> (frontispiece, 2005)

Preceding *Dune* by over two decades and published a year earlier than *Arena*, Peter Schuyler Miller's short story 'The Cave', first published in Astounding in 1943 (Aldiss 1964: 120–37), describes similarly finely balanced ecology to that of *Dune*'s desert planet Arrakis. In Schuyler Miller's story, which is set on Mars, 'a limestone ridge which rose like a giant rounded fin out of the desert' at the base of which is located the eponymous chamber 'less than a hundred feet' in length, 'leached out of the limestone by running water, long before'.

Schuyler Miller tells us that the limestone of the ridge 'was perhaps the oldest exposed rock on the surface of that small old world', laid down 'at a time when there were seas where there were only deserts now'. Alongside details of the traces of vanished seas and the fossil traces of ancient crustacea, Schuyler Miller describes how once 'water, sour with soil acids leached from the black humus of a forest floor' had once seeped through the rock 'eating away the soft stone, widening cracks into crannies and crannies into high arched rooms'. Schuyler Miller's story is both prescient and remarkable in its focus upon such detailed description of geological time. Schuyler Miller devotes over fifteen hundred words at the start of his short story to such description – 'Man' appears only twice, not as a character but as an abstraction – 'a thin man might', 'a man may set foot' once to indicate the height of one of the cave's small chambers and once to indicate the passage of time:

> A man may set foot in the clay of its floor and go away, and another man may come a hundred or a thousand or ten thousand years afterwards and see his footprint there, as fresh as though it had been made yesterday.
>
> (1964: 121–22)

In keeping with tropes of Mars that have persisted ever since Giovanni Schiaparelli's observation of Martian *canali*, the inhabitants of Schuyler Miller's Mars are struggling against complete desertification, but also, struggling to remember, to estimate, to comprehend:

> Most of the planet's surface had been desert for more millions of years than anyone has yet estimated. From the mouth of the cave its dunes and stony ridges stretched away like

crimson ripples [...] they were dust rather than sand: red, ferric ground ever finer by the action of grain against grain, milling over and over through the centuries. It lay in a deep drift in the alcove and spilled down into the opening of the cave; it carpeted the first twenty-foot passage as with a strip of red velvet [...] even in the black silt at the back of the cave, where the air never stirred, there was a soft red bloom on the yellow flowstone.

(1964: 122)

Schuyler Miller's (deserted) desert is only gradually populated as the story progresses: 'The *grak* reached the cave a little after dawn. He had been running all night [...]'. As it does, Schuyler Miller's tale tells of a range of species, including human, seeking shelter from the encroaching desert storm. Although some of the creatures sheltering in the cave would normally be hunter or hunted, the extreme Martian weather enforces a temporary truce in the face of a common enemy:

They were all grekka here – all living things, united in the common battle for existence against a cruel and malignant Nature. They knew the law and the brotherhood, and they would keep the truce as long as the storm lasted. Gradually the nictitating lids [the sentient, tool making *grak* is described as owl like] slipped across his open eyes and he sank into a half-sleep.

Schuyler Miller's exquisite Martian landscape is remarkable in his evocation of a fundamental division between the timescales and needs of living creatures on the one hand and the relentless geological and meteorological processes on the other. Indeed, the human protagonist – a miner from Earth named Harrigan, who seeks shelter from the storm with the other, indigenous creatures in the cave – seals his own fate by failing to share water with all the creatures he finds there, not just the intelligent ones. By failing to do this Harrigan marks himself out in the eyes of the *grak* as one who refuses to side with the struggle of all living things against the hostile landscape and elements of the planet. Schuyler Miller's evocation of a Martian ethos in which '[i]n the battle for life, all living things – all *grekka* – are brothers' (1964: 131) is poignantly misread by an Earth man who not only believes that 'grekka' is a merely a collective noun for his sentient *grak* interlocutor, but has come to mine the sparse remaining mineral deposits that had aeons ago been 'exhausted by a native Martian civilization pursuing its inevitable way to an inevitable end at a time when Adam and Eve probably still had tails' (1964: 126).

Vanishing Horizons, Shifting Perspectives

The geology and climate of Schuyler Miller's imagined Martian desert draws upon referents to be found in the arid badlands of Arizona. As Oliver Morton has documented in his book *Mapping Mars* (2002), during the course of nineteenth and twentieth century American

156

astronomy, the landscape of Arizona has been frequently conflated with that of Mars, despite substantial differences that makes such a conflation arbitrary. Yet Schuyler Miller's short story coincided with a renewed interest in radically re-visualizing the deserts of the South Western United States during the course of World War II.

Georgia O'Keefe's 1940 painting *Red and Yellow Cliffs* presents the striated, eroded Arizona outcrops of the Painted Desert filling the entire frame, without the sky. As the art historian Charles Harrison (1942–2009) remarked this device 'helps to produce an effect of containment that seems at odds with the illusion of distance and space established by other features of the picture' (1994: 221). During the period 1940–45 however, a more sustained re-visioning of the Arizona desert emerged in the work of Frederick Sommer (1905–99) who used photography to document the desert areas of Arizona and Colorado using a large format field camera. Such cameras, which produced a sheet negative 10 inches by 8 inches, allowed for high resolution images to be produced and were the stock-in-trade of many professionals of the time. Sommer's work, however, was radically different in its compositional depiction of the landscape. The adjustable planes of focus and the very high depth of field 10×8 cameras and lenses allowed for – what are technically termed the camera's *movements* – enabled Sommer to create startling perspectives. Capturing such a range of focus and perspective is not one that the human eye is capable of without eye movement and the brain's memory, so the effect of such photography is one of a peculiar ocularity. In one notable picture by Sommer, taken just three years before Schuyler-Miller's story was published, a shark-fin like striated rock rises up from the desert badlands of Arizona. Sommer's photograph, entitled *Petrified Forest National Monument, Arizona, 1940*, (Figure 19) in the collection of The Museum of Modern Art, New York, shows a desert landscape very similar to the one Schuyler Miller describes in 'The Cave' – one of leached limestone striations subject to the depredations of water action over aeons of time and fossilized artefacts laid down in the Late Triassic period. Sommer's image is marked by mostly viewing the landscape looking down from a vantage point far above – the horizon and sky occupy only the top tenth of the picture – creating, in combination with the focusing techniques I mentioned above, a sense of flight. Indeed, in works produced in the immediate years after this one, Sommer began excluding sky and horizon altogether visualizing the desert as immersive fields of detail sometimes inches across, sometimes miles across, all landscapes devoid of the normative figure/ground relations and compositional devices.

The axiomatic encounter between the category of Fine Art and the desert in the twentieth century is frequently held to occur in the Land Art of Nancy Holt, Walter de Maria, Michael Heitzer and Robert Smithson. It has been argued before that the desert land art projects of Smithson, Heitzer et al. were, in part, inspired by the possibility of large structures being photographed from altitude or space: Smithson's *Spiral Jetty* (1970) made at Rozel Point, in Utah's Great Salt Lake, can effectively only be fully viewed by flying over it. However, Sommer's radical visualization of the desert, which evokes a similar sense of in the photographic print, predates the later land art work by over 20 years, marked as it is by the assiduous utilization of photographic skill, but also a formal refusal to conform to what was, at the time, the established conventions of photographic landscape composition. Sommer's work visually surveys the *topos* of the desert as if from above: one is not invited to take one's standpoint *in* the landscape, since the plane of focus is used effectively to *prevent* a clear sense of what one is standing on: in Sommer's photographs, one might just as easily be suspended above the landscape as having any secure or stable foothold on the ground. Sommer's *Arizona Landscape, 1943* (V&A catalogue number E1001–1993) presents a horizon-less view down a small desert gorge, dotted here and there with small rocky outcrops. In the form in which these works were intended to be shown – that is to say, of the black and white 10×8 print, these outcrops appear as apparently randomly distributed slight fluctuations in an otherwise even distribution of mid tone speckles and spots of the desert floor, and the short thin vertical slashes of cacti stems. The print therefore presents a field of abundant pin-sharp detail, within which no single object in particular holds a remarkable position in relation to any other, except perhaps for the small patch of lighter earth mentioned earlier. However, none of these features can be seen to have been 'placed' by the photographer in accordance with any of the traditional compositional rules of photographic composition – neither the so-called 'rule of thirds' or the 'golden section'; two other rocky projections – one in the top most right hand corner of the print and the other placed slightly lower in the top left hand corner, do nothing in terms of framing or compositional balance. On the contrary, these features merely add to the difficulty in establishing a clear sense of recessional depth in the picture: the adjusted plane of focus and maximum depth of field militate against providing the viewer with any strong sense of recessional Renaissance perspective and effectively eliminates any shifts in focus that might assist the viewer in reading the picture easily in accordance with such conventions.

Arizona Landscape, 1943, is perhaps even more challenging. Each cacti stem, naturally darker at the tip than at the base, presents as a miniature scale of the grey tones used in the rest of the image; again, a random, overall scattering of vertical slits across a darker grey speckled, horizonless broad incline.

As with 'Arena' and 'The Cave', at times it might seem that Sommer's images might seem to read the war raging in Europe, North Africa and the Pacific through the struggle for existence in the desert. In images such as *Coyotes, 1945*, the mummified corpses of the hapless coyote pack are framed such that they extend beyond the edges of the photograph, suggesting an unending frieze of emaciation and death contemporaneous with that unfolding in the battlefields, bombed cities and death camps of the time. This visual reference to sculptural frieze or *bas relief* – a theme seen elsewhere in Sommer's photographs – evokes a sense of the 'tragedy of fate' – the classical theatrical form in which human protagonists struggle vainly against the pre-ordained will and cruel indifference of determining forces – either in the form of the gods, or in this case, the extreme conditions of the coyote pack's environment.

In Sommer's work, the desert appears as both a site of the periphery and the peripheralized: during his life, Sommer was not generally acknowledged or accepted within either the community of US photography or its canon. The desert also instigates new forms of looking: as his obituary by Edward Helmore (1999) records, Sommer was excluded from the *f*64 Group because his work was seen as unphotogenic and his parallel practices as an artist working across media – he made drawings, collages and photomontages – left him interpellated as something other than the requisite Modernist purist that critics of his age required. Although linked intellectually and creatively within the community of Surrealist European *émigrés* (he was friends with Max Ernst) Sommer's work – can be seen to draw upon the forms and traditions of scientific survey photography of Timothy O'Sullivan and can be placed antithetically to the picturesque conventions of European conventions of picturing landscape and its American heirs of the Hudson River School of painting and photographers such as Carlton Watkins.

Joel Snyder (1994) argues O'Sullivan's work marks the entry of the photographer as 'technical expert' accompanying the expedition, but nevertheless an artist of landscape. As such, there are analogues here to the position of Klushantsev and Bonestell that I discussed in Chapter 5. Snyder's point is one that differentiates O'Sullivan's practice as one which, effectively liberated by state sponsorship from private commercial pressures, presents a landscape of the American West that does not conform to the picturesque conventions of contemporaneous commercial work of the same region and by doing so, is able to present a landscape not only unfamiliar, inhospitable and terrifying, but, in Snyder's words '*unaddressable* in terms of the evolving practices of photographic landscape' (1994: 199, my emphasis). Snyder goes on to suggest that O'Sullivan's works

[…] mark the beginning of an era – one in which we still live – in which expert skills provide the sole means of access to what was once held to be part of our common inheritance.

(1994: 199)

Snyder's argument is pertinent to the visualization of the desert as a site of testing or scientific research: it places O'Sullivan at a juncture or margin between the categories of pictorial creativity and scientific research and in positing the subject position of 'artist as technical expert' reminds us of the mimetic function of art in replicating the modes of practice or terms of reference found in other categories of human endeavour. This, of course, is something the genre of science fiction itself has always done and continues to do in a wide variety of literary, cinematic, gaming and illustrative forms: to use just one possible example of many one might consider the straight faced delivery of pseudo-scientific jargon or technical explanations.

The radical formal departures of both O'Sullivan and Sommer constituted not only new ways of looking at the desert topos, but through their refusals to abide by pictorial conventions, carry with them a sense of unresolved tension that evokes endlessness and infinity. The framing appears to be random, thereby suggesting any number of alternatives, none of which would bear much difference. In a 2005 monograph of Frederick Sommer's work, Keith F. Davis remarks that 'the vistas of rock and cacti become as sublime as the starry night sky' (2005: 19). Indeed, the random scattering of Sommer's 'fields' of fragments is, I would suggest, not only analogous to the stars in the night sky, but also the immersive darkened cityscapes commonly found in science fiction imagery – myriad fields or towers of lights so vast that they resist any attempt by the viewer to group or identify conventional figure/ground relational reading. In Gestalt terms, looking at fields of rocks, stars or cityscapes produces no sense of closure or resolution on the part of the viewer, but only a sense of endless immersion. As Richard Zaka (2007) remarks in Gestalt theory, '[u]nfinished tasks (non-closure) can cause tension and frustration' (2007: 28).

As such, Sommer's radical break with the precepts and expectations of landscape – in some senses, the conventional 'laws' of landscape – presage those later portrayals of landscapes, cityscapes and skyscapes in which the viewer becomes lost in a dark immensity punctuated by scattered lights to the point of being overwhelmed by tensions and frustrations of immersive disorientation.

The lack of closure or resolution both of the desert and its inhabitants is echoed in the diegesis of Ion de Sosa's *Androids Dream* (2014). Set amidst the immersive banality of an anonymous holiday resort surrounded by barren desert hills, De Sosa's film presents an elegant, radical re-working of Philip K. Dick's *Do Androids Dream of Electric Sheep?*, more famously filmed by Ridley Scott as *Blade Runner* (1982, with various subsequent re-edits). In contrast to the special effects spectacularism of a futuristic Los Angeles China Town for which Scott's film is probably best remembered, de Sosa's film, ostensibly set in the year 2052, begins with documentary-style establishing shots of half completed holiday apartments and residential tower blocks in the real life landscape of a resort predominantly inhabited by an aging population, whiling away their final years amidst the fading glitz of piped-music ball rooms and retirement homes replete with collections of kitsch ornaments. In contrast to the perpetual neon nightscape of Scott's vision, de Sosa's predominant tone is that of a weary diurnal – nocturnal cycle of stillness and silence. Around this suburban agglomeration lie desiccated hills and gullies dotted with sparse vegetation. In establishing shots, the countless bone-white apartment blocks appear to huddle from the encroaching desolation. Enhancing a somewhat minor theme in Scott's film, de Sosa's depiction lingers on the drudge labour sustaining this service economy – cleaners, builders and drug mules – whilst a peripatetic gunman wanders the half built developments and the scrubland outskirts, murdering them. This is a vision of the desert not as distant Other but as something proximal, encroaching and every day. Nevertheless, de Sosa's landscape remains one of paranoia, desperation and growing crisis and conflict: a consumer desert as backdrop to murderous pursuit.

The science fiction literary New Wave of the late 1960s to early 1970s saw a positioning of the alienated in deserts of various forms as romantic anthropology, via the likes of Frank Herbert (*Dune*) and Robert Silverberg (*A Time of Changes*). In Ursula Le Guin's *The Dispossessed* (1974) – subtitled 'An ambiguous utopia' – the Odonian anarcho-syndicalists have been exiled from their lush planet of origin, Urras for two centuries and eke out an alternative society on the desert moon, Anarres. Similar to Earth in the period of the Cold War, Urras is riven by military and political rivalry between capitalist and authoritarian communist blocs: the Anarresti society seeks to obviate the problematics of both by both egalitarian collectivism and a rigorous restructuring of language that obviates individualist or possessive behaviour. The harsh landscape of Le Guin's novel suggests the desert as an unforgiving context for sociological projects – the hero of her story, the scientist Shevek, spends time sharing the work of famine relief rather than pursuing his important research – but as such raises the stakes. In Le Guin's work, the sense of the desert is posited as an acetic leveler of all life, one that engenders a focus upon a mean level of necessity wherein there is no resolution but an ongoing cycle (this is reflected in the chapter sequencing of *The Dispossessed*). However, Le Guin's political framing does place the desert grit as the progenitor of some sort of pearl – in the form of collective social engagement with its challenges, an ongoing existentially affirming engagement with the hardships of life that can be celebrated.

The theme of desert as acetic leveler, as test site and, thereby, as the progenitor of radically revised collective ethics is further distilled in Wanuri Kahiu's intriguing short film *Pumzi* (2009, Figure 20). In Kahiu's film, the protagonist, Asha, is a young woman living in technologically advanced communal habitat, hermetically sealed amidst the dunes of scorching windswept desert extending in all directions outside. Set 35 years after World War III fought over water on an Earth gripped by unfolding ecological catastrophe, the architecture, social conventions and technology of the habitat are all devised to preserve moisture through reclamation, purification and recycling, the energy for at least some of which appears to come from obligatory time spent by the inhabitants on pedalling and rowing machines. This finely balanced, rarefied and rationalized ecology is underscored by the film's dialogue – sparse, abrupt, economic – which, whilst encountered by the film's wilful protagonist at various points as coercive or punitive, is nevertheless responded to with a calm determination to pursue her irrational belief in the possibility of a lush green tree growing outside the habitat, amidst the searing dunes. When a mysterious package arrives at the habitat's virtual museum apparently containing fertile soil, Asha escapes from the habitat. Redolent of Ursula Le Guin's fiction, Kahiu's film evokes the antimonies of landscape and society (figure/ground, community/individuality) with the antimonies of fable, in which dream and memory are lived as an ocular relation with the resistances and histories of the natural world through visitation and hallucination. This act of seeming visionary madness can also be seen as an integral part of what Gerald Vizenor has called 'survivancy' in which stories – in Vizenor's case, specifically stories of the First Nations of the Americas – are an active presence in the reassertion or reversion to a proper relationship with the Earth. For Vizenor, survivance stories are the 'renunciation of dominance, tragedy and victimry' (quoted in Dillon 2012: 143). The character of Asha in *Pumzi* sees the crazy possibility of plant life returning to the landscape, thereby imagining a resurgent biosphere expanded beyond the claustrophobic decreasing circles of the habitat.

Both Kahiu's film and that of de Sosa effectively posit the desert as test site once more, albeit one of social experiment, and in this there is a process of inversion: the desert is no longer subject to human experimentation as much as desertification tests what has become a human experiment.

Breath and Darkness

Within early modern European history, the trope of the expert in the alien desert finds its root in the encounter of the Napoleonic philologist Jean-François Champolion (1790–1832) with the ruins of ancient Egypt. In the European Egyptomania of the early nineteenth century, the desert becomes the holder of not only ancient secrets, but the source of existential anxieties about the fate of empires. If deserts resonate with a Heideggarian existential anxiety of both, being and nothingness then darkness can only double the effect: the two are encountered simultaneously in the first human lunar landings. As Buzz Aldrin recalls:

> We had sixty seconds of fuel left in the descent tanks to either land or abort. I glanced furtively out my window and saw that we were eye level with the moon's horizon. Off in the near distance was nothing but blackness [...] we were moving over the lunar surface like a helicopter coming in for a landing, but we were now in what we sometimes referred to as the 'dead zone'. Any touchdown from higher than ten feet was sure to damage the landing gear. Moreover, if we ran out of fuel at this altitude, we would crash into the moon before our ascent engine could push us back into space. [...] Feelings of elation threatened to overwhelm me, but I dared not give in to them. We still had a lot to do before we could breathe easier. I continued rattling off items from our flight check-list. We didn't want to make any mistakes at this point. 'ACA out of detent', I said, reminding Neil to take the Altitude Control Assembly the joystick with which he had manually landed us on the moon, out of MANUAL and put it back to AUTO for our ascent.

> 'Out of detent. Auto'. Neil replied, matter-of-factly. [...] For the first time I paused and glanced out of my window. The sun was out, the sky was velvety black, and the surface appeared even more desolate than I imagined. The gray-ash colored rocks and pockmarked terrain, which now for the first time in its existence hosted human beings, stretched out as far as I could see and then dipped into the horizon. With our LM descent engine stopped, the pervasive silence seemed surreal 'Okay', Neil said to me. 'Let's get on with it'. Immediately, we were back to business [...] Neil and I went back to work.

> (2011: 516–17)

'Light', writes Emmanuel Levinas in his book *Existence and Existents*,

> whether it emanates from the sensible or from the intelligible sun, is since Plato said to be a condition for all beings [...] whatever may be the physico-mathematical explanation of the light which fills our universe, phenomenologically it is a condition for phenomena, that is, for meaning [...]. Kant's space is essentially a lit up space: it is in all its dimensions accessible, explorable [...] The world, whose existence is characterised by light, is not, then, the sum of existing objects.

> (1978: 47–48)

Levinas goes on:

> Let us imagine all beings, things and persons, reverting to nothingness. One cannot put this return to nothingness outside of all events. But what of this nothingness itself? Something would happen, if only night and the silence of nothingness [...] This impersonal, anonymous yet inextinguishable 'consummation' of being, which murmurs in the depths of nothingness itself we shall designate by the term *there is*. The *there is* inasmuch as it resists a personal form, is 'being in general' [...] We could say that the night is the very experience of the *there is* if the term experience were not inapplicable to a situation which involves the total exclusion of light.
>
> (1978: 57–58. original emphasis)

For Levinas, the darkness of the night 'is not that of pure nothingness' (1978: 58). In this, one might be tempted to differentiate the darkness of night from that of space: interstellar blackness is not the same as the darkness of the night. For Levinas, the struggle to *see* in darkness is what makes darkness an absence of the subjects facility, rather than absence of the Other. As he wrote of making art: 'Painting is a struggle with sight' (1978: 56).

There are many films in which cinematic astronauts find themselves 'struggling with sight' – that is to say, alone, confronted with the infinite blackness space. Since Stanley Kubrick's *2001: A Space Odyssey*, that moment is audibly marked by the sound of the character's breathing, often as if heard over a microphone pick up. Despite its constant uses to the point of cliché, the trope is, regardless of strengths or otherwise in acting, plot or characterization, more often than not effective in its evocation of a soft, vulnerable primate body underneath the space suit, whether floating in the infinite black of space itself or stumbling over a lunar desert under a black sky; and, of course, it is the effective real time measure of the character's emotional state, intimately relayed to the audience when the face might be obscured partially or wholly by space helmet and visor.

In his book *Time and the Other*, Levinas, writing of what he terms 'the tragedy of solitude' emphasizes:

> In the concreteness of need, the space that keeps us away from ourselves is always to be conquered. One must cross it and take hold of an object – that is, one must work with one's hands. In this sense, 'the one who works not, eats not' is an analytic proposition. Toold and the manufacture of tools pursue the chimerical ideal of the suppression of distances.
>
> [...] I am going to pursue the analysis of solitude in the pain of need and work, not in the anxiety of nothinginess.
>
> (quoted in Hand 2003: 39)

Seán Hand (2003) argues that whereas for Heidegger, signification was to be found in existence as a project, for Levinas, it was to be found elsewhere – namely, in obligation to the

Other. For Hand, this suggests a fundamental rift between the two philosophers in their attitude to death: Hand sees Levinas' approach to death not framed by notions of 'virility and authenticity' or the proof of 'mineness' in the manner of Heidegger, but rather, Hand argues that for Levinas, death is the death of the other, that moment 'in which we recognize the limits of the possible in suffering' (2003: 4).

If we are, for the moment, to grant that space flight to moons, planets and asteroids will entail human suffering – immense strains on both the psyche and the body – then perhaps we can imagine Levinas' insistence on *not* speaking about the anxiety of nothingness, as something to be discerned in the space between that nerve-tinged audible breathing of the astronaut and the insistent chirpy communications chatter from mission control: the imperative to 'work the problem', to not allow oneself to be overcome by what Apollo 11 astronaut Buzz Aldrin has termed the 'magnificent desolation' of the black skied lunar surface (2009).

The psychological strain of extraterrestrial landscape is clear to see on a remarkable series of photographs taken in the interior of the Apollo 17 lunar module, *Challenger*, whilst it was on the moon's surface. One of the later so-called 'J Missions', entailing longer periods in space and on the moon itself, the Apollo 17 expedition lasted a total of twelve days. During the mission, Commander Eugene Cernan and Lunar Module pilot Harrison Schmitt spent over three days on the surface of the Moon and a total of 22 hours outside their lander, either walking or travelling by lunar rover on the lunar surface. The photographs show Cernan, sitting in the cramped capsule, having removed his helmet and gloves, but still wearing the rest of his 21-layer EVA suit (Corn 2011: 507), looking with a tired, lined face at the camera. It is a commonplace that the Moon reflecting sunlight against the infinite blackness of its own sky appears pale grey, when in fact its regolith, when brought to Earth, appears quite dark. Nevertheless, the coal-like dust covering board swaths of Cernan's suit seems shocking, as does the weariness on his face.

For Levinas, '[w]eariness does not occur as a judgement about the pain of being, a judgement colored with affective tonality, with a "content" of lassitude. Prior to every judgement, to be tired of everything and everyone is to abdicate from existence. The refusal is *in* weariness. Weariness by all its being effects this refusal to exist. It is, we might say, the very way the phenomenon of the refusal to exist can come about, just as in the order of experience, vision alone is the apprehension of light and hearing alone the perception of sound (1978: 25).

As Michael Holland has observed in his critical reading of Maurice Blanchot's co-option of the Levinasian *il y a*, Levinas recognized various scenes in his friend Blanchot's novels that directly illustrated the notion of *il y a*/'there is':

A night in a hotel room, where, behind the partition, there's endless moving about [...] there's no way of knowing what they're doing next door (2011: 93).

For Holland, what he identifies as Blanchot's 'colonialism' or 'expropriation' (2011: 93) of Levinas' 'there is' is not so much akin to the imperialisms of the modern era – what Holland refers to as 'situations where colonialism is an extension of empire' (2011: 94), but rather a colonization akin to something either 'much further back or much further forward' that puts an end to a state of wandering and dispossession. That suffered by the Jews provides the model from the past, whilst the model from the future can be found in those space wanderers, forced to abandon a dying planet and taking with the remnants of its civilization in order to start up again elsewhere.

(2011: 94)

Holland argues that the impulse for Blanchot's colonization of Levinas' philosophical *il y a* occurred at that point where, for Blanchot, literature, in the form of his vocational novel writing, had become a 'dwindling and disintegrating domain' akin to such a dying planet (2011: 94).

Holland cites Levinas' article 'Heidegger, Gagarin and Us' as an example of how such a science fiction analogy in relation to Levinas' philosophy is not misplaced. Holland's suggestion is that whilst Levinas' monotheism was central to identity as a Jew and his observance of Judaism, for Blanchot the gift of monotheism was primarily that of linguistic constructions whereby humans could place themselves in relation to that which, by way of its infinite distance, excludes relation (2011: 98).

For Levinas, beyond the courage of the world's first cosmonaut and the technological achievement of a viable spacecraft, the significance of Yuri Gagarin's first journey into space in Vostok 1 ultimately lay in its negation of Heideggerian insistence upon place, upon which was founded 'the very splitting of humanity into natives and strangers [...] the privileges of enrootedness and the related sense of exile'. Levinas refuted any suggestion that spaceflight's significance lay in some imagined retrogression to nomadism, the concept of which, he argued, was still bound up with 'a landscape and a climate' (1997: 232). Rather, Gagarin's hour long flight had been a journey 'beyond any horizon' into 'geometrical space', where the opportunity to 'perceive men outside the situation in which they are placed, so that the human face could shine in all its nudity' (1997: 233). To argue thus was, in Levinas' view, Socratic in its extolation of new forms of human interaction: I would also suggest it is the basis of what David Valentine has called an

[...] escape from the assumption (whether rightist or leftist) that the encounter with space will simply produce a repetition, extension, or logical conclusion of history, human sociality, exchange relations or any other human phenomena that have emerged on the surface of our planet.

(2012: 1063)

Solitude, Work and the 'Levinasian Landscape': *The Europa Report*

Themes of darkness, solitude and the concomitant pain of need and work are recurrent themes in four ambitious science fiction films of the second decade of the twenty-first century: Sebastian Cordero's *Europa Report* (2013), Alfonso Cuarón's *Gravity* (2013), Christopher Nolan's *Interstellar* (2014) and Ridley Scott's *The Martian* (2015). Whilst all four films present the vertiginous disorientations of space flight and its concomitant risks in terms of extreme isolation, all of them, I want to suggest here, do so within Levinas' understanding of such in the 'pain of need and work' and not in the Heideggarian anxiety of nothingness. I want to suggest that in all four films 'need and work' is constituted around the imperatives of mission objectives and survival in order to complete these, never as despair or surrender. As the spacecraft pilot Rosa Dasque (Anamaria Marinca) remarks to camera in *Europa Report* '[c]ompared to the breadth of knowledge yet to be known, what does your life actually matter?'

Replete with the contemporary stylistic jump cuts, split screens redolent of CCTV, and overlaid background noise of bleeps, buzzes and communications by-play, Cordero's film nevertheless presents a convincing portrayal of a near future human mission to Jupiter's ice moon Europa, described at the start of the film as the first attempt to send men and women into deep space. As such, the film can be seen as part of the tradition of 'suppositional realism' that I ascribed to much of the work Chesley Bonestell and Pavel Klushantsev in Chapter 5, if not extrapolation, with all the associated contemporary ideological framings such entails: characters speak of the mission's 'legacy' in a telling re-appropriation of a term much overused and diminished in contemporary corporate jargon.

The film begins with a monologue from a Dr Samantha Unger (Embeth Davidtz) suggestive of reflective responses to questions from an unseen interlocutor as part of some video recorded interview. In it, Unger looks back on the parameters of a seemingly failed mission to the Jupiter system and the loss of the six person crew, for whom she clearly feels a sense of responsibility and guilt.

Through the unfolding of a non-linear, episodic diegesis, comprising video diary entries, snippets of dialogue, stream of consciousness mutterings and verbal 'notes to self', the audience learns that the crew lost contact with Earth some time before arrival in Jupiter orbit due to a solar storm. It also emerges that one crew member, James Corrigan (Sharlton Copley), had already died during the journey to Jupiter. Over time we learn that his death was in fact one of self-sacrifice. During extra vehicular activity (EVA) to repair the damage to the spaceship's communications system and hopefully re-establish contact with Earth, Corrigan had been helping his colleague, Andrei Blok (Michael Nyqvist) whose spacesuit has punctured, only to discover that highly toxic hydrazine propellant had contaminated the sleeve of his own space suit. With no means to remove it, Corrigan cannot re-enter the spaceship without contaminating the ventilation system and inadvertently poisoning his crewmates. Having forcibly propelled his reluctant companion into the safety of the airlock, Corrigan releases the tether holding him to the spacecraft and floats away to his death. This incident, and the Unger monologue, ensures that a sombre sense of mourning, but also ethical responsibility to the Other, already permeates the story by the time the spacecraft reaches the surface of Europa.

Cordero's choice of Europa, a Jovian ice moon that actual NASA and ESA probes suggest almost certainly has a subsurface ocean of relatively warm liquid water, jells with the film's overall tone of suppositional realism. In addition, insofar as extant scientific speculation has suggested such an ocean could harbour alien life, the diegesis couples this commitment to its incipient themes of *il y a*, 'need' and 'work'. Appropriately, after the trauma of lost contact and death, one of the crew member's recordings states, 'I started living my life in tune with the mission, which I assumed was still going on'.

As Elizabeth Louise Thomas (2004) has commented, '[i]n *Existence and Existents*, Levinas introduces the other person, not merely as someone hoped for in the height of despair and nausea, but as restoring hope in the midst of despair'. However, Thomas goes on to explain

> There is a sense in which the relation to the other person, described in Time and the Other and Existence and Existents in terms of *eros,* could be interpreted as describing the conditions of possibility for 'power' and 'violence' […] The question of how to think subjectivity in relation to the other, without reducing the other to a functionary of an otherwise powerless subject [was the focus of Levinas' later thought.
>
> (2004: 49)

Thomas' reading of Levinas seems particularly pertinent to the diegesis of *Europa Report*. In the film, the white and russet Europan *topos* is first shown from above, rolling beneath us as the lander disengages from the spaceship and begins its descent from orbit. Once the lander has touched down, the first glimpse we see of the surface as normative landscape is a deep perspective along a deep gully of the same colours – predominantly white but stained with orange brown, pristine under a black sky, overlaid with the reflected face of one of the crew members in the porthole. She is clearly enraptured but presented as insubstantial compared with the hard crystalline certainty of the scene she gazes upon. The next landscape shot reveals blue shadows stretching across the glaring ice overlaid with numerics denoting some sort of telemetric reading and the sublime sight of the thin, striped crescent of Jupiter, which, we are told, is bathing the moon's surface in levels of radiation that would be lethal to any humans facing long periods of exposure. The spacecraft is standing on bed of ice XI (a form of water ice that forms at very low temperatures) and the surface temperature is absolute zero. It is, therefore, through the landscape that *Europa Report* establishes a sombre sense of temporal discrepancy between human time (living memory, life and history) and the mathematized *arche*-fossil in the manner of Meillassoux.

When Katya Petrovna (Karolina Wydra) attempts a surface walk to collect samples, we see her face in close up peering out of her helmet visor intercut with shots of a gibbous Jupiter hanging in the sky surmounted by one for the Galilean moons, and hear not only her whispered bewilderment but momentary fragmentation, multipositionality and displacement: 'I can't believe I'm here…or here…' before a more assertive, 'It's so still out here'. 'Creepy!' one of the crew members still on board the lander suggests in a moment of deflation, but Petrovna demurs: 'I was going to go with cosmically astounding'.

The film's climax develops as transitory luminescence is seen under the ice: first a heated probe that has drilled down through the ice into the water below is lost, having captured some sign of fleeting movement, and then, subsequently, Katya is pulled under the ice, into the ocean. As the remaining crew try to launch into orbit to rendezvous with the spaceship for the return journey, a partial engine failure causes them to fall back to the Europan surface, killing another crew member. The ice, thinned further by the heat of the rocket engines, cracks. Two of the remaining crew attempt to repair the lander outside but fail to do so and succumb in separate fatal incidents, although the second to die manages to repair the communications system sufficiently to allow data to be streamed back to Earth. Aware that the link with Earth has been re-established, that the rest of the crew are dead and she too is doomed, the pilot Rosa Dasque carefully positions cameras and opens the airlock behind her, as the lander sinks into the ocean. In the final seconds of the resulting footage, we see the source of the luminescence – a large octopoid life form native to the depths of the Europan subsurface ocean – briefly but spectacularly emerge into view amidst the maelstrom of surging seawater, establishing the existence of extraterrestrial life in the Solar System and, in the words of Samantha Unger's resumed monologue, thereby 'fundamentally chang(ing) the context in which humanity understands itself'.

Conclusion

Where Otherwise Nothing Has Changed

If we align the 'science fiction imaginary' with the place of the imaginary in psychoanalytical discourse, as I have sought to do in this book, then tensions arise between the sense of self that exists between the normative Law (the superego or the symbolic order) and the unspeakable Real. My use of the 'ur-image', being socially constituted, obviates any implied essential familial reductivism or originary claims, but rather is posited as a nexus of signifiers.

The chapters in this book have thus sought to explore some of those tensions as they are manifested formally by the estranged *topos* of science fiction: through shifts in scale; in the artificial and the virtual; in montage and juxtaposition; in the visualization of collective annihilation; in the slippage between the envisioning of ideology and empirical science; and the last instance, in the anxieties induced in technocratic confidence by darkness and emptiness.

Science fiction's abiding uses – and abuses – of the natural sciences as a model or foundational precept for fantasy that has value or relevance – that is to say, that which is speculatively engaged with futurity located in the 'from here onwards' rather than a maudlin regressive nostalgia, gives it a particular relationship with the potentialities of the lived world. As such, in the spatio-temporal context of landscape, the ocularities of science fiction do not simply project ideals forward into historical time but rather, through the novum, create radical conflations within the present moment and within recognizable spaces.

In Ion de Sosa's film *Androids Dream* (2014), which I discussed in Chapter 6, the novum is entirely located within the dialogue rather than the visuals: a verbal reference to a space-shuttle, a conversation about the exorbitant cost of buying a pet animal, conversations about Earth as if it is one world amongst a number, in a future landscape where otherwise nothing else appears to have changed. Nevertheless, de Sosa's novum is sufficiently effective because it shifts the viewer's perspective in relation to the two key factors that I have argued are constitutive of landscape: on the one hand, time (an anecdote about drug smuggling on a space-shuttle locates the narrative in a future) and the other, space (a conversational intimation that establishes Earth as one habitable planet amongst many). These evocations of displacement through the constitutive elements of landscape create a defining tension in de Sosa's film as powerful as the actual killing spree of the putative 'Blade Runner' assassin: without it, the film would be a thriller, not science fiction. The minimal displacements and resultant uncertainties of the novum in De Sosa's film are arguably indicative of the tensions produced by the landscapes of science fiction generally: for obvious reasons, the constituent elements of the landscapes of science fiction might, on the face of it, appear little different from other genres – the dark forests of folk tales, the high sierras and playas of Westerns, or the nightscape haunts of *film noir*, for example. However, I would contend here that there is a highly significant differentiation to be made insofar as the landscapes of science fiction *dialectically* relate to those of our own world, through the differentiation, however slight, of the novum.

One might, as an analogous example, think of how different visualizations of the past are constituted: either as an idealized unity, an attempt to stop time or shut out the contemporary (as is the case of nostalgia) or as something brought into the present that effects a radical re-reading, where fantasy is brought into play in order to re-articulate our perception of the present and our sense of place. *Mutatis mutandis*, ethical choices arise in relation to visualizations of the landscapes of science fiction.

As I write, popular conceptions of futurity seem focused upon, on the one hand, the precipitous ecology of the planet and, on the other, various spectacles of neo-medievalist revanchism – in real-world politics, the self-proclaimed caliphate of Islamic State, in fiction, the televisual saga of George R.R. Martin's *Game of Thrones* fantasy. Both can be discerned as attempts to obviate the apparently intractable problematics of historical time: the uses and ends of extant modern socio-political formations, technology and ecologies within the extant global polity. Such fantasies seem attempts to escape a state akin to George Steiner's epochal *ennui* I discussed in relation to the 1970s in Chapter 3: that is to say, an obscurantist retreat in the face of the catastrophes, conflicts and instabilities wrought by the schemas of floundering Modernist hegemons that once made such confident claims on the future, only to find the world more complex than they could visualize. Both are played out amidst landscapes of potential hardship and privation: the encroaching desert. This is a world that, as Steiner in his 1971 essay 'The Future' remarked, is 'entangled in a constant web of crisis'. As Steiner goes on, '[w]hether or not our intimations of utter menace are justified is not the issue. They permeate our sensibility. It is inside them that the post culture conducts its fragmented, often contradictory business' (1974: 77). It is worth noting that the same terrible war that has given birth to the Islamic State caliphate has also given birth to attempts to establish a secular polity founded on democratic confederalist principles and gender equality in the cantons of Rojava.

As I have sought to demonstrate in the present book, any dystopic visualizations of 'utter menace' are constitutively bound up with those utopias proffered by the landscapes of other worlds – that is including both other planets and other possible, future Earths. Appropriately, in the same 1971 essay I mentioned above, Steiner sketched a picture of Europe, in the middle of the seventeenth century, exhausted and decimated at the close of the Thirty Years' War and observed how that exhaustion was nevertheless counterbalanced by the incipient energies of Europe's recent discovery of the Americas. 'Entangled in a constant web of crisis' now, who, indeed, does not feel the counterbalancing possibilities of the landscapes of other planets?

Moreover, there is another sense within the terms of reference established by Steiner which I would suggest is relevant here. Within that fragmenting dialectic, one might seek to identify that which is recognizable as knowledge, for knowledge is, as he indicates, constitutive of any ontology of historical progress (1974: 60) – the precept that marks science fiction from other forms of fantasy.

In this context, the inverse is also true: the visualized fever dreams of science fiction continue to generate knowledge, since those fever dreams allow the exploration and evaluations of possibilities, consequences and likelihoods within that ontology of progress. In the second season of the re-imagined *Battlestar Galactica* of 2004–09, Sharon Agathon, one of the Number 8 Cylons played by Grace Park, is repeatedly interrogated by the human Admiral Adama (Edward James Olmos). One recurrent question is why the Cylons hate their human creators so much. Agathon replies, uncertainly, that she believes the root of the Cylons' hate is the refusal of humans to ask themselves why they, as a species, deserve to survive. Of course, whatever the lacunae of the fictional human race of *Battlestar Galactica*, when it comes to the real human species, the Cylons are wrong. The visual culture of the human species reflects a constant self-interrogatory process as to how we might be seen by other eyes – images of destruction, anxieties about artificial intelligence, pollution and despoliation, our relational place in the universe – all reflect back the very self-doubt which the Cylons claim humans lack.

Landscape invites themes of repetitive encounter: human traversals over time lead to recognition, differentiations and taxonomies. That is at the heart of Levinas' differentiation from Heidegger I discussed in Chapter 6. These recurrences lead to both recognition of a plethora of tropes and forms which one has seen many times in mediated form but not previously directly encountered in person. Often the impression formed by those mediated images stretches back into the very distant reaches of the subject's early formative stages. The subject thus feels an interpellative sensation of being 'called home' qua Bloch's *Heimat*, that I described in Chapter 3. However, framed within an ontology of progress, such a sensation does not prevent one from maintaining a critical awareness of the discrepancies between the encountered realities and the mediated ideal: if anything, the impulse to critique is enhanced.

In any figure/ground antimony such as I have discussed in a number of chapters in this book, the viewing subject in question does not necessarily have to be paranoid in order to experience certain tensions that such an antimony produces. If, as I have suggested, time is a constituent but lacunose element within the spatial experience of landscape, it plays this role in evidencing traces of diachronic time. It does this not only positively (the acknowledged presence of historical or geological trace) but, *via negativa*, in the unknowable. This, I would suggest, points to the deep rooted obsessive loyalties of, say, *Star Wars* fans and other devotees of subgenres: what is appealing, reassuring. By signally not establishing any visual novum, De Sosa's *Androids Dream* (2014) stands out for its obstinate refusal of a distinct set of visual forms and as such might be seen as the exception that proves a rule.

A crazed imaginary oscillating between inflated grandiosity and a crushing sense of insignificance – like that of De Sosa's android killer or Philip Dick's rocket powered Nazis that I began this book with – is of course one that remains paranoid and fragmented, subject to unresolved tensions with the space of repetitive compulsion, in which twitching erratic actions and inexplicable verbal ejaculations are performed and rebound, endlessly and violently. Dick's rocket powered Nazis are a case *in extremis*, but they highlight a common trend in the relationship between the imagined human subject and its topographies to be found in many science fiction stories and visualizations – namely, a relation characterized by territorialization and conflict. Sophisticated and successful contemporary science fiction dramas – the 2004–09 reboot of *Battlestar Galactica*, which ran to five seasons, being a good example – owe their success to narratives of war and territorialization: *Caprica*, an interesting prequel not based upon the premise of war but exploring social and political issues across the twelve planets of Kobol 50 years before the interstellar conflict depicted in *Battlestar Galactica*, was cancelled after two seasons due to its failure to win a large enough audience. Arguably, *Caprica* explored the landscapes of its intertwining narratives far more successfully than *Battlestar Galactica*: time and thought had been clearly given to the formative experiences of their homeworlds on the different citizenry of the city and the teenage daughter of one of the key protagonists and her peers were shown immersed in and beholden to the pressures and temptations of a range of richly developed VEs also.

Scientism tends to conflate two conceptions of agency that extend beyond the sphere of the natural sciences – namely historical agency on the one hand and political agency on the other. The science fiction imaginary, both in its utopian/apocalyptic moments of elation as well as its more modulated forms, embodies a faith in the possibility of human history as a *project*. In Chapter 5, I discussed this in terms of the parallels to be found between two artist-denizens of competing polities of the last century. Militarism, like scientism, has pretentions to historical/political agency and, indeed, *Battlestar Galactica* explored the ramifications of this on a democracy in crisis to some considerable success.

Nevertheless, it would be a depressing prospect if the landscapes of science fiction were doomed to forever be seen as passive backdrops to such violence, rather than re-imagined as a time/space nexus wherein a more complex dialectic between the human and its environment can be established. Even if that is the doleful case (although the present book as I hope is clear, aims to reject such a relegation) there would be truth to be had in backdrops. In his essay 'Some Motifs in Baudelaire', Walter Benjamin draws attention to remarks made by Charles Baudelaire's *Salon de 1859*:

> I long for the return of the dioramas whose enormous crude magic subjects me to the spell of a useful illusion. I prefer looking at the backdrop paintings of the stage where I find my favourite dreams treated with consummate skill and tragic concision. Those things, so completely false, are for that very reason much closer to the truth, whereas the majority of our landscape painters are liars, precisely because they fail to lie.
>
> (1999: 187)

Ursula Le Guin's 1992 short story 'The Rock that Changed Things' from her 1994 collection *A Fisherman of the Inland Sea* imagines an oppressive hierarchical society which is as quaintly ridiculous as it is riddled with caste oppression and legalized sexual violence. The scholastic Obls are served by the subservient Nurs, who work as both domestics and builders whilst suffering beatings, imprisonment and rape. Obl towns are constructed on the banks of rivers from tightly arranged patterns of boulders, rocks and pebbles. Revolution follows from a moment when one of the Nurs sees the turquoise colours within a particular stone and establishes by persistence that whereas colour has been ignored/suppressed by the Obls in favour of pattern, the turquoise colouration has an archaic verbal association with concepts of liberation. The Nur's way of seeing the landscape around her therefore represents a paradigm shift in the perception of her environment. The Nur's rebellion against the existing paradigm can be seen as arising from a synchronic moment wherein her vision of the space that she occupies allows the possibility of a re-reading of her temporal, diachronically evolved situation. As Suvin has it:

> [...] the new *epistemé* [...] one of spatiotemporal covariance, simulsequentialism, or humanist relativism and estrangement: in brief, one of alternate historical realities.
>
> (1979: 73–74)

In some sense the above examples – De Sosa's suburban desolate backdrop, Le Guin's creative, indeed revolutionary, re-seen environment, represent a dichotomous opposition – a dyad in terms of how landscape is imagined which demands resolution. In part, this book shares the project of Baudelaire insofar as its focus has been an expanded notion of how we might foreground the background – the topographies and horizons and, indeed, backdrops, by utilizing the affective 'alternative seeing' of science fiction – what I have termed 'ocularity', to allow oneself to cognitively accept the illusions of alternative histories, fantastic environments and value them for the estranged forms of seeing they offer.

Allowing ourselves to see the landscape around us differently to create new interactions within the spatio-temporal nexus that are beyond that of endless backdrops of war and conflict is a project of re-imagining the figure/ground relation. This is not something new. Human culture has long established points of mediation and interaction between the landscape and the body: one ambitious, socially evolved form in which it does so through the project of architecture. With the growth of technology, the project of architecture can be seen as one not only of shelter, but moreover, one that produces nodal points of interface between the body and the landscape.

One might consider the modern hospital as a complex and inspiring paradigm of this interface between body, and landscape, in which the human body in its traumatized, dependent state is connected, by stents, catheters, canulae and all the complexities of modern medical technology to the hospital itself, through which teams of dedicated professionals pursue a relentless war for the life of the species. The development of surgical techniques, such as those found in Interventional Radiology, aimed at minimalizing trauma but optimizing any invasive intervention's effectiveness, is dependent upon the ability to image the body via multiple modalities using a wide range of radiological spectra and the mapping of the body that can be derived from such.

Given the nature of our species' enemies, this is a struggle that can only be fought at all levels, from the domestic staff assiduously cleaning floors and bedframes to the most complex surgery lead by consultants. In contemporary cities, these teams of workers are extremely diverse: but more of everyone is always essential.

If there is an extant visual figure of a cyborg landscape that problematizes simplistic figure/ground relations, it surely presents in this reading of the hospital-in-the-landscape as an expanded field of soma and topos in which both become constitutive and, as such, a radical alternative to the landscape as backdrop to scenarios of conflict and desolation. Insofar as the hospital as I am configuring it here allows for the imaging of such a dialectical interplay of bodies and landscape, I would suggest that it posits the possibility of images of collective, lived experience – a network of human experiences across a *topos*, so that 'the purpose' of species being is no longer pictured in terms of an idealized – and estranged – individual, but rather the collective life of the species as an integral part of a wider ecology, that ecology which, now more than ever, troubles the human conscience, and to which we relate as the landscape around us.

References

Adorno, T.W. (1988), 'Something's missing: A discussion between Ernst Bloch and Theodor Adorno on the contradictions of Utopian longing', in E. Bloch, *The Utopian Function of Art and Literature* (trans. J. Zipes and F. Mecklenburg), Cambridge: MIT Press, pp.

Aldiss, B. (1964), *Introducing SF: A Science Fiction Anthology*, London: Faber.

Aldrin, E. (Buzz) (2011) 'A landing unlike any other: July 1969', in J.J. Corn ed. (2011), *Into the Blue: American Writing on Aviation and Space Flight*, New York: Library of America, pp. 506–19. Originally published 2009.

Alfrey, N. and Sleeman, J. (2009), *Earth-Moon-Earth* Exhibition catalogue, Nottingham: Djanogly Gallery.

Anon. (2011), 'The end of the space age: Inner space is useful. Outer space is history' and 'Into the sunset: The final launch of the space shuttle brings to an end the dreams of the Apollo era', *The Economist*, 30 June.

Apollodorus ([c. 50 BCE] 1998), *The Library of Greek Mythology* (trans. R. Hard), London and Oxford: Oxford University Press.

Armstrong, R. (2015), 'Prototyping starships', Icarus Interstellar' s Starship Congress, https://www.youtube.com/watch?v=F8WIev9Fuzo&feature=youtu.be. Accessed 5 April 2016.

Badiou, A. (2007), *The Century* (trans. A. Toscano), Cambridge: Polity Press.

Beck, J. (2014), 'The purloined landscape: Photography and power in the American west', *Tate Papers*, http://www.tate.org.uk/research/publications/tate-papers/21/the-purloined-landscape-photography-and-power-in-the-american-west. Accessed 6 April 2016.

Benjamin, W. (1999), *Illuminations*, London: Bloomsbury.

Berger, J. (1972), *Ways of Seeing*, London: BBC.

de Bergerac, C. (2008), *Journey to the Moon*, London: Hepsus.

Bjorklund, D.F. (ed.)(2000), *False-Memory Creation in Children and Adults: Theory, Research and Implications*, London and New Jersey: Lawrence Erlbaum Associates.

Bloch, E. (1988), *The Utopian Function of Art and Literature* (trans. J. Zipes and F. Mecklenburg), Cambridge: MIT Press.

Blunt, A. (1958), *Nicolas Poussin*, London: Phaidon.

Borden, I. (1998), 'A performative critique of the city – The urban practice of skateboarding, 1958–1998', *Everything Magazine*, 2:4, pp. 38–43.

—— (2001), 'Another pavement, another beach: Skateboarding and the performative critique of architecture', http://discovery.ucl.ac.uk/26049/1/Borden_Another_Pavement.pdf. Accessed 12 August 2015.

Bourdieu, P. (1990), *Photography: A Middle Brow Art* (trans. S. Whiteside), Cambridge: Polity Press. Oring.

Boyd Haycock, D. (2002), *Paul Nash*, London: Tate Publishing.

Brainerd, C.J. and Reyna, V.F. (2005), *The Science of False Memory*, Oxford Psychology Series Number 38, Oxford: Oxford University Press.

Brassier, R. (2007), *Nihil Unbound: Enlightenment and Extinction*, London: Palgrave Macmillan.

Bridle, J. (2015), *Seamless Transitions*, 6 February–15 April, London: The Photographers' Gallery.

Buck-Morss, S. (1989), *The Dialectics of Seeing: Walter Benjamin and the Arcades Project*, Cambridge: MIT Press.

Bürger, P. (1984), *Theory of the Avant-Garde* (trans. M. Shaw), Minneapolis: University of Minnesota Press.

De Castell, S., Jenson, J., Taylor N. and Thumlert, K. (2014), 'Re-thinking foundations: Theoretical and methodological challenges (and opportunities) in virtual worlds research', *Journal of Gaming & Virtual Worlds*, 6:1, pp. 3–20.

Cathcart, B. (1994), *Test of Greatness: Britain's Struggle for the Atom Bomb*. London: John Murray.

Davis, K.F. (2005), 'Living art: The sources of Frederick Sommer's work', in N. Lyons and J. (eds), *The Art of Frederick Sommer: Photography, Drawing, Collage*, New Haven and London: Yale University Press.

Deighton, L. and Schwartzman, A. (1977), *Airshipwreck*, London: Jonathan Cape.

Derrida, J. (1974), *Of Grammatology* (trans. G. Chakravorti Spivak), Baltimore and London: Johns Hopkins University Press.

——— (1993), *Aporias* (trans. T. Dutoit), Stanford: Stanford University Press.

Dick, P. ([1962] 2001), *The Man in the High Castle*, London: Penguin.

Dillon, G.L. (2012), *Walking the Clouds*: An Anthology of Indigenous Science Fiction, Tucson: University of Arizona Press.

Doyle, D. (2009), 'The body of the avatar: rethinking the mind-body relationship in virtual worlds', *Journal of Gaming and Virtual Worlds*, 1:2, pp. 131–41.

Feuerbach, L. ([1841] 2008), *Essence of Christianity* (trans. G. Eliot), New York: Mineola.

Ficacci, L. (2006), *Piranesi: The Etchings*, London: Taschen.

Foss, C. 20 January 2016 interview.

Freud, S. (1999), *The Interpretation of Dreams,* (trans. J. Crick), Oxford: Oxford University Press.

Frosh, S. (1999) *The Politics of Psychoanalysis*, Basingstoke and New York: Palgrave Macmillan.

——— (2013), *Hauntings: Psychoanalysis and Ghostly Transmissions*, London: Palgrave Macmillan.

Gaiger, J. (2008), *Aesthetics and Painting*, London: Continuum.

Gallagher, C. (1993), *American Ground Zero: The Secret Nuclear War*, Cambridge: MIT Press.

Gregory, R.L. (1998), *Eye and Brain: The Psychology of Seeing*, Oxford: Oxford University Press.

Groys, B. (2008), *Art Power*, London, Cambridge and Massachusetts: MIT Press.

——— (2009), *The Communist Postscript*, London: Verso.

Gwertsman, B. (1981), 'Reagan clarifies his statement on nuclear war', *New York Times*, 22 October http://www.nytimes.com/1981/10/22/world/reagan-clarifies-his-statement-on-nuclear-war.html. Accessed 30 October 2015.

Hand, S. (2003), *The Levinas Reader*, Oxford: Blackwell.

Harrison, C. (1994), 'The effect of landscape' in W.J.T. Mitchell (ed.), *Landscape and Power*, Chicago and London: Chicago University Press, pp. 203–40.

Harvey, D. (2000), *Spaces of Hope*, Edinburgh: Edinburgh University Press.

Hedman, E. R. (2014), 'The Moon or Mars?', *The Space Review*, 14 August.

Helmore, E. (1999), 'Obituary: Frederick Sommer', *The Independent*, 5 February.

Herbert, F. (2005), *Dune*, London: Hodder.

Hillis, K. (1999), *Digital Sensation: Space, Identity and Embodiment in Virtual Reality*, Minneapolis and London: Minnesota University Press.

Holland, M. (2011), 'Let's leave God out of this – Maurice Blanchot's reading of totality and infinity' in S. Hand (ed.), *Facing the Other: The Ethics of Emmanuel Levinas*, New York and London: Routledge, pp. 91–106.

Howell, E. (2012), *Mariner 4: First Spacecraft to Mars*, http://www.space.com/18787-mariner-4.html. Accessed 18 April 2016.

Hughes, R. and Foss, I. (2011), *Hardware: The Definitive SF Works of Chris Foss*, London: Titan Books.

Jameson, F. (2002), *The Political Unconscious*, London and New York: Routledge.

—— (2005), *Archaeologies of the Future: The Desire Called Utopia and Other Science Fictions*, London: Verso.

—— (2013), *The Antinomies of Realism*, London: Verso.

—— (2015), 'In hyperspace', review, *Time Travel: The Popular Philosophy of Narrative*, D. Wittenberg (2013), Fordham: London Review of Books, 37:17, 10 September, https://www.lrb.co.uk/v37/fredric-jameson/in-hyperspace. Accessed 14 September 2015.

Jarvis, W.E. (2003), *Time Capsules: A Cultural History*, Jefferson, North Carolina and London: McFarland & Co.

Jenkins, R., Sas, M., Irving J., Chambers M.. (1995), *Nagasaki Journey: The Photographs of Yosuke Yamahata, Nagasaki, August 10, 1945*, San Francisco: Pomegranate Books.

Kant, I. ([1790] 2007), *Critique of Judgement* (trans. James Creed Meredith), Oxford: Oxford University Press.

Kapterev, S. (2011), Kosmos: Season Introduction, 1 July, British Film Institute Southbank: London.

Klein, Gérard (2001), 'From the Images of Science to Science Fiction' in Patrick Parrinder (ed.), *Learning from Other Worlds: Estrangement, Cognition, and the Politics of Science Fiction and Utopia*, Durham: Duke University Press, pp. 119–26.

Klein, Melanie (1991), 'Mourning and Manic Depressive States' in Juliet Mitchell (ed.), *The Selected Melanie Klein*, London: Free Press, pp. 146–74.

Kollontai, A. (1977) 'Sexual Relations and the Class Struggle' in *Alexandra Kollontai: Selected Writings* (trans. Alix Holt), London: Allison & Busby, pp. 237–49.

Le Guin, U.K. (1980), *The Word for World is Forest*, London: Granada.

—— (1994), *A Fisherman of the Inland Sea*, New York: Harper Prism.

Leonard, Jonathan Norton (2011), 'At White Sands: 1953' in J.J. Corn (ed.), *Into the Blue: American Writing on Aviation and Space Flight*, New York: Library of America, pp. 369–81. Originally published as 'Sacrifice at White Sands: Flight into Space' (1953).

Levinas, E. (1978), *Existence and Existents* (trans. Alphonso Lingis), Hague: Martinus Nijhoff.

———— (1997), 'Heidegger, Gagarin and us' in *Difficult Freedom: Essays on Judaism* (trans. S. Hand), Baltimore: John Hopkins University Press, pp. 231–34.

Marks, David F., (1990), 'On the relationship between imagery, body and mind', in P. J. Hampson, D. F. Marks and J. Richardson (eds), *Imagery: Current Developments*, London: Routledge, pp. 1–31.

Marshall Smith, M. (2002), 'Foreword' in Kitchin, R., and Kneale, J.,eds., (2002) *Lost in Space: Geographies of Science Fiction* London: Continuum, pp xi–xii.

Marx, K. ([1927] 1970), *Economic and Philosophic Manuscripts of 1844* (trans. M. Milligan), London: Lawrence & Wishart.

Marx, Leo (1991) 'The American ideology of space' in S. Wrede and W. H. Adams (eds)., *Denatured Visions: Landscape and Culture in the Twentieth Century,* New York: The Museum of Modern Art, pp. 62–78.

McCurry, J. (2016), 'How Hiroshima rose from the ashes of nuclear destruction', *The Guardian*, http://www.theguardian.com/cities/2016/apr/18/story-of-cities-hiroshima-japan-nuclear-destruction. Accessed 18 April 2016.

McIntosh, J.T. (1977), *Norman Conquest 2066*, London: Corgi.

Meillassoux, Q. (2008), *After Finitude: An Essay on the Necessity of Contingency* (trans. R. Brassier), London: Bloomsbury.

Miles, E.R.C. (1950), *Supersonic Aerodynamics: A Theoretical Introduction*, New York and London: McGraw-Hill.

Millard, D. (ed.) (2014), *Cosmonauts: Birth of the Space Age*, London: London SCALA & The Science Museum.

Miller, R. correspondence with the author, April 2015.

Miller, R. and Durant, F.C. (2001), *The Art of Chesley Bonestell*, London: Collins & Brown/Paper Tiger.

Mitchell, W.J.T. (ed.) (1994), *Landscape and Power,* Chicago and London: Univesity of Chicago Press, pp. 166–74.

Mollon, Phil (2000), *Freud and False Memory Syndrome*, London: Icon.

Moncreiff, Anthony (1984), *Messages to the Future: The Story of the BBC Time Capsule*, London: Futura.

Morris, William (1979), *The House of the Wolfings*, London: George Prior.

———— (1980), *The Wood Beyond the World*, Oxford: Oxford University Press.

Morris-Suzuki, T. (2005), *The Past Within Us: Media, Memory, History*, New York: Verso.

Mortensen, T.E. (2010), 'The player as hedonist: The problem of enjoyment', *Journal of Gaming and Virtual Worlds*, 2:2, pp. 105–12.

Morton, Oliver (2002), *Mapping Mars*, London: Fourth Estate.

Myrone, M. (2011), *John Martin: Apocalypse*, London: Tate Publishing.

NASA Glenn Research Centre Website, www.grc.nasa.gov. Accessed 4 January 2015.

Noys, B. (2010), *The Persistence of the Negative: A Critique of Contemporary Continental Theory*, Edinburgh: Edinburgh University.

Ofshe, R. and Watters, E. (1994), *Making Monsters: False Memories, Psychotherapy and Sexual Hysteria*, Berkeley: University of California Press.

Olasina, G. (2014), 'Exploring how users make sense of virtual worlds using the symbolic interaction theory', *Journal of Gaming and Virtual Worlds*, 6:3, pp. 297–311.

Pace, C. (2008), 'Peace and tranquillity of mind: The theme of retreat and Poussin's landscapes' in P. Rosenberg and K. Christiansen (eds), *Poussin and Nature Metropolitan Museum of Art*, New York: Yale University Press, pp. 73–87.

Parkin, S. (2015), *Death by Video Game: Tales of Obsession from the Virtual Frontline*, London: Serpent's Tail.

——— (2015a) 'Eve Online: How a virtual world went to the edge of apocalypse and back' *The Guardian*, https://www.theguardian.com/technology/2015/may/12/how-virtual-world-edge-of-apocalypse-and-back-again. Accessed 5 February 2016.

Paul-Choudhry, S. (2011), 'The joy of starships new scientist culture lab', *New Scientist*, September, https://www.newscientist.com/blogs/culturelab/2011/09/chris-foss-the-joy-of.html. Accessed 31 January 2016.

Prokhorov, G. (1995), *Art Under Socialist Realism: Soviet Painting 1930–1950*, Roseville East NSW: Craftsman House.

Rafman, Jon (2014), Performative Lecture, 4 September, Istanbul, https://www.youtube.com/watch?v=qqDy_VRLWd8. Accessed 4 February 2016.

Rennie, D. (2005), 'World War Three seen through Soviet eyes', *The Daily Telegraph*, http://www.telegraph.co.uk/news/worldnews/europe/poland/1504008/World-War-Three-seen-through-Soviet-eyes.html. Accessed 10 November 2012.

Rhodes, R. (1988), *The Making of the Atomic Bomb*, New York: Simon & Schuster.

——— (1995), *Dark Sun: The Making of the Hydrogen Bomb*, New York: Simon & Schuster.

Robinson K.S. (2009), *Red Mars*, New York: Random House.

Rose, J. (2005), *Sexuality in the Field of Vision*, London: Verso.

Rosen, E. (trans.) (1967), *Kepler's Somnium: The Dream, or a Posthumous Work on Lunar Astronomy*, Madison, Milwaukee and London: University of Wisconsin Press.

Sallis, J. (1987), 'Imagination and presentation in Hegel's philosophy of spirit', in P. G. Stillman (ed.), *Hegel's Philosophy of Spirit*, New York: State University New York Press, pp. 66–88.

Sawyer, A. (2005), 'Notes', in H.G. Wells (ed.), *The War of the Worlds*, London: Penguin.

Schuetz, Melvin H. (1999), *A Chesley Bonestell Space Art Chronology*, Parkland: Universal Publishers.

Shanahan, M. (2015), *The Technological Singularity*, Cambridge and London: MIT Press.

Shaviro, S. (2010), *Post Cinematic Affect*, Winchester and Washington: Zero Books.

Sidorov, A. (1992), 'The thaw – Painting of the Kruschev era' in M.C. Brown and D. Elliott (eds), *Soviet Socialist Realist Painting 1930s–1960s*, Oxford: Museum of Modern Art, pp. 30–40.

Silver, M. (2010), 'Framing the ruins' in D. Stahl and M. Williams (eds), *Imag(in)ing the War in Japan: Representing and Responding to Trauma in Postwar Literature and Film*, Leiden and Boston: Brill.

Smith, Cordwainer, (2003), *The Rediscovery of Man*, London: Gollancz.

Snyder, J. (1994), 'Territorial photography', in W.J.T. Mitchell (ed.), *Landscape and Power*, Chicago and London: University of Chicago Press, pp. 175–202.

Stapledon, O. (1999), *Last and First Men*, London: Victor Gollancz.

Steiner, G. (1974), *In Bluebeard's Castle: Notes towards a Redefinition of Culture*, London: Faber & Faber.

Sterling, Bruce (2003), *Tomorrow Now: Envisioning the Next 50 Years*, New York: Random House.

Stross, C. (2007), http://www.antipope.org/charlie/blog-static/2007/06/the_high_frontier_redux. html. Accessed 2 December 2015.

Suvin, D. ([1974] 1979), *Metamorphoses of Science Fiction: On the Poetics and History of a Literary Genre*, London and New Haven: Yale University Press.

—— (1988), *Positions and Presuppositions in Science Fiction*, London: Macmillan.

Swift, J. ([1726] 2001) *Gulliver's Travels*, London, Wordsworth.

Tanner, R. (2006), *A History of Air-to-Air Refuelling*, Barnsley: Pen & Sword Aviation.

Thomas, E.L. (2004), *Emmanuel Levinas Ethics Justice and the Human Beyond Suffering*, London: Routledge.

Turkina, O. (2014), *Beyond Zero*, London: Calvert 22 Foundation.

Valentine, D. (2012), 'Exit strategy: Profit, cosmology and the future of humans in space', *Anthropological Quarterly*, 85:4, pp. 1045–68.

Vaughan, W. (1994), *Romantic Art*, London: Thames and Hudson.

Verran, H. (2014), 'Number' in C. Lury and N. Wakeford (eds), *Inventive Methods: The Happening of the Social*, London and New York: Routledge, pp. 110–23.

Virgil (1999), *The Eclogues and The Georgics* (trans. C. Day Lewis), Oxford: Oxford University Press.

Virilio, P. (2006), *Speed and Politics* (trans. M. Polizzotti), Los Angeles: Semiotext(e).

Vizenor, G. (1994), *Shadow Distance: A Gerald Vizenor Reader*, Hanover and London: Wesleyan University Press.

Von Braun, W. and Ordway, F.I. (1975), *History of Rocketry and Space Travel*, New York: Crowell.

Wall, J. (2007), *Selected Essays and Interviews*, New York: Museum of Modern Art.

Wark, M. (2007), *Gamer Theory*, Cambridge and London: Harvard University Press.

Watney, S. (1982), 'Making Strange: The Shattered Mirror' in Burgin, V. (ed.), *Thinking Photography*, London: Palgrave Macmillan, pp. 154–176.

Weart, S.R. (1988), *Nuclear Fear: A History of Images*, Cambridge and Massachusetts: Harvard University Press.

Wells, A. (1977), 'Introduction' in *21st Century Foss*, Brighton: Dragon's Dream Publishing, pp. 6–9.

Wells, H.G. ([1904] 2010), *The Food of the Gods*, London: Gollancz.

Willett, N. (2013), 'Mars versus the Moon', *The Mars Society* (Issue 19), 1 July.

Zakia, R.D. (2007), *Perception and Imaging: Photography – A Way of Seeing*, Oxford: Focal Press.

Zupančič, A. (2008), *The Odd One in: On Comedy*, Cambridge: MIT Press.

Illustration Copyright Acknowledgements

Figure 1:   Image used with permission of the Metropolitan Museum of Art, New York © Metrolopolitan Museum of Art.

Figure 2:   Image courtesy the Imperial War Museum, London. © IWM.

Figure 3:   Image used under the terms of under the fair dealing exception S.30, of the Copyright, Designs and Patents Act 1988 and Article 5 3.(d) of Directive 2001/29/EC of the European Parliament and of the Council, for the purposes of criticism, review and quotation.

Figure 4:   Image courtesy Keiichi Matsuda © Keiichi Matsuda.

Figure 5:   Image of The Game of Pelota ©Museo Nacional del Prado.

Figure 6:   Henk Snoek / RIBA Collections © RIBA.

Figure 7:   Image reproduced courtesy of Chris Foss/DACS ©ChrisFossArt/DACS.

Figure 8:   Image reproduced courtesy of Chris Foss/DACS ©ChrisFossArt/DACS.

Figure 9:   Image reproduced courtesy of Chris Foss/DACS ©ChrisFossArt/DACS.

Figure 10: Reproduced by permission of the Random House Group Ltd.

Figure 11: Image reproduced courtesy of Shogo Yamahata © Shogo Yamahata.

Figure 12: Image reproduced courtesy of *The Daily Telegraph*.

Figure 13: Image reproduced courtesy of Shogo Yamahata © Shogo Yamahata.

Figure 14: Image reproduced courtesy of Bonestell LCC. © Bonestell LCC.

Figure 17: Image reproduced with permssion of the Metropolitan Museum of Art, New York © Metropolitan Museum.

Figure 18: Used with the kind permission of the White Sands Missile Range Museum. New Mexico. © US Department of Defense.

Figure 19: © Frederick and Frances Sommer Foundation. Digital image © 2017 Museum of Modern Art./SCALA Florence.

Figure 20: Production still image courtesy of Wanuir Kahiu reproduced © Wanuri Kahiu.

Index

A

Abdeslam, Salah, 53
accelerationism, 78, 87–89
Active Worlds (VR environment), 52
Adorno, Theodor, 12, 73
Aelita (film), 134
Airshipwreck (Deighton and Schwartzman), 36–37
Akira (anime), 110
Akira (film), 115–116
al-Qaeda: The Third World War (TV series), 113
Alamogordo. *See* Trinity Test Site
Aldiss, Brian, 85, 90
Aldrin, Edwin 'Buzz', 142, 162
Alexander the Great, 27, 42
Alien (franchise), 9
Alien (1979 film), 33
Aliens (1986 film), 30–31, 33–34, 137
Allen, Irwin, 33–34, 41, 46–47
'Alpha Ralpha Boulevard' (Smith), 13, 35
Althusser, Louis, 20, 58, 124
Ambika P3 (London), 60
Anarres (fictional planet), 160–161
Anderson, Michael, 106
Anderson, Paul Thomas, 149
Anderson, Poul, 88
Androids Dream (film), 160, 161, 171–172, 173–175
Andromeda (Yefremov), 137

apocalyptic landscape
atomic tests and, 106–108, 114–115
in film and television, 96–97, 100, 105–106, 108–109, 110–111, 113
nuclear war as false memory and, 111–115
regeneration of, 115–117
threat of nuclear war and, 109–111
time capsule projects and, 99, 106
utopian imaginary and, 95–99
Yamahata's *Nagasaki* and, 100–106, 108, 111–112, Fig.:11, 13
Apollo 18 (film), 18
Apollo and Daphne (Poussin), 14
Apollo moon landings, 18, 29
Apollodorus, 28, 46
aporia, 98
Arcadia, 28, 37
The Architectural Uncanny (Vidler), 142
"Arena" (Brown), 154
Ares Vallis, 17
Arizona, 156–158
Arizona Landscape, 1943 (Sommer), 158
Armstrong, Neil, 162
Arnold, Jack, 41
Arrakis (fictional planet), 155
The Art of Chesley Bonestell (Miller and Durant), 126–127
Artificial Intelligence (AI), 70–74
artist's impression (artist's concept), 19, 78–80. *See also* Foss, Chris
Asimov, Isaac, 34, 82, 86–87, Fig.:9

Asteroids (computer game), 51
Astounding Analog Reader (Foss), 82
Astounding Science Fiction (magazine),
    154, 155
Astronomical Art, 129
Atari, 51
Athshe (fictional planet), 43–45
Attack of the 50 Foot Woman (film), 41
Augmented Reality, 52–53
Autumn Landscape (Nestorov), 133
Avatar (film), 30–31

B
B-29 (bomber), 100
Baastrup, Mads, 136–137
Badiou, Alain, 125, 145
Ballard, J.G., 88, 90
Barthes, Roland, 102
Battlestar Galactica (1978 film), 51
Battlestar Galactica (2004–09 television
    series), 42, 115, 116–117, 173, 174
Baudelaire, Charles, 174
Beck, John, 154
Beneath the Planet of the Apes (film), 106
Benjamin, Walter, 7–8, 77, 97, 174
Between the Eyes (Levi Strauss), 113
Bible, 25–26, 33, 57, 153–154
Bikini Atoll, 107–108
'Black Destroyer' (Van Vogt), 33
black sky, 146, 163, 167
Blade Runner (film), 4, 9, 160, 171–172
Blair Witch Project (film), 18
Blanchot, Maurice, 164–165
Blefuscu, 40. *See also Gulliver's Travels* (Swift)
Blind Orion Seeking the Sun (Poussin), 29–30,
    31–32, Fig.:1
Bloch, Ernst, 8, 10–12, 14, 90, 92, 142,
    145, 173
Blunt, Anthony, 13–14, 27
Bock's Car (bomber), 100
Boeing, 78
Bogdanov, Alexander, 134
Bolsheviks, 134–135, 137

Bonestell, Chesley
    apocalyptic landscape and, 107
    astronomical time and, 145–146
    Earthlike planets and, 140–143, 145
    extrapolation and, 123–124, 126–127,
        Fig.:14
    Friedrich's *Rückenfiguren* and, 138–140
    ideology and, 124–126
    instrumentalization of art and, 129–131
    Ley and, 131–133, 136–137
    O'Sullivan and, 159
    photo-realism and, 128–129
    reception of, 121–123
    science fiction and, 124
    Suppositional Realism and,
        132–133, 166
Bonneville Salt Flats, 153
The Book of Dragons (Nesbit), 34
Borden, Iain, 58
Borden, William Liscum, 107
Bourdieu, Pierre, 19–20
Bradbury, Ray, 59
Brand, Amelia (fictional character), 144
Brassier, Raymond, 145, 146
Braun, Wernher von, 133
Brezhnev, Leonid, 133
Bridle, James, 59–60
British Aerospace, 78
British Broadcasting Corporation (BBC), 78,
    99, 104, 108–109, 113
Brobdingnag, 39–42, 45
Brown, Fredric, 154
Brunelleschi, Filippo, 60
Brutalism, 80
Buck-Morss, Susan, 7–8
Bukharin, Nikolai, 135
Bürger, Peter, 79, 85, 130
Burgin, Victor, 60
Burke, Edmund, 105

C
C-57D (starship in *Forbidden Planet*),
    149–150

Cameron, James, 30–31, 33–34, 137
Campaign for Nuclear Disarmament
    (CND), 109
Campbell, John W., 154
canali (Mars), 155–156
A Canticle for Leibowitz (Miller), 105–106
Capa, Robert, 63
Caprica (television series), 174
Castle Howard, Yorkshire, 99
Cathcart, Brian, 114–115
"The Cave" (Miller), 155–157
CCTV (Closed-Circuit Television), 166
Cedalion, 29–30, 31–32
Cernan, Eugene, 164
Chaffey, Don, 34
Challenger (Apollo 17 Lunar Excursion
    Module), 164
Champollion, Jean-François, 162
Channel Islands, 89
chiasmus, 19
Christ, 139, 153–154
Christianity, 103, 139. *See also* Bible
chronoslip, 70
Church, Frederic Edwin, 127–129
Clarke, Arthur C., 88
Cloverfield (film), 18
Cold War, 43, 98–99, 100–101, 105–114,
    116, 160–161
colour, 29
Comfort, Alex, 88
Communism, 121. *See also* Soviet Union
conception, 63–64
Contact (film), 27–28
Conversations on the Plurality of Worlds
    (Fontenelle), 68
Copley, Sharlton, 166
Cordero, Sebastián, 143, 165–168
Cornwall, 89
cosmonauts, 30–31, 138, 165
Costanza's number, 56
Côt, Pierre-August, 13
Coyotes, 1945 (Sommers), 158
Crash (Ballard), 90

Cronos (Saturn), 28
Crossroads (nuclear tests), 107
Crowd Control Productions, 51–52
Cruise, Tom, 96
Crypt of Civilization, 99
Csikszentmihalyi, Mihaly, 55–56, 58
Cuarón, Alfonso, 143, 165–166
cyberpunk, 37
Cyclopes, 27, 28, 32–33
Cynics, 26–27
Cyrano De Bergerac, Savinien de, 25–27, 32,
    44, 46

D

Daily Telegraph (newspaper), 107
Damon, Matt, 143
Danby, Francis, 105
Däniken, Eric von, 81
Dark Sun (Rhodes), 110
darkness, 162–165
Darwin, Charles, 13
Dasque, Rosa (fictional character), 166, 168
Dassault, 78
Davidtz, Embeth, 166
Davis, Keith F., 159
The Day After (film), 108–109
The Day After Tomorrow (film), 100
The Day of His Judgement (Martin), 100
'The Day We Embarked for Cythera'
    (Aldiss), 90
Deighton, Len, 36–37
'The Deliverers of Their Country' (Nesbit), 34
Denatured Visions (exhibition), 17
Le Dernier Homme (Grainville), 96
Derrida, Jacques, 65, 98
desert landscape
    in *Android's Dream* (film), 160, 161
    darkness and, 162–165
    in *Europa Report*, 165–168
    photography and, 157–160
    in *Pumzi* (film), 161, Fig.:20
    in science fiction novels, 160–161
    speed and tests in, 149–155

desire, 90–91

The Destruction of Herculaneum (Martin), 100

Devon, 89

The Dialectics of Seeing (Buck-Morss), 7

Diana, 29–30

Dick, Philip K., 3–5, 9, 66–67, 160, 173–174

difference, 65

Diogenes, 26–27, 42

The Dispossessed (Le Guin), 160–161

Do Androids Dream of Electric Sheep? (Dick), 4, 66–67, 160

Doctor Faustus (Marlowe), 72

Dodd, Lancaster (fictional character), 149–150

Dornier, 78

Dorset, 89

dromology, 153

Dune (Herbert), 155, 160

Durant, Frederick C., 126–127

E

Earth Is Room Enough (Asimov), 82, 86–87, Fig.:9

The Economist (magazine), 122

Edgerton, Harold, 152–153

ego development, 6–7

Egyptomania, 162

eidon, 12–13, 91

The Eighty Minute Hour (Aldiss), 90

eikon, 12–13, 91

Eliot, George, 139

Elson, Peter, 45–46

Emerich, Roland, 100

The Empire Strikes Back (film), 30–31

ennui, 78, 91–92, 172–173

Ernst, Max, 159

erotics, 34, 69, 90–91

eSports, 54, 67

Essence of Christianity (Feuerbach), 139

Europa (moon of Jupiter), 166–168

Europa Report (film), 143, 165–168

EVA (extra vehicular activity), 166

EVE Online (computer game), 51–52

Everest, Mount, 126

Existence and Existents (Levinas), 162–163, 166–167

The Exploration of Mars (Ley and von Braun), 133

Exploratorium (San Francisco), 111–112

extrapolation
    artist's impressions and, 19, 78–79
    Bonestell and, 123–124, 126–127
    Klushantsev and, 123–124, 126, 127
    role of, 14–15

F

f64 Group, 158–159

Failsafe (film), 105–106

False Memory Syndrome, 111–115

The Family of Man (exhibition), 107

Fantastic Voyage (film), 41

Fat Man (atomic bomb), 100–101, 105, 106–107

'Feminism and the Psychic' (Rose), 95–97

Feuerbach, Ludwig, 139

Ficacci, Luigi, 47–48

First Lightning test (1949), 107

A Fisherman of the Inland Sea (Le Guin), 174–175

fission, 152–153. *See also* nuclear weapons and nuclear apocalypse

Fleischer, Richard, 41

Flexible Response, 110

flow, 55–56, 58

Fontenelle, Bernard Le Bovier de, 68

The Food of the Gods (Wells), 34–35, 37–39

Forbidden Planet (film), 9, 149–150

Foss, Chris
    accelerationism and, 87–89
    book covers by, 82–87, Fig.:8, 9, 10
    erotics and, 90–91
    LYDD and *Astounding Analog Reader* by, 81–82, Fig.:7
    montage and juxtaposition in work by, 77–78, 79–81, 85–86

four minute warning, 109–110

Frakes, Jonathan, 141

'Framing the Ruins' (Silver), 102

French Revolution, 105

Freud, Sigmund, 46–47, 112

Friedrich, Caspar David, 105, 133, 138–139, Fig.:17

'From the Images of Science to Science Fiction' (Klein), 12–13

Frosh, Stephen, 7, 111

Furtseva, Yekaterina, 138

fusion, 106. *See also* nuclear weapons and nuclear apocalypse

'The Future' (Steiner), 172–173

G

Gadget (nuclear test device), 105

Gagarin, Yuri, 136, 165

Galilean moons, 167

Galileo, 13–14

Gallagher, Carole, 154

The Game of Pelota (*El Juego de Pelota a Pala*) (Goya), 53–54, 57–60, 63, 68, 73, Fig.:5

Game of Thrones (television series), 172

gamespace

garden, 68

Gassendi, Pierre, 26

Gattaca (film), 9

Gautier, Théophile, 92

Ge (Gaia), 28

genius loci, 81–82, 90

Georgics (Virgil), 28, 32–33

Gestalt theory, 160

giants and giantism, 25–35, 37–39, 46–47. *See also Gulliver's Travels* (Swift)

Gibson, William, 4, 6, 37

Gigantes, 28, 32–33

Giger, H.R., 34

Goble, Warwick, 35–36

Goddard, Robert H., 129, 151

The Goddess of Discord Choosing the Apple of Contention in the Garden of the Hesperides (turner), 27

The Gods Themselves (Asimov), 34

Google Street View, 62–63

Gorgon (anti ballistic missile), 153

Goya, Francisco, 28, 38, 53–54, 57–60, Fig.:5

Grabar, I.E., 133

Grainville, Jean-Baptiste Cousin de, 96

Grand Theft Auto (computer game), 64

graphic novels, 64

Gravity (film), 143, 165–166

'The Great Ennui' (Steiner), 91–92

Great Kantō Earthquake (1923), 100

The Great Oath (Gerasimov), 130

Gregory, Richard, 60

Grierson, John, 103

Grimshaw, John Atkinson, 128–129

Group for the Study of Reactive Motion (GIRD), 136

Groys, Boris, 131

The Guardian (newspaper), 115

Guggenheim, Daniel, 151

Gulliver's Travels (Swift), 32, 39–41, 45

H

Hammaguir, 153

Hand, Seán, 163–164

Harrison, Charles, 157

Harrison, Harry, Fig.:10

Harrison, M. John, 85

Harvey, David, 68, 69–70, 74, 140

Hathaway, Anne, 144

Hauer, Rutger, 4

HD114762b (exoplanet), 141

Heavy Metal, 100

'Heidegger, Gagarin and Us' (Levinas), 165

Heidegger, Martin, 163–166, 173

Heimat, 142, 145, 173

Heitzer, Michael, 157

Helmore, Edward, 158–159

Herbert, Frank, 155, 160

Heston, Charlton, 96

Higashi, Jun, 101, 108

High-Rise (Ballard), 90

Hillis, Ken, 55–56, 57, 59, 62, 63–65, 67–68

Hindenburg (airship), 36–37
Hines, Barry, 108
Hiroshima, 100–102, 104, 105, 106–107, 108, 115. *See also* Nagasaki
Hiroshima Peace Memorial Museum, 115
Hoffman, Phillip Seymour, 149
Holland, Michael, 164–165
Holm, Ian, 33
holodeck, 60–62
Holt, Nancy, 157
horror films, 18
hospital, 175–176
The House of the Wolfings (Morris), 4
Hoyle, Fred, 88
Hubbard, L. Ron, 149
Hudson River School, 127–128, 145, 159
humanism, 104
Hume, David, 63
Hungarian Uprising (1956), 134
Hunter, Mel, 88
Hurricane (nuclear test), 114–115
Hurt, John, 33
hydrogen bomb
Hyper Reality (video), 53, Fig.:4

I

I Am Legend (film), 96
iatrogenic disorder, 112–114
ice XI, 167
ideality, 34
ideology, 124–126
il y a (Levinas), 164–165
imaginary, concept of, 3–4
The Incredible Shrinking Man (film), 41
The Interpretation of Dreams (Freud), 46–47
Interstellar (film), 15, 143, 144, 165–166
Islamic State, 172

J

J Missions (Apollo moon landings), 18, 29
Jackson, Mick, 108
Jameson, Fredric, 3–4, 9, 16, 18, 20, 33, 97, 127
Jarvis, William E., 98–99

Jason and the Argonauts (film), 34
Jenkins, Rupert, 102–103
Johnson, Michael, 81
jouissance, 79, 84–85, 138
Journey to the Moon (Cyrano De Bergerac), 25–27
The Joy of Sex (Comfort), 88
El Juego de Pelota a Pala (*The Game of Pelota*) (Goya), 53–54, 57–60, 63, 68, 73, Fig.:5
Jupiter (planet), 125–126, 140
Jupiter (Zeus), 28
Juran, Nathan, 41
juxtaposition, 77–81, 85–86

K

Kahiu, Wanuri, 161
Kant, Immanuel, 97
Kapterev, Sergei, 131, 134
Kazakhstan, 153
Kepler-186f (planet), 141
Kepler, Johannes, 13–14, 25
Kepler space telescope, 140–141
Kershner, Irvin, 30–31
Kertesz, André, 91
Kishimoto, Yoshita, 115
Kitty Hawk, 150
Klein, Gérard, 12–13, 20, 91
Klein, Melanie, 6–7
Klushantsev, Pavel
    astronomical time and, 145–146
    Earthlike planets and, 140–143, 145
    extrapolation and, 123–124, 126, 127, Fig.:15–16
    Friedrich's *Rückenfiguren* and, 138–140
    giantism and, 30–31
    ideology and, 124, 125
    instrumentalization of art and, 129–131
    Korolev and, 136
    O'Sullivan and, 159
    photo-realism and, 128–129
    reception of, 121–123
    Suppositional Realism and, 132–133, 166

Kneale, Nigel, 81, 85
Kollontai, Alexandra, 137
Korolev, Sergei, 136
Kracauer, Siegfried, 77
Kronkite, Walter, 137
Kruschev, Nikita, 109, 133–134
Kubrick, Stanley, 14, 15, 78, 84–85, 88, 163

L
Lacanian psychoanalysis, 3–4
Land Art, 157–158
Land of the Giants (TV series), 33–34, 41, 46–47
Landscape with Polyphemus (Poussin), 27, 28, 29, 67
landscaping, 4
Laputa, 41–43
Larionov, M.F., 133
Larson, Glen A., 51
Last and First Men (Stapledon), 73–74
The Last Man (Martin), 95
The Last Man (Shelley), 96
Le Guin, Ursula, 43–46, 160–161, 174–175, Fig.:3
Le May, Curtis, 110, 150
The Leader, Teacher, and Comrade (Shegal), 130
League of Legends (computer game), 54
Lee, Ang, 65
Lefebvre, Henri, 58
Lem, Stanislaw, 44–45
Lenin, Vladimir, 134
Lensman series (Smith), 84
Leonard, Jonathan Norton, 151–152, 154
Levania, 25
Level 7 (Roshwald), 106
Levi Strauss, David, 113
Levinas, Emmanuel, 16, 162–167, 173
Levitsky, Rafail Sergeevich, 128
Levitsky, Sergei Lvovich, 128
Ley, Willy, 131–133, 136–137
Life of Pi (film), 65
Lilac Bush in Flower (Larionov), 133

Lilliput
Lily (fictional character), 141
Limited Test Ban Treaty (1963), 106
Little Boy (atomic bomb), 100–101, 106–107
Lockheed-Martin, 78
Loftus, E.F., 114
Logan's Run (film), 106
loneliness, 137
Lucas, George, 106
Lumet, Sidney, 105–106
Lunacharsky, Anatoly, 134
LYDD (Foss), 81–82, Fig.:7

M
Mac, Kurt J., 66–67, 69
Mach, Ernst, 150–151
Mach's number, 151
Mad Max (franchise), 106
Mad Max: Beyond Thunderdome (film), 106, 115
Maetzig, Kurt, 105–106
Making Monsters (Ofshe and Watters), 113
'Making Strange: The Shattered Mirror' (Watney), 91
The Man in the High Castle (Dick), 3–4, 5
The Man in the High Castle (series), 5
Man Ray, 91
Mapping Mars (Morton), 17, 156–157
Maralinga, 153
Maria, Walter de, 157
Marinca, Anamaria, 166
Mariner 4 (spacecraft), 70–71
Marks, David F., 13, 91
Marlowe, Christopher, 72
Mars (planet)
    Bonestell and, 126, 127, 132–133
    as earthlike planet, 140, 141–142
    Klushantsev and, 132–133
    Miller and, 155–157
    Morton on, 17
    pictures of, 70–71
    robotic space probes and, 122
Mars (film), 133, 138, Fig.:15

The Martian (film), 143–144, 165–166
The Martian (Weir), 143–144
Martin, George R.R., 172
Martin, John, 95, 98, 100, 102, 103–104, 105
Marx, Karl, 8, 139
Marx, Leo, 15–16, 17
Massively Multiplayer Online Games
    (MMOGs), 51–52, 54, 55, 67–68
The Master (film), 149
Matheson, Richard, 41
Matsuda, Keiichi, 53, Fig.:4
McCarthy, Cormac, 104
McCurry, Justin, 115
McIntosh, J.T., 82–86, Fig.:8
McNamara, Robert, 110
Mechs, 30–31
Meillassoux, Quentin, 13, 132, 146
Mercury (god), 14
Mercury (planet), 14
Meridian 59 (computer game), 67–68
Merope, 30
Metal Gear Solid (computer game), 64
Metal Gear Solid (video game), 59
Metamorphoses of Science Fiction (Suvin),
    10–11
Meunier, John, 80, Fig.:6
Michael, A.C., 36, 38, 45
Michino-o (district of Nagasaki), 101
Milky Way galaxy, 141
millenarian ideologies, 96–97
Miller, Peter Schuyler, 155–157
Miller, Robyn and Rand, 54–55
Miller, Ron, 124–125, 126–127, 131–133
Miller, Walter J., 105–106
Milne, Julie, 100
Minecraft (video game), 66–67, 69
Misrach, Richard, 154
Mitchell, George William, 80
Mitchell, W.J.T., 4, 17–18, 58, 71, 144
MMOGs (Massively Multiplayer Online
    Games), 51–52, 54, 55, 67–68
Modernism, 71–72, 77, 81–82, 104, 159
Moholy-Nagy, László, 91

Mollon, Phil, 112
Moncrieff, Anthony, 99
montage, 77–81, 85–86
Moon
    Aldrin and, 162
    Apollo moon landings and, 18, 29
    Challenger and, 164
    as earthlike, 142
Moon (film), 137–138, Fig.:16
Morbius, Dr (fictional character), 149–150
More, Thomas, 51
Morris-Suzuki, Tessa, 111–112, 114
Morris, William, 4, 11, 149
Mortensen, Toril Elvira, 55
Morton, Oliver, 17, 156–157
Mostow, Jonathon, 100
'Mourning and Manic-Depressive States'
    (Klein), 6
music, 138
Myrone, Martin, 100
Myst (computer game), 54–55

N
Nagasaki
    destruction of, 100–101, 106–107
    regeneration of, 115–117
    Yamahata's photographs and, 100–106,
        108, 111–112, Fig.:11, 13
Nagasaki Journey (Jenkins et al.), 102–103
Napoleon, 91
NASA (National Aeronautics and Space
    Administration), 70–71
Nash, Paul, 35, 81–82, 91, 92
The Nation (magazine), 114
Native American cultures, 153–154
NATO (North Atlantic Treaty Organization),
    100, 110, 113–114
Nazi Germany, 3–5, 99, 102, 115, 129, 137,
    150, 173–174
Neo Tokyo (fictional city), 115–116
Nephilim, 33, 47
Nesbit, Edith, 34
Nestorov, M.V., 133

Neue Sachlichkeit, 104
Neumann, John von, 150
Nevada, 153
Nevinson, C.W.R., 35
New York World's Fair (1939–40), 99
Newsweek (magazine), 114
Nicoll, Andrew, 9
1984 (Orwell), 131
Nishikado, Tomohiro, 51
Nixon, Richard, 111
Nolan, Christopher, 15, 143, 144, 165–166
Norman Conquest 2066 (McIntosh), 82–86,
    Fig.:8
novum
    Android's Dream and, 171–172
    Bloch on, 8, 10–12
    Suvin on, 10–12, 88, 90
Noys, Benjamin, 87–88
Nuclear Test Ban Treaty (1963), 100
nuclear weapons and nuclear apocalypse
    atomic tests and, 106–108, 114–115
    destruction of Hiroshima and, 100–102,
        104, 105, 106–107, 108, 115
    destruction of Nagasaki and, 100–101,
        106–107
    nuclear war as false memory and,
        111–115, Fig.:12
    threat of nuclear war and, 109–111
    Yamahata's *Nagasaki* and, 100–106, 108,
        111–112, Fig.:11, 13
nuclear winter, 109
Nyqvist, Michael, 166

O
object relations, 6–7
Oblivion (film), 96
Obls (fictional race of beings), 174–175
ocularity, 4–8, 70–71, 152–153
Oculus Rift, 64
Oddworld (computer game), 54–55
Oddworld Inhabitants, 54–55
Oedipus Rex (Sophocles), 47, 98
Ofshe, Richard, 113

Oglethorpe University, 99
O'Keefe, Georgia, 157
Olasina, Ghobolahan, 52
Olmos, Edward James, 173
The Omega Man (film), 96
'On the Relationship between Imagery, Body
    and Mind' (Marks), 13
One Step from Earth (Harrison), Fig.:10
Operation Crossroads (nuclear tests), 107
Operation Sandstone (nuclear tests), 107
Oradour-sur-Glane, 115
Orford Ness, 153
Orion, 29–30, 31–32
Orwell, George, 131
ostranenie, 91, 104
O'Sullivan, Timothy, 159
The Other World (Cyrano De Bergerac),
    25–27
otium cum dignitate ('leisure with dignity'), 68
Otomo, Katsushiro, 115–116
Our Banner in the Sky (Church), 128
Ovid, 68
Øvredal, André, 18, 32

P
Pace, Claire, 68
The Pall Mall Magazine (literary magazine),
    36
Pan, 28
Pan Am (Pan American World Airways), 78
Paris terror attacks (2015), 53
Park, Grace, 173
Parkin, Simon, 51, 54, 62, 66, 67, 70
parkour, 58–59
Parris, Tom (fictional character), 61
Passagenwerk (Benjamin), 7–8
The Past Within Us (Morris-Suzuki),
    111–112, 114
Paul, Frank R., 88
perception, 63–64
Peredvizhniki (Russian itinerant painters),
    127–128, 145
periphery, 106

Perry Rhodan series, 84

Persson, Markus, 66

Petrified Forest National Monument, Arizona (Sommer), 157, Fig.:19

Petrovna, Katya (fictional character), 167

Phoenix, Joaquin, 149

photo-realism, 128–129

The Photographers' Gallery (London), 59–60

Picard, Jean-Luc (fictional character), 15, 141

picturesque, 30

Piper, John, 81

Piranesi, Giovanni Battista, 47–48, 90–91

Planet of Storms (film), 30–31, 137, 138

Planet of the Apes (film), 96, 106

plutonium

Poe, Edgar Allen, 154

Poland, 113–114, Fig.:10

The Political Unconscious (Jameson), 16, 97

politics, 95–96

Polyphemus, 27, 28, 29

Polyphemus Derided by Ulysses (Turner), 27

Pop Art, 81

Positivism, 129

Post, Ted, 106

postcolonial melancholia, 111

Poussin, Nicolas, 13–14, 27, 28, 29–30, 31–32, 57, 67, 68, Fig.:1

power, 29–30, 41

Prepper movement, 116

Prokhorov, Gleb, 130

prosopography, 123

Protozanov, Yakov, 134

psychoanalysis, 3–4

Pumzi (film), 161, Fig.:20

"The Purloined Letter" (Poe), 154

R

Rafman, Jon, 51, 52, 62–63

Reactive Scientific Research Institute (RNII), 136

Reading Capital (Althusser), 20

Realism, 97–98. *See also* Suppositional Realism

Reconstructive Retrieval, 114

Red and Yellow Cliffs (O'Keefe), 157

Red Mars (Robinson), 34

reductio ad absurdum, 95

religion, 97. *See also* Bible

Rephaim, 33

'The Representation of Wish-Landscapes in Painting, Opera and Poetry' (Bloch), 90

The Revolution Betrayed (Trotsky), 135

Rhodes, Richard, 70, 101, 104, 105, 107, 110

Riot Games, 54

The Road (film), 104

The Road (McCarthy), 104

The Road to the Stars (film), 136–137

Robbie the Robot, 149–150

Robinson, Kim Stanley, 34

Robocop (film), 31

'The Rock that Changed Things' (Le Guin), 174–175

Rockets (Ley), 131

Rococo, 90

Rolls-Royce, 78

Roman Catholic Church, 12–13

Romanticism, 97–98

Rome, 47–48, 90–91

Rose, Jacqueline, 95–97, 115, 117

Rosen, Edward, 25

Roshwald, Mordecai, 106

Rückenfiguren (back turned figures), 19, 105, 133, 138–139, Fig.:17

Rudeaux, Lucien, 124

Russian Artists' Union, 134

S

Sacrifice at White Sands (Leonard), 151–152

Sagan, Carl, 27–28

Sallis, John, 20

Salon de 1859 (Baudelaire), 174

SALT (Strategic Arms Limitations Talks), 110

San Francisco Earthquake (1906), 100

Sandstone (nuclear tests), 107

satellite telescopy, 140–141
Saturn (Cronos), 28
Saturn (planet), 146, Fig.:14
Saturn Seen from Mimas (Bonestell), 146,
    Fig.:14
Sawyer, Andy, 36
scale
    collisions and, 36–37, Fig.:2
    giantism and, 25–35, 37–39, 46–47
    in *Gulliver's Travels* (Swift), 39–43, 45
    in illustrations of Wells' novels, 35–36
    in Le Guin's fiction, 43–46
    in Piranesi's etchings, 47–48
schemas, 127
Schiaparelli, Giovanni, 155
Schmitt, Harrison, 164
Schuetz, Melvin, 126–127
Schwartzman, Arnold, 36–37
'Science Fiction and Utopian Fiction' (Suvin),
    9–10
Scientology, 149
Scott, Ridley, 4, 5, 9, 33, 143–144, 160,
    165–166
Seamless Transitions (exhibition), 59–60
Second Life (VR environment), 52, 62–63
sensation, 63–64
A Sense of Place (exhibition), 60
September 11, 2001 attacks, 113, 114
September Snow (Grabar), 133
Serge, Victor, 135
Serov, Vladimir, 134
Seven of Nine (fictional character), 61
Shanahan, Murray, 53, 70, 71, 72
Shaviro, Steven, 88
Sheffield, 108
Shegal, Grigory, 130
Shelley, Mary, 96
Shimerman, Armin, 60
Shippey, Tom, 4
The Shrinking Man (Matheson), 41
Sidorov, Aleksandr, 133–134
The Silent Star (*Der Schweigende Stern*)
    (film), 105–106

Silver, Mark, 102–104
Silverberg, Robert, 160
skate culture, 58–59
Skotak, Robert, 137
Skywalker, Luke (fictional character), 141
Smith, Cordwainer, 13, 35
Smith, E.E. 'Doc', 84
Smith, Michael Marshall, 15
Smith, Will, 96
Smithson, Robert, 157–158
Snyder, Joel, 159
social media, 69–70
Sojourner, 17
Solaris (Lem), 44–45
'Some Motifs in Baudelaire' (Benjamin), 174
Sommer, Frederick, 157, 158–160, Fig.:19
Somnium (Kepler), 25
Sony, 69
Sophocles, 47, 98
Sosa, Ion de, 160, 161, 171–172, 173–175
'A Sound of Thunder' (Bradbury), 59
Soviet Union
    Peredvizhniki in, 127–128, 145
    science fiction in, 134–136
    space travel and, 129
    See also Klushantsev, Pavel
Space Invaders (computer game), 51
space shuttles, 78, 171
space travel, 129, 136, 137
Space War (computer game), 51
Spaces of Hope (Harvey), 140
Speed and Politics (Virilio), 150–151, 153
Spiral Jetty (Smithson), 157–158
sports and games, 54, 57–59, 67
Spring (Vinogradov), 133
Sprint (anti ballistic missile), 153
Stalin, Josef, 130
Stalinism, 134–136
Standardized Casualty Rate, 101
Stapledon, Olaf, 73–74
The Star Dreamer (film), 136–137
Star Trek: Deep Space Nine (TV series), 60
Star Trek: First Contact (film), 141

Star Trek (franchise), 88, 110, 144
Star Trek: The Next Generation (TV series), 15, 60
Star Trek: Voyager (TV series), 60–62, 65
Star Wars (franchise), 51, 144
StART (Strategic Arms Reduction Talks), 110
steampunk, 37, 77, 78
Steichen, Edward, 104, 107
Steiner, George, 78, 91–92, 172–173
sterility, 106
Sterling, Bruce, 116
Stewart, Patrick, 141
The Storm (Côt), 13
Strategic Arms Limitations Talks (SALT), 110
Strategic Arms Reduction Talks (StART), 110
Suppositional Realism, 132–133, 166
Surrealism, 81, 159
survivancy, 161
Sutherland, Graham, 81–82
Suvin, Darko, 9–12, 88, 90, 126, 134, 136, 137, 144
Swift, Jonathan, 13, 32, 39–43, 45

T
Tambora, Mount, 96
Tarrant Rushton airfield, 80
Tatooine (*Star Wars* planet), 141
Taylor, Peter, 113
team sports, 54
Terminator 2 (film), 137
Terminator 3 (film), 100
Terminator series, 31
terror attacks, 53, 113, 114
Theogony (Apollodorus), 28
There Will Be No Time (atomic bombs), 107
Thomas, Elizabeth Louise, 167
Thorne, Kip, 143
Threads (TV series), 104, 108, 109
Thunderbird mythos, 153–154
THX1138 (film), 106
Time and the Other (Levinas), 163
time capsule projects, 99, 106

A Time of Changes (Silverberg), 160
Tinian Island, 107
Trinity Test Site, 105, 151–153
Troll Hunter (film), 18
Trollhunter (film), 32
Trotsky, Leon, 134–135
Truman, Harry S., 107
The Truman Show (film), 9
Tsiolkovsky, Konstantin, 129, 136
Tularosa Basin, 151–152, Fig.:18
Tularosa Frontier (film), 152, 155
Turkina, Oleysa, 136
Turner, J. M. W., 27
Turner, J.M.W., 86
Turner, Tina, 106
Two Men Contemplating the Moon (Friedrich), Fig.:17
2001: A Space Odyssey (film), 14, 15, 78, 84–85, 88, 90, 163

U
UFO sightings, 153–154
Unger, Dr Samantha (fictional character), 166
Ur-images, 103
Ur-past, 8
Uranus, 28
Urras (fictional planet), 160–161
utopia
    apocalyptic imaginary and, 95–99
    Bloch on, 12
    Virtual Reality and, 51, 53, 74
The Utopian Function of Art and Literature (Bloch), 11–12

V
V-2 rockets, 129, 150
Valentine, David, 165
Van Vogt, A. E., 33
'Vaster than Empires and More Slow' (Le Guin), 44–45
Vaughan, William, 138–139
Venus (planet), 140, 141–142

Vereshchagin, Vasily, 127–128
Verhoeven, Paul, 31
Verran, Helen, 56
Vesterholt, Sonja, 136–137
Vidler, Anthony, 142
Vietnam War, 43–44, 45–46
Vinogradov, S.A., 133
Virgil, 28, 32–33, 46
Virilio, Paul, 150–151, 153
Virtual Reality (VR) and Virtual
    Environments (VEs)
  Artificial Intelligence and, 70–74
  Augmented Reality and, 52–53
  detail in, 62–66
  digits and, 54–56
  as 'failed utopias', 51–52
  The Game of Pelota (Goya) and, 53–54,
    57–60, 63, 68, 73
  holodeck of *Star Trek Voyager* and, 60–62
  Minecraft and, 66–67, 69
  retreat and detachment in, 67–69
  sports and games and, 54, 67
  time and space in, 69–70
Vizenor, Gerald, 161
volcanic winter, 96
Voltaire, 13

W
W-53 (nuclear warhead), 100
Wall, Jeff, 16
The War Game (film), 105–106, 108–109,
    110–111
The War in the Air (Wells), 36
The War of the Worlds (Wells), 8–9, 35–36
Wark, McKenzie, 51, 55–56, 65–66
Watkins, Carlton, 159
Watkins, Peter, 105–106, 108–109, 110–111
Watney, Mark (fictional character), 143–144
Watney, Simon, 91
Watteau, Jean-Antoine, 90
Watters, Ethan, 113
We (Zemyatin), 131

Weart, Spencer R., 107
Weir, Andy, 143–144
Weir, Peter, 9
Weissman, Susan, 135
Welles, Orson, 8
Wells, Angus, 80, 85
Wells, H.G., 8–9, 34–36, 37–39, 46
Westinghouse Time Capsules, 99
White Sands, 150, 151–153, Fig.:18
Wilcox, Fred, 9, 149–150
Wilson, Harold, 78
Wölfert, Friedrich Hermann, 37
women, 40–41
Woodard, Alfre, 141
Woomera, 153
The Word for World Is Forest (Le Guin),
    43–46, Fig.:3
World War II. *See* Hiroshima; Nagasaki; Nazi
    Germany
World War III, 115–116, 141, Fig.:12
Wright Brothers, 150
Wydra, Karolina, 167–168
Wyndham, John, 81, 85

X
X planes, 151

Y
Yamada, Eiji, 101, 108
Yamahata, Yosuke, 100–106, 108, 111–112,
    115, Fig.:11, 13
Yefremov, Ivan, 137
YouTube, 66–67

Z
Zaka, Richard, 160
Zamyatin, Yevgeny, 131
Zemeckis, Robert, 27–28
Zeus (Jupiter), 28
Zipes, Jack, 11–12
Zupančič, Alenka, 46